The Internet *Imaginaire*

The Internet *Imaginaire*

Patrice Flichy

Translated by Liz Carey-Libbrecht

The MIT Press
Cambridge, Massachusetts
London, England

First MIT Press paperback edition, 2008
English translation © 2007 by the Massachusetts Institute of Technology

This work originally appeared in French under the title *L'Imaginaire d'Internet*.
© 2001 Editions La Découverte, Paris, France

This book was set in Sabon by Binghamton Valley Compostion, LLC.

Library of Congress Cataloging-in-Publication Data

Flichy, Patrice.
[Imaginaire d'internet English]
The internet imaginaire / Patrice Flichy ; translated by Liz Carey-Libbrecht.
   p. cm.
Translated from the French: L'imaginaire d'internet.
Includes bibliographical references and index.
ISBN-13: 978-0-262-06261-9 (hardcover : alk. paper), 978-0-262-56238-6 (pb)
1. Internet—Social aspects. 2. Computers and civilization. 3. Cyberspace—Social aspects. 4. Virtual reality.   I. Title.
HM851.F56   2007
306.4'6—dc22
                                                              2006027603

Contents

Introduction

Communication techniques are like some department stores: there's always something new. For the past thirty years we've been hearing about "new communication techniques." Initially the term referred to the VCR or cable television; later, to the microcomputer and now to the Internet. Every time people believed that the new device was going to impose itself and oust existing ones, that self-media would replace mass media, that all individuals would be able to express themselves without the usual intermediaries, and, finally, that new communities would bring together individuals in different parts of the world. But promises of a communication revolution have a long history, dating back to the advent of radio in the late nineteenth century when these promises flourished.

A reading of the discourse that attended the birth of new means of communication sometimes gives the impression that history stutters. Time after time, the same social reformers cherish hopes of solving problems of education or reviving the functioning of democracy, the same Cassandras perceive new media as a threat to culture or citizens' rights, the same ideologists see the dawn of a new civilization. Should we denounce these false prophets with their short memories, who repeatedly forget to compare today's technical trends with yesterday's prophecies? Or should we take a stand, espouse the ideologists', realists', or skeptics' cause, and separate the wheat from the chaff in these discourses accompanying the birth of new communication technologies?

The social sciences have studied these discourses, but often either superficially or else condescendingly, with irony. In the former instance they are assumed to tell the truth about a new technology, although that truth may eventually be belied by the technology's successors or sellers;

in the latter, they are seen as no more than a fable, at best the product of literary analysis. This book approaches the question from an entirely different angle. We consider these discourses as an integral part of the development of a technical system, and we study them as such.

The Internet, the main subject of this volume, is a prime example of the *imaginaire* surrounding a technique. Discourse on the Internet abounds, but this profusion cannot simply be interpreted as the effect of some fad or as an extreme case. The Internet *imaginaire* is closely related to the role of this new technology in Western societies, especially in North America. The purpose of this book is to show how an entire society is tilting into a new technological era.

Why have actors as different as computer scientists who design software, managers and employees who have to produce and coordinate within their firm, individuals who interact and entertain themselves at home, or politicians who dialogue with citizens, all agreed to adopt this technology? Why did computer scientists, sometimes voluntarily, design this technique rather than another one in the first place? Why have ordinary people agreed to learn about and then use the Internet for activities as commonplace as communicating with their family or friends, conducting information searches, or listening to music, as well as for design, administrative, or managerial work? In the final analysis, what we need to look at are the social actors' justifications for their engagement in the Internet project and the frame of representation of the new technique that has enabled designers and users to coordinate their actions.

Science and Technology Studies and Social Imagination

The project of this book coincides in certain respects with other sociological and historical studies of techniques. Most contemporary studies in this domain have definitively abandoned the traditional perspective in which the inventor's work was seen as the concretization of an initial intuition. In that approach it was believed that one particular technical alternative would triumph, owing to its intrinsic superiority. The initial idea was therefore crucial. This is the main point on which I focus my analysis. To this conventional linear perspective of technical development, the sociotechnique network approach, developed essentially by

Bruno Latour,[1] opposes a model in which innovation can start at any point and not necessarily in the fertile brain of a brilliant inventor. Following a series of translations, it attracts an increasing number of allies. It is the extent and soundness of the network, and not the relevance of the technical solution, that explains the success of an innovation. This constructivist approach has radically renewed the sociology of techniques. However, by focusing on alliances and opportunities, this research current cuts out the study of initial intentions and innovative projects. Although it is necessary to take into account the entire system of construction of a technique, does that mean that the characteristics of the initial project have no relevance?

Specialists in management extensively use the project concept.[2] The project team is the place in which a new technical device is formulated. One of the characteristics of management by projects, introduced into many firms, is the objective. Whereas the team and its leader have a large degree of autonomy and can choose their means, they have to attain a set objective. The principle of the project structure contrasts with the traditional rationalist model that radically separates design and execution. There is no simple, rigorous method for succeeding. Successful projects are the result of constant compromises with the different actors who have specific competencies and come from various departments in the firm. There is a continuous play of negotiation and interaction. The project leader has to be able to assert the identity of his or her project and discuss each of the elements with different experts involved in the operation. This idea of negotiation, compromise, and innovation induced by opportunities and ad hoc agreements is not too far from Latour's model. It nevertheless differs insofar as tension is constantly present between the wish to assert the project's identity and the openness to negotiation and compromise with partners both inside the firm and outside.

Finally, there is another current of sociological research that has also raised the question of coordination in technical development. Interactionist sociologists of science and techniques have examined how actors belonging to a distinct social world, with different visions of the same object, cooperate. Star and Griesemer introduced the boundary-object concept to study scientific or technical devices that are situated at the intersection of several social worlds but meet the needs of each world.

"They are objects which are both plastic enough to adapt to local needs and the constraints of the several parties employing them, yet robust enough to maintain a common identity."[3] The boundary-object allows cooperation to be organized between actors with different points of view and knowledge, without overlooking their individual competencies, by adopting a common approach. These two authors show that in the design and development of a joint research project, two types of boundary-object are created: a common vision that structures the project, and collective working methods.

These three theoretical currents have the same perspective: scientific or technical innovation that requires the coordination of many actors and the development of a series of compromises and adjustments. It is through these operations that innovation takes shape. Yet unlike Latour's sociology of translation, the other two currents consider that a new technical object has to be articulated around a specific identity, a common vision. Note that this collective representation of the technical project is not preestablished; it is the outcome of a collective construction. In other words, the technical collective is constituted not only through a series of local adjustments but also through the production of a common purpose.

When we leave "the short-term dimension" of technical development, that is, a specific project, and consider a more long-term dimension such as electrical light and power, high-speed trains, Internet, and so forth, we encounter more than simply a project or common intention; what we witness is a collective vision or *imaginaire*. This vision is common to an entire profession or sector, rather than to a team or work collective. It concerns not only designers but also users, which is one of the strong points linking these two types of actors of technical activity. Hence, if intentions and projects, as well as utopias and ideologies, play a part in the creation of technical systems, the contribution of the history of techniques will be useful to our study of the subject.

History of Innovation

Thomas Hughes's work on electric networks and on more contemporary projects like Arpanet is crucial. His technological system approach is very broad, and in *Networks of Power* he shows how a technical network necessarily intersects with larger social, political, and economic networks. For instance, electrical systems include not only utility companies, but also manufacturing firms or investment banks. Hughes was keenly interested in "project management." He distinguished two types of technological project management: the modern, hierarchical kind used by Edison and Ford, with a bureaucratic structure and a specialization of scientists and engineers; and the postmodern one used in technological and scientific undertakings of the post–World War II era, with a flat organization, a collegial community, and interdisciplinary cooperation among engineers.[4]

Arpanet, the Internet ancestor, is a good example of this kind of management. Bright and self-motivated researchers can reach decisions by consensus. Heads of the projects are "not just managers," but they have technical competences for which they are well known.

Finally, the organization of Arpanet was based primarily on the values of the academic world. By focusing on the management of technical projects, we see to what extent the construction of the technical object is connected to the values of the environment in which it was born. We come across another concept in the study of innovation, that of the "design ambience," that John Staudenmaier tells us highlights "the many ways in which technological praxis is inextricably part of the larger human fabric."[5] The design ambience approach opens an interesting avenue. It shows that, contrary to the position of externalist historians, we cannot study the role of ambience without analyzing technical design. That is why the chapters of this book on Internet designers' *imaginaire* also consider their technical choices.

There is also a whole research tradition in the history of techniques that studied the question of *imaginaire*. Leo Marx pointed out a long time ago the "rhetoric of the technological sublime"[6] that appeared in the mid-nineteenth century with the steam engine. The vocabulary of the sublime, used to describe nature in the eighteenth century, was adopted in the industrial age to describe the "technological sublime." From these images a hymn to progress was built, an optimistic vision of these new technologies that was to facilitate their diffusion and use. Rosalind Williams has shown just how diverse and often contradictory these technical visions were. For instance, for some the steam engine symbolized power; for others it was hell.[7]

Several studies have investigated technological *imaginaires*: Carolyn Marvin on electricity, Susan Douglas on the wireless, and Joseph Corn on aviation.[8] Susan Douglas's objective is close to mine—namely, to analyze "the ideological frameworks within which emerging technologies evolve."[9] Corn clearly shows the interest of these different historical studies for furthering our understanding of technological development, when he writes: "The most naïve fantasies about machines and their possible impact are part of the same cultural milieu in which actual invention takes place and technology is adopted and diffused."[10] This *imaginaire* can thus mobilize both designers and users. It is precisely this question of the mobilization of actors that is at the heart of Charles Bazerman's and Joanne Yates's work.

Bazerman studies how Edison gives electrical light and power sense and value and incorporates it into existing cultural systems of meaning. Edison and his associates were not only making electricity, "they were also making meanings."[11] This creation of meaning has to take place in various arenas: laboratory, patent system, investment bankers, journalists, families, and so on. At the end of the process, meanings and value are permanently set. Thus, in the realm of representations, we find the same black-boxing phenomenon as sociology studied in the case of the technical object.

This question of the mobilization of individuals has also been studied with regard to the introduction of an information and communication technique, the first data processing machines (typewriters, calculators, etc.) in the nineteenth century. Yates has shown[12] that the model of coordination by writing and use of these new machines would not have spread without a specific setting in which mediation and incentives could change. The first business schools and the managerial literature that developed at the time proposed management methods and advised on the use of office machines. For this new managerial ideology, the written procedure was the most appropriate for establishing efficient coordination between the different actors in a firm.

Uses of the Internet are, however, far more diverse than those of the first office machines. One of the main difficulties in studying this type of communication system derives from its complexity. Some analyze it as a new addition to the media, others as an interpersonal communication tool or new system of corporate organization, and others as a device facilitating trade. All these facets of the Internet are rarely studied simultaneously, yet individuals are present on several scenes of the Internet at the same time and the justifications for their engagement are global. It is in this respect that this study differs from Rob Kling's[13] study on computerization. Although I believe, as he does, that there are key ideological beliefs which help to legitimize the take up of computers, the starting point of my analysis is not social movements concerning computing but a corpus of discourses.

Before embarking on the study of the Internet case, it seems important to set out the key concepts of my analysis and to present my corpus.

Myth, Utopia, Ideology

The authors who celebrate or denounce discourse on the Internet readily use terms such as *myth*, *utopia*, or *ideology*. These concepts need to be clarified.

Myth

Although in the ethnographic tradition myths relate to the founding narratives of a culture, it is rather in the semiological sense that I use the term. For Barthes, the myth is a metalanguage that takes an existing sign as signifier and gives it another meaning as signified (*signifié*). The author of *Mythologies*[14] applied this approach to his study of advertisements or magazine photos that signify more than what the photographer's camera immediately shows. The meaning of a particular event recorded by a photographer or recounted by a writer gradually becomes poorer, eventually fading away. That initial meaning thus loses its value but retains a life sustained by the myth. Eventually the myth transforms a particular story into a natural representation.

Take the example of the anecdote that appeared several times in the first books on the Internet, in which two Internauts living at opposite ends of the United States, who had met on the Internet, decided to marry. By becoming a myth, this story took on another meaning. It was no longer the personal history of two individuals but an account showing that the Internet helped to construct a new social link, to create an intimate relationship between two strangers who for a long time had never actually met each other face-to-face.

In this perspective the myth is distinguished from symbols insofar as it is based on a real event. "It is full of a situation,"[15] said Barthes. It is also distinct from ideology in that it does not hide the real: "Its function is to deform, not to do away with."[16]

Utopia, Ideology

The notion of a myth is often associated with that of utopia. In that case it is presented as a dream, a chimera. Paul Ricœur associates it with the notion of ideology and constructs an interesting conceptual frame in which he articulates the two. Although this analysis was designed to study nineteenth-century political thinking, Ricœur's frame is rich enough to be imported into the technical domain. Let us have a closer look at it.

At the center lies the idea that an ideology or a utopia should not be defined in relation to reality. Contrary to the entire Marxist tradition, ideology is not opposed to the real, for reality is symbolically mediat"Where human beings exist," says Ricœur, "there cannot be a non-symbolic mode of existence, and even less so, a non-symbolic kind of action."[17] Likewise, the current view which opposes utopia and reality overlooks the fact that reality is not a set condition but a process. On the other hand, utopia and ideology are the two poles of the social *imaginaire*, one trying to maintain social order and the other trying to disrupt it. Hence, there is constant tension between stability and change.

Ricœur's dialectic between utopia and ideology functions at three levels (table I.1).[18] At the first and most obvious level, an ideology, which is a distortion of the real, is opposed to a utopia, which constitutes a "totally unrealizable phantasmagoria." Then, "when we dig down, we reach the level of power"[19]—clearly the level that interests Ricœur most. Ideology legitimizes power, whereas utopia constitutes an alternative to the power in place. At the third and last level, we see the positive function of these two sides to social imagination appearing "to preserve the identity of a [social] group," in the case of ideology, and "to explore the possible," in that of utopia.

In the final analysis, the philosopher's conviction is "that we are always caught in this oscillation between ideology and utopia, . . . we

Table I.1
The three levels of Ricœur's Concepts

	Ideology	Utopia
First or current level	Distortion of reality	Escape
Second or political level	Legitimization of power	Alternative to power; undermining authority
Third or social function level	Group identity Integration	Exploration of possibilities

must try to cure the illnesses of utopia by what is wholesome in ideology—by its element of identity— . . . and try to cure the rigidity, the petrification of ideologies by the utopian element. It is too simple a response, though, to say that we must keep the dialectic running. My more ultimate answer is that we must let ourselves be drawn into the circle and then try to make the circle a spiral."[20] It is in this dynamic perspective that I wish to use Ricœur's schema to construct a model for the analysis of the technical *imaginaire*.

The subversive function of utopia, that allows the full range of possibilities to be explored, can be put at the start of the process. This is probably one of the most inventive phases but also the most unmethodical. In the process of gestation of innovation this phase corresponds to what I have called the "catch-all object."[21] The projects conceived of here are widely diverse, often opposed, sometimes simply juxtaposed. They belong to different social worlds. It is also in this period that some actors of technology discover the questions or projects of others. These improbable encounters among different technical devices or between designers and users can be passing occurrences or profoundly fertile events. In such cases, I refer to a *watershed utopia* (figure I.1).

In the second phase, a real alternative to existing technical devices is constructed as the models roughed out in the preceding phase become full-blown projects. We witness a change of meaning in the concept of a model, significant of this evolution. Whereas in the preceding phase a model meant tension toward an ideal, it now becomes the formalized schema of a technique to realize. At the end of this phase utopian reflection can evolve in two ways. Either it is embodied in an experimental

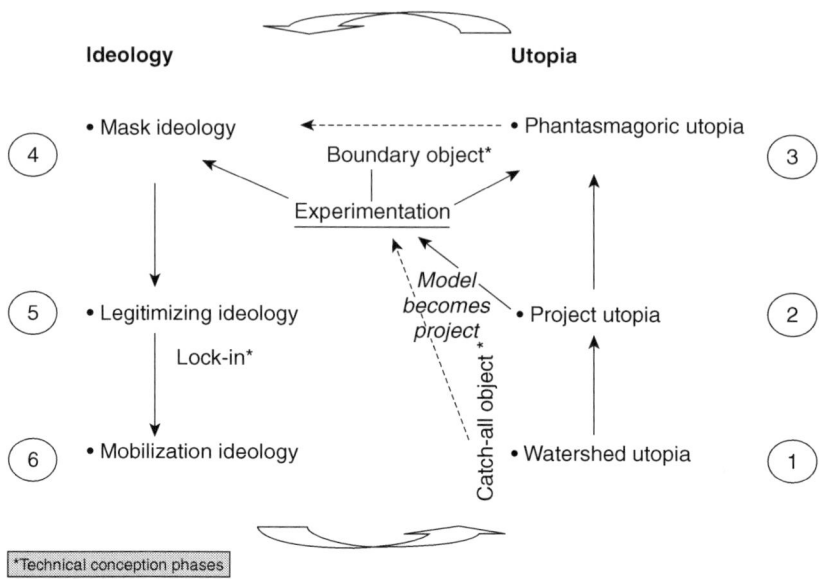

Figure I.1

project, or it becomes pure fantasy. The first possibility, the *project utopia,* is a peculiarity of the technical utopia. The author of this utopia often tries to concretize his or her project by building a mock-up or performing a technical test. This incarnation of the utopia is even easier to accomplish in the case of the computer techniques studied in this book. Very few tools are required to write computer software, compared to those needed to create a prototype in the mechanical or energy fields. What's more, software can be duplicated instantaneously and disseminated on a telecommunications network. It is therefore one easy step from design to use. By contrast, the *phantasmagoric utopia* is an escape, a way out, a refusal to face the technical reality.

When utopians become experimenters they are confronted not only with the technique but also with other social actors who have a different view of it. If they want to ensure that their experimentation gets beyond their workshop or, in the case of interest to us here, their computer, they need to construct a boundary-object, a compromise that can be used to associate multiple partners sufficiently loosely for everyone to benefit, yet sufficiently rigidly for the device to function. This object situated on the boundary of several social worlds is different to the initial catch-all object.[22]

The experimental phase is not only a time for construction of the technique and its uses but also a phase in which the utopian discourse is reconstructed and bases its claims on the exemplarity of the trials performed. To attain their goals, utopians have to diffuse their new technology far and wide. The successful experiment will then become a myth. The particular social context that made the experimentation possible is forgotten, and this local technique is presented as the basic technique of a new social functioning. This shift performed by the myth will eventually transform the utopia into an ideology. In this new phase, aspects of reality are readily concealed in order to promote the new technique. In this case, I refer to a *mask ideology*.

The technical ideology will make it possible to legitimize the new technical system. As it becomes increasingly rigid, alternatives are cast aside and what economists call technological lock-in results. In this case, I use the term *legitimizing ideology*. Finally, since the positive function of this ideology is to mobilize the actors concerned—both the producers of the technology and its users—I call it a *mobilization ideology*.

These six types of utopian or ideological discourses allow us to separate different functions of the discourses of *imaginaires*. These functions can be used to characterize certain texts but may also coexist in the same document. The different types of discourse also follow one another in a temporal cycle. In some cases, the steps are crossed successively; in others, some never appear, or the process may even stop and the technical project never reaches maturity. In the case of the phantasmagoric utopia, the abundance of *imaginaires* prevents the technique from ever being set in reality; in other cases, the absence of a legitimizing ideology precludes the technique from occupying any significant place in engineers' options and users' ways.

Since this schema of the evolution of the technical imagination does not always exist in such a complete form, we can consider it an ideal-type. Yet there is always an articulation between utopia and ideology. The one is more evident in periods of technical conception and the other in periods of diffusion of the technology. In this book, we see several cases of articulation between the different types of technical imagination, situations in which a technical utopia, unable to develop into a project, becomes a mask ideology. We also examine cases where, on the contrary, a utopia becomes a project that spreads throughout society after a long experimental phase. Finally, we see experiments that become the base of a new myth, and discourses that certain authors use to create a watershed utopia or, in other cases, a mask ideology.

A Corpus of U.S. Texts

U.S. literature on the Internet is recent but abundant. If we limit ourselves simply to books with the word Internet in the title, we find 1 or 2 per year from 1984 to 1991, 11 in 1992, 37 in 1993, 181 in 1994, 465 in 1995, 1,014 in 1996, and 1,395 in 1997. It is naturally out of the question to study all these books! For the purposes of my study here, I selected a number of reference texts that have two main origins: documents written by academics and computer scientists, and press articles. The first corpus includes writings by the founding fathers of information highways, the Internet, and virtual reality. To find these documents I relied on the first U.S. historical books and on certain collective volumes available in hard copy or online. I first selected texts which defined the main lines of the technical project and its intended uses, then others which described the first effective uses and inferred possible development scenarios. In order to avoid retrospective constructions as much as possible, I primarily used texts written before or during the early development of the technique, which therefore correspond to the actors' initial projects.

The second corpus consists of observations and comments by academics, experts, and journalists. For my guideline I chose the magazine *Wired*, the main U.S. magazine for reflection and debate on the Internet and digital techniques. I identified authors who had written or been interviewed or simply commented on in *Wired*. I then noted what these intellectuals of digital technology had published in *Wired* and which books they had written.

As far as the press is concerned, I selected all relevant articles in *Wired* that were written by intellectuals or journalists. For comparison, and to be able to study how the Internet *imaginaire* diffused from specialists toward the public at large, I also selected articles on digital techniques in the three main U.S. news magazines: *Time, Newsweek,* and *Business Week*. These four magazines were studied systematically from 1991 to 1995. For the following years, I carried out an in-depth study of *Wired* and added a few important articles from *Business Week* on the new economy.

A corpus like this obviously favors certain actors rather than others. It allows more space to academics, intellectuals, and journalists, and largely overlooks the discourses of entrepreneurs and users.

Historical and Thematic Analysis

These different texts cover two main domains of the technical *imaginaire*: the utopias and ideologies associated with the elaboration and possibly the diffusion of technical devices, and the description of an imaginary virtual society. As regards the former, I studied the representations of technical systems, the dreams and experiments that developed around information highways, the Internet, Bulletin Board Systems (BBS), and virtual reality. Concerning the latter, I propose a kind of treatise on the digital society, containing chapters on the individual and the body, communities, politics, economics, and representations of the past and future. These two approaches each constitute a section of this book. For the sake of fluidity in the presentation of these different issues, I have included reflection on virtual communities in the chapter on BBS and a presentation of virtual reality in the chapter on the body.

This work would not have been possible without Stanford University, which enabled me to constitute the corpus of documentation on which my study is based. In particular, I wish to thank Ralph Hester, who hosted me in his department. My reflection also benefited from the comments and advice of my colleagues at LATTS, Marne-la-Vallée University.

I

Designers' and Promoters' *Imaginaire*

1

Information Highways, or the Difficulty of Transforming a Utopia into a Technological Program

Who knows what the proposed National Information Infrastructure will be? Will it be a scheme for hundreds of video channels over cable? Will it become a way to bring the Internet out of the universities and into our homes and public schools?

Will it be primarily a commercial endeavor or a public service?

Will the government regulate its growth and content? Will it be a part of the telephone or cable-television system? Should I worry that local bulletin boards won't have access? Will the government further subsidize an industry that's making lots of money already?

The answer is yes to all the above and more.

—Clifford Stoll, *Silicon Snake Oil: Second Thoughts on the Information Highway*

Not all technical utopias reach the experimental project stage; far from it.[1] It therefore seems appropriate to start this first part on designers' *imaginaire* by considering a utopia that was never realized in the form of a technical achievement. Information highways, a catch-all object, are a fine example. Several actors from the political and industrial worlds built utopias that were partly convergent but led to different projects. That divergence precluded the definition of a boundary-object common to the different protagonists. Unable to develop into a project, the utopia took a turn and mutated into a mask ideology. As the imaginary project was gradually emptied of its substance, it found another content: the justification for a telecommunications liberalization policy. We examine first this shift from a watershed utopia to a phantasmagoric utopia, and then its transformation into a mask ideology.

Birth of a Technical Utopia

An Old Concept

In May 1970 the weekly *The Nation* published an article entitled "The Wired Nation." Ralph Lee Smith wrote: "In the 1960s, the nation provided large federal subsidies for a new interstate highway system to facilitate and modernize the flow of automotive traffic in the United States. In the 1970s it should make a similar national commitment for an electronic highway system, to facilitate the exchange of information and ideas."[2] The electronic highway metaphor thus appeared in the literature from the early 1970s. A new infrastructure was associated with the new electronic world, but the technology to which Smith and many others were referring at the time was the cable.[3] This new network would allow interactive television, movies-on-demand, and telechat, while home voting would usher in the era of teledemocracy. The theme of the cabled city, cabled nation, and cabled world became a new communication utopia. Teledistribution operators believed in the "cable revolution,"[4] as did militants of the alternative video.[5]

The theme of a networked society reappeared at the end of the decade among computer scientists, at a time when microcomputing and the Internet were still in an embryonic stage. It was believed that "the network nation could re-unite individuals and groups dispersed over wide distances by the jet plane and car, and recreate emotional bonds among family members, friends and professional colleagues whom fate has separated."[6] One computer scientist saw it as "a revolutionary network where each node is equal in power to all others."[7] At the time the information society became a topic of academic reflection and debate, and the idea of convergence among television, telephone, and computers started to spread. It was in this context that Anne Branscomb laid the foundations for the first reflection on government policy concerning an information infrastructure. She wrote: "A national system of electronic superhighways is not likely to emerge without the exercise of collective will through substantial government involvement at least in the planning process."[8]

A Network for Education and Research

The term "information highways" appeared in 1985 in a book written by librarians.[9] In 1987 the educational organization Educom published a paper on the advantages of network communication: "Faculty in all disciplines have a need to use networks for communications among their peers and within research projects. Networks which provide a new way of collaborating and disseminating information are affecting publications and libraries. A network for higher education can be seen as a *new national highway system* linking universities, colleges, libraries, research and industry organisations, for the transport of information rather than goods."[10] At about the same time, the National Research Council (NRC) also called for the construction of a "national research network."[11]

In the following year several educational institutions, including Educom, proposed the creation of a National Research and Education Network (NREN). The project was taken up in the political sphere, and in 1989 the *High Performance Computing Plan* drafted by the White House's Science and Technology Policy Office provided for development of the network. In parallel, the Senate, primarily on the initiative of democratic senator Al Gore, drafted a bill that was eventually passed in 1991 and approved by President George Bush.

The *High Performance Computing Act* was designed to "provide American researchers and educators with the computer and information resources they need, and demonstrate how advanced computers, high-capacity and high-speed networks, and electronic databases can improve the national information infrastructure for use by all Americans."[12] This preamble summed up various objectives that were not always compatible. The network was to be above all an educational and research tool requested by the academic world. It was not a physical network, but a network of networks, like the Internet. The law simply provided for a continuation of current government policy in this respect. The second objective corresponded to a technological research program in the computer and network sector, and it was essentially to this area that federal funding was to be directed. Last, the law was to prepare a national information infrastructure for American society as a whole. Although this was the first official reference to information highways, this utopian project was not expressed in any concrete operational terms in the law. The definition of this utopia had to be found elsewhere.

In a speech prior to the passing of this law,[13] Al Gore defined the NREN as an information highway, that is, a high-capacity, fiber-optic network. The information highway utopia was thus based on a specific technical project. Gore had first proposed the construction of this type of network in the early 1980s. He saw fiber optics as a profound technological revolution comparable to the transistor: "It will change the way we view our world, just as the Copernician Revolution did." Democratic congressman Rick Boucher expressed similar views: "The NREN is a major step on the road to the future information infrastructure of the nation. This future ubiquitous network for voice, video and data communications of all kinds will connect homes, schools, and workplaces. It will constitute an essential ingredient for our future economic competitiveness and will open new worlds of information and services for all of our citizens. The NREN . . . will form the backbone of the new network—the interstate highways."[14] In the official discourse, information highways thus seemed to be the instrument of a new information revolution that would spread from universities throughout society. It was this vision that was echoed by the press in comments on the 1991 law.[15]

Similar projects were also launched by various states, especially Ohio and Iowa.[16] As is often the case in the United States, politicians requested the input of university think tanks during the development of these projects. At Harvard the information infrastructure project was founded for this purpose in 1989.

In a document published several years later, James Keller, one of the coordinators of the project, defined the characteristics of these future highways as follows: "Network use should not be limited to the passive receipt of information. . . . Even the most basic connection should enable users to act as information sources as well as destinations. In this way, development of the NII offers a potential paradigm shift in communications, publishing and human interaction comparable to that effected by the Gutenburg press. Information Infrastructure is an enabler of both free speech and efficient markets. It can help overcome barriers of information and create opportunities to convene regardless of geographic, physical or financial constraints."[17] We thus see the emergence of a doctrine that could be called liberal (in the political and economic sense of the word): information highways. It was believed that these highways would make it easier for citizens to express themselves, thus enhancing democracy, and would open up new economic possibilities, for example, by improving performance and pooling competencies.

An economist proposed calculating the impact of information highways. The Economic Strategy Institute considered that a national fiber-optic network would generate annual productivity gains of 0.4 percent. By 2010 the GDP would have increased by $320 billion.[18]

In 1991–1992 a debate on industrial policy ran through the intellectual and political world. Whereas in France the government had often been an active player in industry, the same did not apply to the United States. Yet with the economic recession that followed the Gulf War and the need to convert part of the military industry after the Cold War, certain currents of public opinion saw a technological and industrial policy as a necessity. The profoundly liberal *Business Week* wrote: "The nation needs a plan to nurture growth. . . . Government can become a key player in the knowledge economy. It should boost research. . . . It can enhance productivity by building up infrastructure, especially by encouraging the development of high-speed communications networks."[19]

Two thrusts of government intervention were envisaged: investments in public infrastructure, in the New Deal tradition, and financing of civil research programs as a substitute for military research that was expected to decline as a consequence of the end of the Cold War. The former was exceptional in U.S. history and corresponded more to a democratic approach. The latter, easier to accomplish, amounted to officializing aid to high-tech industries masked until then by military programs. Since information highways could simultaneously correspond to both thrusts, public discourse often confused the two.

Al Gore's Utopia

It was in 1992, during Bill Clinton's and Al Gore's election campaign for president and vice president, respectively, that discourse on information highways became more coherent. Various issues, raised in the academic and research world, in the political or economic reflection of think tanks, and in the federal or state governments' early political projects, were combined. This theme started to occupy a prime place in public debate[20] and in the media, where "information highways" became the most commonly used term to refer to this type of project. Gore, whom the media saw as the author of the project, constructed his own genealogical account. He explained that he had been thinking of this project for over ten years and that he had chosen the name to honor the memory of his father who, as a senator, had played an important part in launching the interstate highway program in the 1950s.

The metaphor was essential in this technical utopia. Through it the project was synthesized in a single word and inscribed in the land and in history—not only in Gore's personal history but also, and above all, in that of the state's circulation and intervention in this domain. Gore explained that after World War II the state had built a federal network of highways to meet the demand of new owners of cars. "Today," he said, "commerce rolls not just on asphalt highways but along information highways. And tens of millions of American families and businesses now use computers and find that the two-lane information pathways built for telephone service are no longer adequate."[21]

The comparison with highways and reference to the actions of Gore's father, used to obtain the government funds required for the construction of the network, also set this project in another historical tradition, that of the New Deal. Like that of the automobile society, this information society infrastructure had to be funded by the state.

The first writings of Clinton and Gore as president and vice president defined the main characteristics of this new utopia. The idea was to design an interactive network for both entertainment and work. To achieve that goal it would be necessary to build "a fiber-optic network capable of transmitting billions of bits of information in a second."[22] Among the multiple uses of these technologies, Clinton and Gore cited the following: "A doctor who needs a second opinion could transmit a patient's entire medical record—x-rays and ultrasound scans included—to a colleague thousands of miles away, in less time than it takes to send a fax today. A school child in a small town could use a personal computer to reach into an electronic Library of Congress for thousands of books, records, videos, and photographs. At home, viewers could choose whenever they wanted from thousands of different television programs of movies."[23] These documents defined a vision of the future, ten or fifteen years ahead, according to Gore.[24]

This vision clearly corresponded to a technological utopia. It explored new fields of possibilities (telemedicine, tele-education, telework, etc.) and presented alternatives to physical circulation and a one-directional mode of transmission of information. Some observers saw this as more than simply a technological program. For example, John Schwartz of *Newsweek* noted: "The data highway is essentially an act of faith: if we build it, they will come."[25] We are thus looking at a project utopia that, as Robert Samuelson notes in the same magazine in relation to "pipe dreams,"[26] could become a phantasmagoric utopia.

Clinton and Gore wanted to ensure that information highways were not simply an election campaign slogan, and that the utopia was transformed into a concrete program. Less than two months after their arrival at the White House they set up the Information Infrastructure Task Force to prepare what would henceforth be called the national information infrastructure. The public debate was open.

The Catch-All Object

The Industrial Arena

Before its appearance on the political agenda the information highway debate had also been initiated in other areas. In the industrial world similar utopias had developed. For example, Robert Allen, chairman of the telecommunications giant AT&T, called for the development of a "new Renaissance."[27] He pointed out that just as the treasures of ancient Greek and Latin literature remained hidden in monasteries in the Middle Ages, so too modern day libraries and universities were packed with insufficiently diffused knowledge. The NREN could make that knowledge available for all. Several electronics firms in Silicon Valley created the association "Smart Valley" to use new communication infrastructures to offer educational and health services.[28]

In parallel with these utopias designed by individuals or small groups, official spokespersons of the industrial world, who in the early 1990s had already launched reflection on these subjects, made their positions known in 1993. The documents put out by the main employee unions of the telecommunications[29] and computer industries,[30] or representatives of industry as a whole,[31] all presented a "vision" of the information society and information highway. This term was used in all the reports. For computer scientists, for example, "the information infrastructure of the future will revolutionize the way individuals relate with one another by enabling us to work together, collaborate, and access and generate information without regard to geographical boundaries. It will enable fundamental changes in the way we educate our children, train and retrain our workers, earn a living, manufacture products, deliver services of all kinds, and interact with family and friends."[32] This infrastructure was much more than a network; it was also a set of applications and services available to all, at any time and in any place. In macroeconomic terms, "there is no doubt that information infrastructure helps create jobs and drive economic growth."[33] But it was also seen as the best way of treating a number of urgent social problems such as health, education, and pollution.

These documents clearly defined the respective role of industry (building and commercializing information highways) and the state. The state first had to develop a common vision of information highways, in cooperation with industry, and to mobilize the nation. One of the employer's unions suggested that the president "declare the national information infrastructure a new national technology challenge."[34] The state should then act as a driving force and an example by defining a regulatory framework, boosting research, and using these technologies itself. Its power should thus impact more on supply than on demand.

Apart from these general perspectives, firms participated more closely in the debate launched by the presidency by presenting their own technical views on the development of information highways. Each industrial sector made specific proposals that took into account its role in the field and its technological competencies. However, these proposals soon proved to be contradictory and within a few months a utopia had turned into an industrial conflict. In reality, this conflict had already started to develop in the 1990s, when technological progress had allowed the use of cabled networks for telephony, and the telephone network was adapted to the transmission of television. Eventually the two networks started to invest in a new technique, fiber optics. In a political context where deregulation was a key orientation, the government wanted to create competition in local networks dominated by monopolies.[35]

To prepare this new era of convergence between telephone and cable, companies in both sectors started to launch various experiments.[36] Despite their opposition, they shared the same vision of the short-term information highway markets that these experiments were supposed to prefigure. Television on demand (choice of a program in a base for immediate viewing) and e-commerce were the two "killer applications," as marketing people put it. In some cases distance games, video telephony, and video conferencing were added.[37] This common vision and the fact that companies often lacked competencies in areas that historically were not part of their core business, sometimes transformed competition into union.

During the fall of 1993 several mergers and buyouts were prepared between telephone and cable companies. This "cable-phone mania" received extensive media coverage, especially since the planned merger between Bell Atlantic and TCI was to be the biggest in the history of the U.S. stock exchange. Although it foundered a few months later, these huge financial maneuvers enhanced the credibility of information highways. From all this agitation the national press concluded that if such industrial restructuring was envisaged to prepare for information highways, it was because the stakes were very high.[38]

In the final analysis, companies perceived information highways not only as a grand project offering attractive prospects that the state had to boost, but also as a challenge to the boundaries among telecommunications, the broadcasting media, and computers, namely, as technological convergence. Some companies that were not leaders in technological change wanted to safeguard their positions; others adopted a more offensive approach and tried to obtain competitive advantages in the new legislative framework accompanying the establishment of information highways.

The Civil Society Arena
Some representatives of civil society had also been mobilizing for a long time to promote network computing. We have already mentioned

Educom in the education field, which, like Computer Professionals for Social Responsibility (CPSR), was a key player in public debate. But many other institutions in civil society also participated. In July 1993 about forty organizations took the initiative to create a roundtable on telecommunications policy. This national coordination was soon joined by over two hundred organizations. It organized public conferences and circulated many documents that were debated on the Internet.

Even though, as the CPSR noted, there was consensus on the fact that the national information infrastructure had to meet public interest objectives, the play of particular interests was likely to cause this general principle to be forgotten. James Duderstadt, chancellor of Michigan University and member of Educom, proposed that the network be built by a state enterprise and financed by taxing users. He considered this to be the only way of ensuring that the network was truly universal.[39]

Four other topics regularly appeared in proposals by civil society:

• the *diversity of information sources*: information must not be controlled by a few operators; network managers must not choose the information that circulates by favoring certain content suppliers or blocking others' access;

• commercial trade must not replace *free noncommercial communication*: there must be a free space for public debate at the center of information highways, a burgeoning of new electronic public forums;

• *information of public interest* supplied by the state or by citizens must remain freely available;

• finally, the network must guarantee the *privacy* of the data transported.

Negotiation among Different Social Worlds

Gore associated the information highway utopia, widely diffused during the presidential campaign in the latter half of 1992, with a relatively precise project: the state would finance and build a national fiber-optic network while the services would be provided by the private sector under public sector supervision.[40] This schema is very similar to the one that served to finance the Internet. However, the project was no longer set in the world of research, the traditional area of federal government investments; it had moved out into American society where a basic infrastructure was to be built for all. This clearly corresponds to the tradition of electric networks developed at the time of the New Deal.[41] The state's project to provide tomorrow's infrastructure was associated with an industrial policy design. A member of the Clinton administration's provisional team commented: "I think the telecommunications industry is not moving very rapidly. If the Federal Government sets out to build a high-speed digital infrastructure, that will be a kind of competitive spur. You will have competition between private and public sectors and that would be a wonderful thing for the infrastructure."[42]

But competition created in this way was unacceptable to national telecommunication operators such as AT&T which thus lost an opportunity to diversify. In December 1992, during a meeting between the future Clinton administration and industrial leaders, AT&T chairman Robert Allen fiercely criticized Gore.[43] The year 1993 was to be one of renegotiation of the Democrat's project in order to take industrial players' positions into account first, with those of civil society taking second place.

In February a blueprint of the new government's technology policy, co-signed by the president and vice president and made public in Silicon Valley, stipulated that information highways would be "constructed by the private sector but encouraged by federal policy and technology developments."[44] A *Newsweek* journalist commented: "Clearly the administration hasn't discouraged the rhetoric of revolution. But the most far-reaching ideas have quietly disappeared."[45]

To implement the policies announced in February, a task force on information infrastructure was set up. It submitted a report (the Agenda for Action) in September, proposing several priorities for federal policy. The first consisted in promoting investment by the private sector and in modifying the legislative framework accordingly. The second concerned equality of access, thus responding to one of civil society's preoccupations: "As a matter of fundamental fairness, this nation cannot accept a division of our people among telecommunications or information haves and have-nots. The administration is committed to developing a broad, modern concept of Universal Service—one that would emphasize giving all Americans who desire it easy, affordable access to advanced communication and information services, regardless of income, disability or location."[46] The third priority concerned innovation. In addition to research grants, the report suggested financing experimental services. This point corresponded to a broad consensus in all interest groups. Finally, the last priority proposed that the state make a large part of public information available online. This was also something that certain companies and many civil society organizations wanted. Several states had already launched similar policies.

This total modification of the initial technical project was the result of the process of negotiation engaged in by Gore and the Clinton administration with representatives of the industrial lobbies and organizations in civil society. Behind a largely shared utopia, the projects of the different actors were so antagonistic that consensus could be reached only on a small part of the program concerning the environment of information highways. One could say that the boundary-object that was negotiated was virtually empty. Apart from changes to the law, the new financing provided for in the program for experimentation was minimal, approximately $30 million per year. Only about 100 projects were funded compared to the 1,000 grant applications filed in 1994 and 1,800 in 1995.[47] Even though the information highway utopia resulted in no nationwide program, it did mobilize many actors.

From Technical Utopia to Political Ideology

A Slogan in Search of a Mission

Even when consensus has been reached, it is still possible to expand the debate. The Agenda for Action took on board the proposal of several lobbies to create a national information infrastructure council. This body was created by the government at the beginning of 1994. All the actors in the debate (telecom operators, television networks, film companies, unions, and organizations from civil society) were represented on it, but its influence was weak since the information highway project had been abandoned. The members of this council consequently produced a federative utopia grouping together elements of each party's individual utopia, but this discourse lacked the mobilizing force characterizing that of the previous year. We thus see that the role of the technological *imaginaire* differs, depending on its position in the decision-making process.

Before the decision the utopia can lay the foundations for a great project and mobilize actors. Afterward, it often simply accompanies a project decided on other bases, and it becomes a legitimizing ideology. Despite their differences, all the members of the council shared the same vision of the future: they considered that a highly computerized society was better than a less computerized one. But this discourse also served as an illusion, masking reality. Even though there were no more grand technological projects, and even though the great fiber-optic network was never built, reference to information highways remained frequent. It was a slogan in search of a mission.[48]

Other utopian perspectives nevertheless appeared, those of local communities which largely replaced the discourse on industrial policy of 1991 and 1992. The information superhighway was no longer a grand national project; instead, it was believed that it would "first be built and used and . . . generate its greatest effect at the community level."[49]

In one of its documents[50] the council tried to promote community uses. It cited many edifying examples of old people, groups of Boy Scouts, isolated college students, and Navajo Indians who were connected to information highways. The technology used was not always specified; it may have been a CD-ROM or, most likely, the Internet.

What we have here is a prospective and imaginative discourse that explores the various possibilities of an information society presenting alternatives to existing techniques. The idea is no longer to launch a grand national network managed or financed by the state, but to allow initiatives launched by businesses or communities of interest to flourish. Whereas in the former case the idea was to push back frontiers, to send a man to the moon, in the latter the utopia was one of small is beautiful. In fact this tension between large and micro projects is a common feature of American culture. After all, the Western frontier epic was a combination of a multitude of small personal epics, those of all the individual pioneers on their land. This longstanding tradition has reappeared today in the high-tech world.

Information Highways, a Liberal Ideology

While the advisory council on information infrastructure organized hearings, Gore explained the Clinton government's new policy as defined by the Agenda for Action. The information highway utopia was henceforth part of a social and technological revolution. From a social point of view, Gore emphasized that, unlike current trends in the mass media, citizens would become the suppliers of information and would add value to the community and the economy.[51] From a technological point of view, the revolution would result from the convergence of telecommunication, computer, and broadcasting technologies.

On all these points, Gore noted that consensus existed among the different actors and that it was up to the government to set clear objectives in order to be a catalyst of common actions. He hoped that state institutions and industries would unite "to connect and provide access to the National Information Infrastructure for every classroom, every library and every hospital and clinic in the entire United States of America."[52] To concretize this alliance between public and private that replaced formerly conflictual relations between the two, Gore proposed five main principles: private-sector investments; competition; a flexible regulatory framework; open access; and a universal service. These principles clearly had no direct link with the construction of information highways. In reality, they were the underpinnings of a telecommunications liberalization policy that had been launched by the preceding Republican governments, along with a specifically Democratic position on universal access. In just over one year, Clinton and Gore had abandoned their grand technological program. They relied on the effervescence triggered by the announcement of this project to revive the telecommunications reform bill that had been lying dormant in Congress.

In subsequent months, the term "information highway" became synonymous with telecommunications liberalization. The technological utopia became an ideology used to legitimize a liberal policy that had difficulty being fully accepted. The term "national information infrastructure" concealed a liberalization policy behind an interventionist façade. Discourse was no longer intended to define the future, to mobilize an entire nation, as in the utopian mode; on the contrary, it was designed to legitimize a policy by distorting reality. In the framework of the new liberal and anti-interventionist government policy, it is difficult to see the sense of a grand technological ambition—unless we consider, like John

Malone, chairman of TCI (one of the first cable operators), that "the government should be mainly a cheer-leader."[53]

But it was probably at an international level that the ideological function of the discourse on information highways was most obvious. Here Gore had built the concept of a global information infrastructure, the international counterpart to the national information infrastructure. In a speech to the International Telecommunications Union (ITU) in Buenos Aires, he emphatically defined the role of information highways: "In a sense, the GII will be a metaphor for democracy itself. . . . The GII will not only be a metaphor for a functioning democracy, it will in fact promote the functioning of democracy by greatly enhancing the participation of citizens in decision-making. And it will greatly promote the ability of nations to cooperate with each other. I see a new Athenian Age of democracy forged in the fora the GII will create."[54]

To realize this utopia and promote democracy, development, and peace, Gore simply proposed that the ITU adopt the five political principles he had set down a few months earlier. The ideological message of this speech can be summed up as follows: democracy = information highways = deregulation. In this sequence of translations, the first relates to an idea of technical determinism (a new technique promotes democracy), and the second to a political choice (deregulation promotes the construction of that technique). The shortcut (democracy = deregulation) aims to produce an illusion, a mask ideology.

The Internet, the Latest Avatar of Information Highways

U.S. industrialists managed to persuade the Clinton administration to abandon its project to build fiber-optic networks capable of transporting vast quantities of data. While the idea was that they would take care of this new technology themselves, we may rightly wonder what exactly the private sector has actually accomplished. It has been content to undertake market studies and to run about forty experiments.

In the fall of 1993, the huge annual ICT trade fair in Las Vegas, Comdex, afforded an opportunity to take the industry's pulse. Behind the euphoria of information networks disillusionment started to show. One consultant commented: "We talk as if all this was going to happen tomorrow, but that's not the case."[55] A study found that movies on demand, then considered as the leading product of information highways, would not exceed two million consumers within five years.[56] Nor were the results of the first experiments much cause for optimism. In Colorado, guinea pig subscribers viewed an average of 2.5 movies per month—fewer than the monthly average rented from video stores.[57]

A few months later *Business Week* concluded an article on technical problems encountered in the Orlando experiment with the following comment: "Nothing is sure, except that there will be a lot of delay and disillusionment before information highways exist."[58] It was in this context of disenchantment that we began to witness the emergence of another medium, born not in a market context but in a culture of free exchange: the Internet. As *Time* noted in late 1993, what cable and telephone operators planned to sell, the "Internet was already providing free-of-charge."[59]

At the same time *Business Week* wondered whether information highways were "not part of the wrong direction." In reporting on a book on communities of Internauts, the journalist highlighted the following sentence: "People don't want more information and entertainment, they want to spend their time getting to know each other in cyberspace."[60] Within a few months, the Internet was to become the main subject of interest as regards ICT. Between September 1993 and November 1994, the three main U.S. news magazines all devoted a special section to it,[61] although *Time* and *Newsweek* had already published special issues on information highways in the spring of 1993.[62] Figure 1.1 clearly shows that from the spring of 1994 on, the Internet was cited more than information highways in the English-language press. By early 1995 the ratio was one to four.

Themes in the media discourse had totally changed. In the autumn of 1995 journalist Steven Levy summed up this development as follows: "If the dream of having 500 TV channels is an outdated future, the new future is Internet on your computer screen." To stress the point, he compared the Internet to an iceberg that had sunk the *Titanic* of interactive five-hundred-channel television.[63] Although the Internet was generally

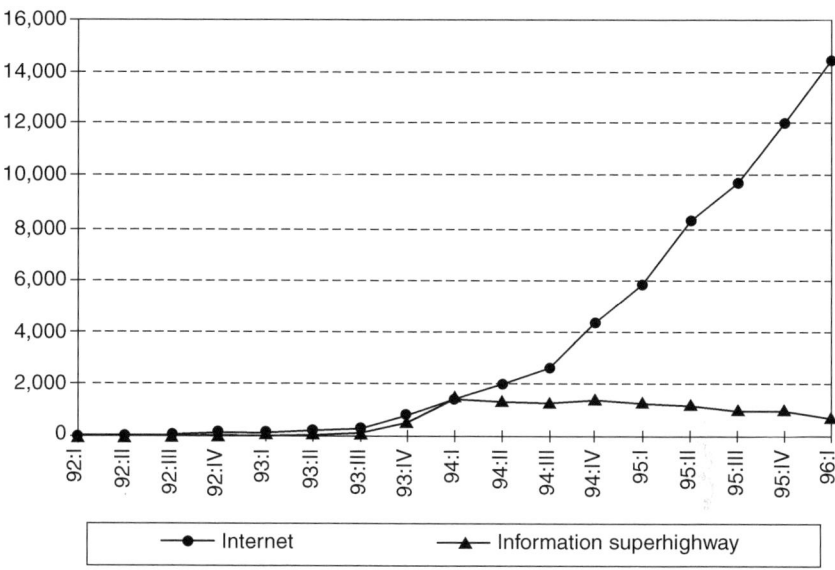

Figure 1.1
Number of articles on the Internet and information highways in the fifty most read English-language newspapers and magazines (per quarter, from 1992 to 1996). *Source*: Majpap Nexis Library Archive, quoted in Kahin, "The U.S. National Information Infrastructure Initiative," p. 185.

seen as a substitute for the preceding mode, some journalists linked the two systems and presented the Net as the prototype of information highways.[64]

The White House was willing to endorse this new definition of information highways, and both the president and vice president obtained an email address in June 1993. After a year they received 10–15 percent of their mail that way.[65]

As is frequently the case in the history of communication techniques,[66] one project was replaced by another that had been developed in a different context. But the communication *imaginaire* is general and malleable enough to adapt to different technical systems. The shift was particularly easy to achieve in this case since some of the founding fathers of discourse on information highways were themselves children of the Internet world (academia, think tanks) or knew of its existence (Gore). Yet the assertion that the Internet was the first information highway masks the failure of a project, that of interactive television defended by cable operators, and the success—at least for a while—of a free and convivial conception of communication defended by the first Internauts. The last avatar of information highways still has two faces: one utopian and the other ideological.

2

The Internet, the Scientific Community's Ideal

The Internet, at the forefront of the media scene in early 1994, was not a potentially new technology or technical project that could be substituted for information highways; it was a technical system that had been developing underground for almost three decades. Its use was, however, still very limited. A survey in October 1993 found that 6 percent of Americans used online information services at home and 8 percent at work. In 1989 these figures had stood at 1.7 percent and 2.5 percent respectively.[1] Thus, the Internet, which accounted for only a part of online services at the time, was largely unknown to the general public.

During its first twenty years of existence (1969–1989), the new technology developed in very specific circles: initially among researchers in computer science, then throughout the entire academic community and, at the same time, in counterculture communities. The innovation framework was therefore very particular: a nonmarket community in which the designers were also the users, so that during the entire period the creators of the Internet were under no pressure to sell their technique in the market. All they had to do was develop a system capable of meeting their own needs, within the limits of a budget based essentially on government funding. In this type of innovation representations of a technique are relatively uniform; they correspond to specific social worlds. Moreover, the usual tension between designers' and users' *imaginaire* is absent since the two groups overlap.

In this chapter,[2] I study the creation of this new framework of use. Unlike the preceding chapter, we see not the *imaginaire* of politicians or company directors, but the discourses and practices of the actors directly involved with the technique, especially those that Hughes called the "system builders."[3] Finally, and this is the main difference compared to information highways, the utopias that I present were to be embodied in a technical system that worked and really was used.

From Calculation Computing to Network Communication

If we are to understand the intentions of the creators of the Internet, we need to consider the situation of computer science in the early 1950s and 1960s, in relation to which they defined their approach.

Time-Sharing Computers and Man-Computer Symbiosis

At the end of the 1950s, computers were still rare. There were only about five thousand in the world, and they were expensive, and access was never direct. After writing their programs, programmers used punch cards to load them onto their machines. If the programs ran as expected they would take the results and hand the machine over to the next person. If, however, there was a mistake, they would have to adjust the program and reintroduce it later. Computers were therefore simply tools for doing the calculations presented to them. Moreover, the central processing unit (CPU) was active for part of the time only. To improve the performance and efficiency of the calculation, computer scientists conceived of time-sharing, in which machines would carry out several tasks simultaneously, thereby giving all users the impression that they were using the computer independently. For Maurice Wilkes, lecturer at Cambridge University: "Time-sharing will enable the super-fast machines now being constructed to be fully loaded."[4] Other researchers saw this technological change as an opportunity to alter computer scientists' work: "[They will] communicate directly to the high-speed elements, to add instructions, to change a program at will or to obtain additional answers from the machine on a time-sharing basis with other programs using the machine simultaneously."[5] Finally, in a broader sense, some saw time-sharing as interactive use of a computer not by a single programmer but simultaneously by several, each with a specific terminal subservient to the machine (slave-master relationship).

The concepts of communication and interaction with computers that appeared along with initial reflection on time-sharing were also present, although less systematically, in Joseph Licklider's programmatic article

"Man-Computer Symbiosis." This psychophysiologist who worked with computer specialists as an expert on the human factor had the opportunity to use one of the first minicomputers, the PDP-1. With this machine, far smaller than any other computer at the time, it was possible to enter programs and data on a strip of paper, so that interaction became possible: "The PDP-1 opened me up to ideas about how people and machines like this might operate together in the future," he recalled in the 1980s.[6] These ideas were gathered together in his article, in which he reflected on the process of intellectual work, noting that "thinking time was devoted mainly to activities that were essentially clerical or mechanical . . . and that can be performed more effectively by machines than by men." The solution, he suggested, could be "to create a symbiotic relation between a man and a fast information-retrieval and data processing machine, however, it seems evident that the cooperative interaction would greatly improve the thinking process."[7] Despite its originality, Licklider's thinking corresponded to the perspective of some of the large projects already under way at MIT for the defense force, and in which he participated. In particular, he worked on the computer interface design of the SAGE system (computer assisted antiaircraft defense network), devised to associate humans and machines in a large unified technological system.[8]

The following year, at a conference held at MIT on the future of computer technology, Licklider again described what computers could do for intellectual work: "In due course it will be part of the formulation of problems; part of real-time thinking, problem solving, doing of research, conducting of experiments, getting into the literature and finding references. . . . And it will mediate and facilitate communication among human beings."[9] Licklider's project contrasted with a prevalent belief at the time, that the computer ought to be an autonomous intelligent tool capable of replacing the human brain. John von Neumann, one of the founding fathers of computer technology as we know it today, had, in fact, designed his machine as a copy of the human brain, which would eventually be able to replace humans. The idea of man-machine symbiosis, argued by Licklider, is somewhat different. With it we leave the world of artificial human brains and enter that of human-machine collaboration. The purpose is "to think in interaction with a computer in the same way that you think with a colleague whose competence supplements your own."[10] Finally, he wrote, "The hope is that, in not too many years, human brains and computing machines will be coupled together very tightly, and that the resulting partnership will think as no human brain has ever thought and process data in a way not approached by the information-handling machines we know today." He added: "Those years should be intellectually the most creative and exciting in the history of mankind."[11] Linguist Y. Bar-Hillel[12] expressed similar ideas in his paper on man-machine dialogue at a conference at MIT.

Two years after publication of his article, Licklider was put in charge of the Information Processing Techniques Office (IPTO) and the Behavioral Sciences program by the Advanced Research Projects Agency (ARPA), the new Defense Ministry research agency. At the time, the Cold War was at its peak and the U.S. defense administration played a key role in funding university research. In 1965 it supplied 23 percent of all academic research funds, as opposed to 13 percent from the civil National Research Foundation.[13] Licklider thus had substantial budgets. From the outset he gave a series of lectures on computers for military purposes, in which he argued that "a computer should be something anyone could interact with directly, eliminating computer operators as the middlemen in solving their problems."[14] He used the programmatic guidelines of "man-computer symbiosis" to get his former university colleagues in Boston to agree to certain projects. "I wanted interactive computing, I wanted time-sharing. I wanted themes like: computers are as much for communication as they are for calculation."[15]

Apart from these very general objectives, Licklider had no particular project with set aims. Instead, he supported the leading universities in computer technology. That was how, with his help, MIT computer specialists launched the Multiple Access Computer (MAC) project to enable a large number of users to use the same machine. Licklider was so enthusiastic about the project that he took charge of it shortly after leaving ARPA. The MAC project was more than a new generation of computer technology, it was a more collective way for computer scientists to practice their profession. Programmers were confronted with their colleagues' work, which got them thinking about writing programs that others could reuse. As Fernando Corbato and Robert Fano, the first leaders of the MAC project, wrote: "The time-sharing computer system can unite a group of investigators in a cooperative search for the solution to a common problem, or it can serve as a community pool of knowledge and skill on which anyone can draw according to his needs."[16]

It was with this project and similar research conducted in other universities, especially in California, that the idea of a computer network or of an intergalactic computer network, as described by Licklider, started taking shape. To illustrate the concept, Licklider took the example of a researcher with a set of digital data to analyze, who tries by trial and error to find the curve that will accurately explain the data. In order to do so, he will try different available programs, and once he has found the right curve, he will archive everything so that the connection established between the results of the experiment and the theory may be accessible to other researchers. This network project also contained the wish to construct common tools for an entire research community, and to build on the experience and computer programs of all its members. Licklider believed this goal could best be achieved by developing research on man-machine interaction, time-sharing, and computer networks.[17] Seven years later he reviewed his action: "After joining Project MAC [in 1967], I began to realize that the then-prevalent man-computer communication via typewriter was rather far removed from the fast-response graphic interaction of which my dreams were made and that the 'online community' was not so much a community of users as an in-group of computer programmers. . . . It seems to me that the efforts of the 1960s fell somewhat short of what is needed and achievable in very close man-computer interaction . . . and quite short of the dream of an 'online community.'"[18]

Although Licklider's visions had not yet become reality, significant research had been done in the 1960s. The fruit of that groundwork was to be reaped in the following decade in the areas of interface tools and network computing.

The Interface and Enhancing Intelligence
In the early 1970s, a number of technological perspectives similar to Licklider's appeared in the writings of various specialists, particularly mathematicians or computer scientists who recommended "close man-computer interaction"[19] or imagined computers as "extending

man's intellect."[20] But it was unquestionably Douglas Englebart, a California researcher, who considered the question in greatest depth. According to Howard Rheingold's hagiographic account, when Englebart entered Stanford Research in 1957, he presented "his ideas on getting computers to interact with people, in order to augment their intellect:

How many people have you already told about that? asked [his interlocutor].
None, you're the first I've told.
Good. Now don't tell anyone else. It sounds too crazy. It will prejudice people against you.[21]

Despite this warning, Engelbart wrote an ambitious document on the subject, entitled "Augmenting Human Intellect." In the introduction he described the project:

By "augmenting human intellect" we mean increasing the capability of a man to approach a complex problem situation, to gain comprehension to suit his particular needs, and to derive solutions to problems. Increased capability in this respect is taken to mean a mixture of the following: more-rapid comprehension, better comprehension, the possibility of gaining a useful degree of comprehension in a situation that previously was too complex, speedier solutions, better solutions, and the possibility of finding solutions to problems that before seemed insoluble.[22]

After describing the characteristics of human intelligence, he showed that computers could be used to increase performance. He saw them not as calculating machines, but as tools for symbolic manipulation; they would be able to augment intellectual capacities. He believed that machines should enable people to perform very simple intellectual operations, such as writing and correcting a written text. Individuals could thus spend less time drafting texts and devote part of their energy to more complex intellectual tasks. The best way of organizing or reorganizing words in a text was by being able to touch them, to transform them manually. Engelbart explains: "Symbols with which the human represents the concepts he is manipulating can be arranged before his eyes, moved, stored, recalled, operated upon according to extremely complex rules—all in very rapid response to a minimum amount of information supplied by the human, by means of special cooperative technological devices."[23] His interest in these small material devices led Engelbart to focus on interfaces.[24]

The question of graphics was already of interest to ARPA. In 1962 Sutherland, Licklider's successor at the military research agency, developed the first graphics software package, Sketchpad. After his appointment at the head of ARPA he financed Engelbart's research team, called the Augmented Human Intellect Research Center. Their laboratory developed and tested individual workstations linked to a computer on a time-sharing basis. Each of the stations had a visual display unit and several dialogue tools: alphanumerical keyboard, mouse, and five-key chord keyset. Other interfaces that had been tried, such as the light-pen, were not retained. The principle of "windows" by "cutting a hole" in the screen and seeing an image in that space was tested. But the laboratory's most original feature was that it not only produced technological tools, it also ran experiments with them. "Thus the research group is also the subject group in the experiment. . . . This 'bootstrap' group has the interesting assignment of developing tools and techniques to make it more effective at carrying out its assignment."[25] For instance, after using the word processor, one of the designer-users noted: "I find that I write faster and more freely, pouring thoughts and trial words onto the screen with much less inhibition, finding it easy to repair mistakes or wrong choices."[26] Experimental uses were not only individual but also collective. For example, certain documents were accessible collectively on the computer system. Similarly, the laboratory experimented with online conferences, commented on at length in a new reference document cosigned by Licklider and Taylor, at the time head of the computing department at ARPA: "In a few years . . . men will be able to communicate more effectively through a machine than face-to-face. That is a rather startling thing to say, but it is our conclusion."[27] They also introduced the idea of online communities: "They will be communities not of common location, but of *common interest*. . . . The impact of that fact will be very great both on the individual and on society. First, life will be happier for the online individual because the people with whom one interacts most strongly will be selected more by commonality of interests and goals than by accident of proximity. Second, communication will be more effective and productive, and therefore more enjoyable."[28]

The Computer Network
While time-sharing had enabled a group of about one hundred computer scientists to use the same machine, the computer network seemed to be

the next step allowing thousands of users to share the same resources. ARPA, in particular, wanted to link the seventeen research centers with which it was working. Tom Marill, who conducted one of the first experiments linking two computers, commented that there is no "common ground for exchanging programs, personnel, experience, or ideas."[29] In 1966 he launched the first study on this subject. The report concluded that "the principal motivation for considering the implementation of a network is that a user of any cooperating installation would have access to the programs in the libraries of all the other cooperating installations."[30] Insofar as his aim was to put an end to incompatibility among computer systems, he noted in another report that "participating in the network will not require adhesion to a particular norm."[31]

Similar projects were also developed by the computer manufacturers IBM and Control Data. In 1968 Control Data opened an international network called Cybernet, connecting a number of computing centers.[32] However, these computer companies had a different vision of computing; they developed computer-dependent software, ruling out all communication among different machines. They had also opted for a star-shaped structure, with a center and a periphery, where sites were not all equal.

Toward the end of 1966, the directors of ARPA agreed to Taylor's plan to build a computer network. Taylor justified the project by the fact that it would obviate the need constantly to buy new equipment for university departments working for the Pentagon. Each team would thus have access to the most powerful computers and to machines or programs produced by other manufacturers (since in those days different computers were incompatible).[33]

Apart from this wish to enhance the productivity of computers, there was also the goal of strengthening cooperation among computer scientists. Robert Fano, one of the leaders of the time-sharing project MAC, subsequently recalled "friendships being born out of using somebody else's program, people communicating through the system and them meeting by accident and saying 'oh, that's you.' All sorts of things. It was a nonreproducible community phenomenon."[34] It was precisely these communities that Licklider and Taylor wanted not to reproduce but to extend. In their 1968 article they note:

Today the online communities are separated from one another functionally as well as geographically. Each member can look only to the processing, storage, and software capability of the facility upon which his community is centered. But now the move is on to interconnect the separate communities and thereby transform them into, let us call it a supercommunity. The hope is that interconnection will make available to all the members of the communities the programs and data resources of the entire supercommunity.[35]

To implement this project, the ARPA team made highly innovative technical choices concerning networks. Unlike the telephone where the user is given a connection for a certain amount of time, project leader Lawrence Roberts[36] opted for transmission by packets, which seemed better suited to computerized data. Each message was divided into small packets of data that were then transmitted in a fraction of a second on the telephone network, not necessarily by the same route. Upon arrival, the message was reconstituted. This system had several advantages: first, it meant that users did not have to rent a specific telephone line for long periods since packets of different origins could be mixed; second, it was highly flexible because in the event of problems on a line, messages could automatically be rerouted on another. This network architecture seemed to have been inspired by research carried out at MIT by Leonard Kleinrock[37] (1964) and, to a lesser extent, by a report written prior to that by Paul Baran from Rand Corporation for the Defense Department. The latter report had a very different aim, however, insofar as the authors' mission had been to design a network capable of withstanding a Soviet nuclear attack.[38]

Roberts made a second essential choice: he decided to place a specific computer, the Interface Message Processor (IMP), as the interface between the network and the host computers. This technical architecture left a large degree of autonomy to each computer site that could organize itself as it wished, regarding equipment and software, and could even create a subnetwork linking several machines. The only constraint was the need to be able to link to the IMP. These technical choices to decentralize would be repeated in the organization of work required for the development of a network to be known as Arpanet or "Resource Sharing Computer Networks."

Arpanet was built by a small Boston company, BBN (Bolt, Beranek and Newman), that had close ties to MIT. The organization was closed and academic. Frank Heart, the head of the team, was "not just man-ager"; he had technical skills as well and spoke of his team as "a labor of love," while his engineers referred to their work as "fun." [39]

BBN did not involve itself in technical problems posed by data exchange beyond the IMP, which it saw as the universities' responsibility. Unlike the time-sharing system with its master-slave relation between the central computer and its terminals, in Arpanet the host computers were on an equal footing. Communication protocol between hosts therefore had to be defined in a cooperative manner. The universities entrusted young graduates or students with the task of developing these protocols. A task force (Network Working Group), consisting of representatives from the four universities concerned,[40] was soon formed on a cooperative and egalitarian basis. To highlight these principles, the minutes of its meetings were called "Request for Comments" (RFCs). This was an open system since "notes may be produced at any site by anybody,"[41] in which the rules of the game were set from the start. The content was open, without any constraint on presentation: "philosophical positions without examples or other specifics, specific suggestions or implementa-tion techniques without introductory or background explication, and explicit questions without any attempted answers are all acceptable."[42] This was a scientific world where scientific skills predominated over hier-archy. "We hope to promote the exchange and discussion of considerably less than authoritative ideas,"[43] said the authors of the founding text who had been influenced by the anticonformist and antiauthoritarian climate of West Coast universities in the late 1970s.

Apart from scientific work, interpersonal relations subsequently devel-oped among members of the group. Three members noted in the follow-ing year that "the resulting mixture of ideas, discussions, disagreements, and resolutions has been highly refreshing and beneficial to all involved, and we regard the human interaction as a valuable by-product of the main effort."[44]

Twenty years later, one of the participants in the Network Working Group attested to this way of working: "For me, participation in the development of the Arpanet and the Internet protocols has been very exciting. . . . There were a lot of very bright people all working more or less in the same direction, led by some very wise people in the funding agency. The result was to create a community of network researchers who believed strongly that collaboration is more powerful than competition among researchers."[45] These same principles can be found in technical choices. An NWG document noted: "Restrictions concerning character sets, programming languages, etc., would not be tolerated and we avoided such restrictions."[46] The Arpanet community likewise demanded that BBN, the network constructor, share the source code, although BBN initially refused.[47]

Development of a Network of Computer Scientists

A Tool for Interaction

Arpanet did not remain at the experimental stage for very long. A year after its creation, in January 1970, the network already consisted of thirteen research centers. In April 1972 this figure had swelled to twenty-three, and by July 1975 to fifty-seven. In 1971 the project leader, Lawrence Roberts, considered the network to be operational and decided that "true user activity could usefully begin."[48] The first application proposed by the network was file transfers. It thus became possible to use the computer resources of other research centers as originally planned. As Roberts and Wessler had noted in 1970: "Currently, each computer center in the country is forced to recreate all of the software and data files it wishes to utilize. In many cases this involves complete reprogramming of software or reformatting the data files. This duplication is extremely costly. . . . With a successful network, the core problem resources would be severely reduced."[49]

In reality, this use was very limited. It is estimated that in 1976 under 15 percent of computer activity stemmed from distant queries.[50] As Arpanet historian Janet Abbate notes, the majority of the network's capacity remained unused in the early years because computer teams were reluctant to lend outsiders use of their machines. Moreover, it was difficult for anyone other than the designers of the network to use it. An outside consultant noted in a 1972 Arpanet Study Final Report that "the network user, new and established, is probably the most neglected element within the present development atmosphere. The mechanisms for assisting and encouraging new members are relatively informal or nonexistent."[51]

Another potential use of the network had not been included in the initial project: electronic mail. Roberts considers that "it was not a major motivation for a scientific computer network."[52] Yet an email system was developed informally. Although an email program existed in time-sharing computers, it took on an entirely new dimension when users were geographically distant. This use of Arpanet was particularly successful. According to an ARPA study, in 1973 email accounted for three-quarters of all traffic on the network.[53] Observers at the time commented: "A surprising aspect of the message service is the unplanned, unanticipated, and unsupported nature of its birth and early growth. It just happened, and its early history has seemed more like the discovery of a natural phenomenon than the deliberate development of a new technology."[54] Email spread all the more naturally because it allowed users to short-circuit what they called "the teletypewriter priesthood of traditional electronic mail systems, such as Telex, TWX, and most facsimile services."[55] Despite this success, email was not mentioned at the time in the different presentations of Arpanet, as if it were not serious enough for a scientific network or, on the contrary, as if this usage had become so natural that it was not worth mentioning.

It was only later, in the late 1970s, that this new practice was discussed, prompting Licklider to revise his analyses. Whereas in 1968 he foresaw the development of online communities and machine-mediated communication, ten years later, in a new document written with Albert Vezza, he compared the computer network to the telephone and demonstrated its superiority:

It soon became obvious that the Arpanet was becoming a human-communication medium with very important advantages over normal U.S. mail and over telephone calls. . . . The formality and perfection that most people expect in a typed letter did not become associated with network messages, probably because the network was so much faster, so much more like the telephone. . . . Among the advantages of the network message services over the telephone were the fact that one could proceed immediately to the point without having to engage in small talk first, that the message services produced a preservable record, and that the sender and receiver did not have to be available at the same time.[56]

This informal electronic communication was particularly intense because use of the network was free (IMPs had no billing function[57]) and messages were exchanged between people who knew one another. Thus, in 1975 Arpanet had about one thousand electronic addresses[58] and most of the traffic was local. An estimated 60 to 80 percent of the messages at the time were transmitted by people belonging to the same geographic site.[59] An Arpanet community was thus formed. As an "Arpanaut" remarked: "The closed community of the Arpanet and its research orientation yield a situation different from what could be expected outside."[60] Some started to imagine that this new medium could possibly be diffused outside, and create new social relations: "We in the ARPA community (and no doubt many others outside it) have come to realize that we have in our hands something very big, and possibly very important. It is now plain to all of us that message service over computer networks has enormous potential for changing the way communication is done in all sectors of our society: military, civilian government, and private."[61] Although this project took over ten years to realize, Arpanauts started in the latter half of the 1970s to explore nonacademic uses. Two California researchers created the game Adventure, the first computer version of Dragons and Dungeons, a highly complex role-play game.[62]

When all is said and done, Arpanet was used primarily to communicate, rather than to supply computer resources from a distance as its promoters originally intended.[63] It was as if the designers of the network wanted to maintain the type of cooperation they had developed when defining the technical system. This is a very specific characteristic of the new medium. Not only were its designers its main users for a long time, but the cooperative model on which its design was based constituted the actual content of its use.

A Tool for Cooperation

In parallel with the construction of Arpanet, Licklider's reflections, and Engelbart's experiments, a trial Computer Assisted Conference was held in 1970. Once again, the system had been developed with public funds, not from the military but from a government agency responsible for dealing with emergency situations. The Emergency Management Information System and Reference Index (EMISARI) was used to control the freezing of prices and wages decided by the Nixon administration. The idea was for participants to have access to the same data, for data to be transmitted from the various regions to Washington, for them to be annotated, and then for deferred, distant debates to be held. Eighty terminals linked by the telephone network participated in the operation. Murray Turoff, one of the main designers of this project, commented a few years later: "I think the ultimate possibility of computerized conferencing is to provide a way for human groups to exercise a 'collective intelligence' capability."[64]

We have here a computer tradition that I have not yet mentioned: the management tool. Turoff adds another dimension, that of a device which, by connecting people, creates collective intelligence. At the time, certain computer scientists developed operations research tools for corporate use, that is, methods of calculation used to choose parameters linked to one another by different constraints, for maximizing a mathematical function—a common situation in economics and management. Turoff was also in search of an optimum, although he thought that computers could be used to achieve it not through mathematical calculation but by making cooperation among individuals more effective. Such cooperation, however, required long and complex learning about the tools. The Electronic Information Exchange System (EIES) program, which replaced EMISARI, required eight hours of training and twenty hours of practice.[65]

Despite the highly confidential nature of this system, Murray Turoff published a book with Hiltz in 1978, entitled *The Network Nation: Human Communication via Computer*. In the preface the authors described their vision of the future: "We believe that [computer conferences] will eventually be as omnipresent as telephone and as revolutionary, in terms of facilitating the growth and emergence of vast networks of geographically dispersed persons who are nevertheless able to work and communicate with one another at no greater cost than if they were located a few blocks from one another."[66]

Indeed, of all the communication technologies invented in the twentieth century, none were adapted to group communication. Computer conferencing, on the other hand, enabled everyone to send and receive information at the time and place of their choice: "These systems allow a person meaningful, frequent, and regular communications with five to ten times more people than is possible with current common communication options. . . . When such systems become widespread . . . we will

become the Network Nation, exchanging vast amounts of both information and social-emotional communications with colleagues, friends and
strangers who share similar interests, who are spread out all over the
nation."[67]

The book then presented effective or expected uses of computer conferencing: teaching, political debate, family relations, friendships, science
and technology, and management. The latter uses were considered in
more detail. In the scientific field, small communities of researchers specialized in a particular domain constituted what certain sociologists
called "invisible colleges."[68] Researchers met one another from time to
time at conferences, exchanged preprints, and cooperated on certain
projects. Computer conferencing seemed particularly well-suited to this
type of cooperation. By contrast, in the corporate world it often met with
resistance: "By changing the communication channels in an organization, . . . we are also threatening the power of those whose positions in
the organization depend on control over the generation and dissemination of the information that flows through these channels. Such an innovation is thus likely to be seen by many as a usurpation, a threat."[69]
Behind the computer conference project appeared another ambition, that
of reshaping labor relations. It is probably this hope of reform that
explains the book's success. The computing magazine *Byte*, for example,
presented EMISARI as the founding software: "The history of computer
conferencing after EMISARI reads like the Bible's first chapter of
Mathew: EMISARI conceived . . . Discussion. Discussion begat EIES.
EIES begat Participate."[70] The origins of computer conferencing thus
became a legend in itself.

Use of network computing for scientific work was also theorized, in
the same year as *Network Nation*, by Joshua Lederberg. This Nobel
Prize winner for medicine was a skilled user of computers and, in his
own words, "an enthusiastic user" of Arpanet. He explained how,
thanks to email and the circulation of files, network computing enabled
scientists to work more efficiently. He showed that it had numerous
advantages compared to the telephone. Based on an experiment in the
medical research field, he pointed out that this new technology "has been
indispensable for the division of labor in drafting and criticizing compli-
cated research proposals: twenty people may be closely involved in a
product of 250 print pages."[71]

This experiment with cooperative scientific work was carried out at roughly the same time by Lynn Conway, an engineer at Xerox Park. Conway was the leader of a community of researchers in microelectronics, who wanted to define a new method for designing chips. The network made it possible to disseminate knowledge fast in the community concerned and to integrate immediate amendments: "The network provides the opportunity for rapid accumulation of sharable knowledge."[72] This system simultaneously facilitated collaboration and intense competition: "Students and researchers at MIT, Stanford, Caltec, Berkeley, etc., could visualize the state of the art of each other's stuff. These factors stimulated competition, which led to many ambitious projects."[73] Fifteen years later Mark Stefik, who published this text, considered that it was a paradigmatic example illustrating the stories of the Tower of Babel and Pentecost. Before Conway's project, specialists in microelectronics were all working on their own, with different tools. The highlight of the operation was its creation of a common language for describing chips. As a result, by the end of the project a scientific community existed. This process of collaboration/competition made possible by Arpanet also facilitated the constitution of the network, as previously shown. Thus, scientific cooperation was situated at the very core of the Arpanet.

A Community of Computer Scientists, Unix

In the 1970s most academic computer scientists used a computer language called Unix, developed by Bell laboratories, AT&T's research center.[74] This was the first system programmed in a language that was independent of the machine (C language). In addition, Unix was constructed as an assemblage of modules, each with its own particular function.[75] This computer operating system that had the unique capability of functioning on different types of computer was created for the needs of Bell, then the country's leading research center in the electronics industry.

Since U.S. legislation prohibited AT&T, the parent company of Bell laboratories, from marketing computer products, Bell sold Unix licenses very cheaply to the universities, its usual partners. The transaction was virtually noncommercial since AT&T supplied only the source code, without any documentation. Some universities published Unix manuals as a way of appropriating the new software.

This principle of open diffusion enabled the academic world to suggest or even to make amendments to programs, which could then be circulated throughout what was to become the Unix community. This mode of cooperative research was, moreover, part of software creators' projects. Fifteen years later one of them recounted: "What we wanted to preserve was not just a good programming environment . . . but a system around which a fellowship could form. We knew from experience that the essence of communal computing, as supplied by remote-access, time-shared machines, is not just to type programs into a terminal instead of a keypunch, but to encourage close communication."[76] In this context a group of Unix users (Usenix) from different universities started to form.

In 1978 a new version of Unix provided for the transmission of files from one machine to another. The protocol was called Unix to Unix Copy Program (UUCP). Bell laboratories were the first to use this new function, but the network also spread to the universities.[77] Unlike Arpanet, it used only telephone lines rather than a mixed network consisting of a backbone and telephone lines.

Usenet, the Poor Man's Arpanet

In the late 1970s and early 1980s, students from Duke University and University of North Carolina adapted the UUCP protocol to allow for document transmission. They launched a network between the two universities, called Usenet, short for "Unenix Network," although they had also thought of calling it Chaosnet or Spidernet.[78] The designers of this network, who presented their project at Usenix conferences, pointed out in one of their papers that "a goal of Usenet has been to give every Unix system the opportunity to join and benefit from a computer network (a poor man's Arpanet, if you will)."[79] The aim of Usenet was thus to facilitate cooperation within a community of computer scientists not connected to Arpanet. The documents exchanged, called articles, were grouped together in what were called newsgroups, as in newsletters. These newsgroups were in fact files into which the computer system sorted all articles sent on a given subject, and then sent to the people registered as members of the group.

This new computer network grew extremely fast. In 1982, three years after its creation, four hundred sites were linked to Usenet.[80] During the

Table 2.1
Distribution of newsgroups by subject in 1982 (in %)

	Usenet	Arpanet
Computing	40	56
Organization of newsgroups	12	9
Science and technology	14	13
Leisure	15	9
Sport	8	—
Debate, miscellaneous	11	13
No. of newsgroups	92	23

same period, Arpanet had only two hundred sites. The reason for Usenet's growth was that it catered to a potentially larger community, Unix users, and subsequently all computer specialists since the acronym Usenet changed its meaning to "User's Network." This community, excluded from Arpanet, managed to build a bridge between the two networks in 1982. "Usenauts" thus had access to the newsgroups that already existed on Arpanet. Traffic subsequently rose to about fifty texts (articles) per day.[81]

Owing to the archives that were constituted[82] it was possible to retrieve messages, examine group lists, and thus get an idea of the use made of the network. Over half the groups were involved in computing or organizing the network itself. Authors of new software used the network to make their work known. Everyone could ask for information or advice. Since the demand was collective, the requester's chances of receiving a reply were increased. Moreover, because that reply was archived, it could also serve other users.

The newsgroups (table 2.1) were also opportunities for debate on the respective advantages of a new system or protocol. There were, for example, groups on the bugs in different versions of Unix or on problems with the Usenet/Arpanet connection. Within Arpanet a group discussed a new protocol, the Tcp/Ip, subsequently to become a key element in the definition of the Internet. Nonprofessional uses also appeared, although more frequently on Usenet than on Arpanet which still lay in the shadow of the military. The subjects debated primarily concerned science and technology, which was hardly surprising for engineers, mathematicians, astronomers, and specialists in transport techniques. Even leisure activities were considered from a technical point of view: hackers, computer games (chess, video games), electroacoustic music. Both networks also included a group of science fiction fans and groups on diverse subjects, such as classified advertisements, job seeking, funny stories, and so on, as well as debates on subjects of general interest (e.g., taxes, suicide). These uses were not fundamentally different from those of the Arpanet mailing lists.[83] Ray Tomlinson, who developed the first message service software for this network, commented: "For most of the people with access to email, the word 'computer' figured prominently in their resume. Topics ranged from bug reports and meeting announcements to recipes for pretzels."[84] Arpanet mailing lists, like Usenet newsgroups, were also a medium for the publication of electronic journals. The head of a conference on computer networks in 1976 remarked: "It is interesting to note that many of the abstracts and several complete papers were delivered via electronic mail. . . . This practice is becoming quite common for some journals and newsletters, and is proving to be a viable medium for such tasks."[85] The idea of electronic journals started to circulate in the computing world. People started talking of a virtual journal,[86] and one of the subjects of the "net.usenix" newsgroup was the creation of an electronic newsletter on Unix.[87] Computer specialists on Unix were used to working together: "People often look at each other's code, comment on it in person and through interuser communication facilities, and take pieces of it for their own use. The ideas of programming teams and egoless programming fit into the Unix environment well, since they encourage sharing rather than isolation."[88] In this context of sharing and collective writing, "some programs have always been 'owned' by one or two people, [while] many others have been passed around so much that it is difficult to tell exactly who wrote them."[89]

Even in groups not working on computing as such, it was never very far away. Thus, in "human-nets," "netters" talked of their own use of the network: "I think/feel that computer communications (done between humans via computers) lie somewhere between written and verbal communications in style and flavor. There is an ambience of informality and stream-of-consciousness style that pervades it but coupled with ideas that are well thought out (usually) and deeper in insight than average verbal communications."[90]

Usenet was not only the medium of intellectual interaction between computer specialists, but also the result of continuous technical
cooperation. Whereas Arpanet was financed and developed by ARPA,
with the support of a group of computer scientists, Usenet was an independent initiative, a cooperative structure without its own funding. The
administrators of the system were computer specialists who participated
on a voluntary basis, freeing space on their computer hard disks to
record messages (news) and organizing the transfer by telephone. Some
machines, to which users of small sites could connect to retrieve the
newsletters to which they subscribed, became the backbone of the system. The most important points in the backbone[91] were either academics
or those who worked for one of the two firms that played a key part in
the development of Unix: AT&T and Digital Equipment Corporation
(DEC).[92] The activity of the site was, however, largely dependent on the
person in charge of the operation, and the site would sometimes lose its
importance when that person moved on.[93] The institution left things to
happen rather than initiating the operation: "Much of the netnews distribution within Bell labs is done without any explicit approval, commented a Netter.[94] Sometimes the heads of the operation even had to
contribute personally: "When I was at cincy [Cincinnati University] we
had a HARD fight to get the administration to pay the bill."[95]

Usenet, from Computer Debate to Free Public Debate

Growth in the number of groups required reorganization in the hierarchy of group names. This was undertaken in 1986–1987. Six main
themes were selected. The first two items corresponded to academic
subjects: *computing*—the field in which Usenet was founded—and *science.* The following three concerned nonprofessional themes: *society*
(social and possibly political debates), *recreation* (leisure, hobbies),
and, last, *miscellaneous* (comprising mainly classified advertisements).
Finally, *news* concerned organizational debates on Usenet itself. A sev-
enth domain, *talk,* was created for debates on controversial subjects.
The administrators of the servers saw this as a way of grouping
together controversial forums that they would be able to censor. Thus,
despite the existence of this area of free talk, the administrators could
refuse to distribute certain forums. A system of parallel distribution

was therefore set up. That was how the eighth subject domain, called *alternative,* was born. Brian Reid, who played an essential part in the creation of this parallel device, justified his choice as follows: "In retrospect, this is the joy of the alt network: you create a group, and nobody can kill it. It can only die when people stop reading it. . . . I don't wish to offer an opinion about how the net should be run. . . . Nobody has any control over it, regardless of what opinions they might have."[96] This libertarian position, which played a key role in the new development of Usenet, was nevertheless moderated by the fact that the site administrators' selection of newsgroups was, on the whole, accepted: "Usenet has adjusted in the past to this site by site selection of hierarchies. It has made Usenet less unified and more patchy over time, but that's part of the anarchy and freedom Usenet has always striven for."[97]

The new division of subject domains accompanied a change in Usenet. The number of newsgroups swelled and scientific themes became relatively less important. In 1987 there were 250 newsgroups, and by June 1992 this figure had risen to 3,260.[98] "Recreation" was the field in which the most articles were received (25 percent). Those forums with the most readers proposed lists of jokes: rec.humor.funny (220,000 readers) and rec.humor. "Computing" came second, with 21 percent of the articles sent. "Alternative" accounted for 16.5 percent of the documents transmitted,[99] and the most frequently visited forums were alt.sex (220,000 readers) and alt.sex.stories, as well as certain heterodox academic subjects such as hypertext. The domains "society," "talk," and "science" received 10, 5, and 4 percent of all articles, respectively. Finally, although the categories "miscellaneous" and "talk" received few articles, they were read by a large number of people. The two groups with the most readers were classified advertisement forums (misc.jobs.offered and misc.forsale) with 280,000 and 250,000 readers, respectively. The groups news.announce.newusers and news.answers, which provided advice to new users, each had over 100,000 readers.[100] Thus, the scientific forums that accounted for the major share of Usernet activity in 1982 accounted for between a third and a quarter only, ten years later. Usenet became, above all, a site for open debate. Exchange was, however, unequal. According to a survey carried out in 1994 on six newsgroups, only one to two percent of the people registered had sent a message during the month. Of those messages, about half were answers. Only one-third of the initial messages initiated an exchange; the rest remained unanswered.[101]

In spite of everything, Usenet, because of its open organization and the diversity of subjects addressed, was to be the first computer network in the academic world to open up to the outside. The first interconnections were made in 1988.

Toward a World-Wide Research Network

Networks Open to All Scientists

Arpanet, as we have seen, linked up only a small number of university computing departments (an eighth in 1979). Its success led academic authorities to consider the construction of a network for all the universities concerned. In 1974 the National Science Foundation (NSF) advisory committee concluded a report on the subject by recommending a service that "would create a frontier environment which would offer advanced communication, collaboration, and the sharing of resources among geographically separated or isolated researchers."[102] This proposal was, however, rejected. In 1977 the University of Wisconsin developed the small Theorynet network that provided about a hundred computer scientists with email. Two years later the same university, in collaboration with others, proposed to the NSF the construction of a Computer Science Research Network (Csnet). The project was approved in 1981, after much discussion, and became operational in the following year. Different levels of services were proposed, from email to data transfer. In 1983 the network linked more than half the university computer science departments, and, in 1986, all of them.

Two East Coast universities, in cooperation with IBM, launched the Bitnet network in 1981. The acronym initially stood for "Because It's There," relating to the fact that the protocol was already present on IBM computers, but was subsequently changed to "Because It's Time."[103] This project was strongly supported by the association Educom. Bitnet, like Csnet, developed pathways to interconnect with Arpanet. In the mid-1980s the wish to be linked to a computer network was expressed in other university departments, and this new mode of communication started to spread outside computer science departments. The NSF designed a new Nsfnet network opened in 1985, organized on three levels. A national backbone, financed by the NSF, linked five supercomputers that could be used by other universities, and about twelve points of interconnection. These provided the interface with regional networks that had to find their own funding. Finally, each university built a local network on its own site, mostly with NSF grants. The foundation, which wanted to promote the network in all the disciplines, demanded that "the connection . . . be made available to ALL qualified users on campus."[104]

Internet or the Metanetwork

Development of the Arpanet required the creation of more robust and universal protocols than those defined at the beginning. Robert Kahn, one of the main members of the BBN team that had set up the Arpanet, had subsequently taken charge of another ARPA project consisting of the construction of a network of data transmitted in packets, via ground or satellite radio link. It soon appeared that each of these networks had its own peculiarities and that the Arpanet protocol could not be applied to all. Kahn, with Vinton Cerf (one of the main designers of the preceding protocol), conceived of "an internetworking architecture," that is, a metaprotocol by means of which networks designed differently would be able to interfunction. The concept of an open architecture left each network totally autonomous so that it would not have to change its existing mode of operation; the metaprotocol concerned only the exchange between networks. Cerf and Kahn defined the first principles in a text published in 1974.[105] The basic idea was similar to that chosen for the transport of goods by container: all the boxes are identical but can contain very different objects, which then circulate on different networks (train, cargo, truck). In the present case, the computer data (texts, sounds, or images) are encapsulated in packets or datagrams.

The detailed elaboration of the protocol mobilized Arpanauts fully for a fair amount of time. The system chosen had two parts: the Transmission Control Protocol (TCP), responsible for fragmenting messages into packets at the start and reconstituting them on arrival, detecting transmission errors and sending back missing elements; and the Internet [working] Protocol (IP), responsible for organizing the circulation of packets and providing each host machine with an address in order to organize the routing. The TCP/IP protocol was tested in 1977. The Defense Ministry chose it in 1980. On January 1, 1983, Arpanet switched to the new system,[106] which was henceforth called the Internet.[107]

In the same year, the computer science department at Berkeley, which had played an important part in the diffusion of Unix in the academic community, created a TCP/IP version for Unix. Suddenly the new protocol became accessible to 90 percent of all university computer science laboratories.[108] At MIT researchers subsequently developed a version for PC.

In 1983 Arpanet also split into two networks, Milnet for military use, and a new Arpanet for research, which was to link to Csnet. Nsfnet chose from the outset to use the TCP/IP protocol. Thus, in the mid-1980s the Internet managed to federate a large proportion of the computer networks in the United States. The number of networks that had adopted the Internet protocol rose steeply from then on, from fifteen initially to over four hundred in 1986.[109] All these networks using the same language could interconnect in a network of networks that also became known as the Internet.

The links that had been created extended well beyond national borders to foreign universities, thus creating an international network. In 1975 Arpanet had established a satellite link with the United Kingdom. Usenet linked up to Canada in 1981 and then to Europe in the following year. The authors of one of the first books on Usenet was thus able to say in 1986: "Your link to the Unix network becomes your link to the world and the world's link to you."[110] In the mid-1980s Bitnet and Csnet established links with Europe and Japan. The international computing network thus had connections to U.S. universities. All this together formed what John Quarterman, in 1990, in the first reference book published on computer networks, called the matrix: "The *Matrix* is a worldwide metanetwork of connected computer networks and conferencing systems that provides unique services that are like, yet unlike, those of telephones, post offices, and libraries. It is a major tool in academic and industrial research in computer technology, physics, and astronomy, and increasingly in biological, social, and other sciences.[111] The Internet thus became a network of networks. (See table 2.2 for a history of the Internet.)

Table 2.2
History of the Internet: Some key dates

Arpanet (ARPA Network)
1969: first link
1983: Milnet, specifically military network, split off
1990: closing of the network

Usenet (Usenix Network)
1979: beginning of the network
1982: gateway between Usenet and Arpanet

Csnet (Computer Science Network)
1982: opening
1983: gateway between Csnet and Arpanet

Nsfnet (National Science Foundation Network)
1983: opening

Internet
1983: the system is operational

World Wide Web
1990: diffusion of the software
1993: Mosaic navigator

Access to Knowledge

The founding fathers of the Internet conceived of not only a network of cooperation and exchange between machines (file transfers) and people (message services, newsgroups), but also one providing access to universal knowledge. Thus, when Licklider joined ARPA he wrote a paper on future libraries. In the preface he cited an article by Vannevar Bush which, although published in 1945, guided his thinking twenty years later.

Bush, who had developed an analog calculator, had been in charge of the administrative services running the scientific war effort. After the war he wanted to ensure that the scientific cooperation developed during the conflict would be kept alive. The main problem was that "publication has been extended far beyond our present ability to make use of the record."[112] Bush considered that the hierarchical organization of information in existing libraries did not correspond at all to the functioning of the human mind, for our thinking is above all by association; it advances in a "web of trails."[113] He therefore suggested grouping together documents and mechanizing information searches. He designed an individual workstation called Memex, used to consult all sorts of data recorded on microfilm. Users keyed in the references of the document they wished to consult; they were then able to move about in the text (skip pages, return to contents page, etc.) and to move on to other, related documents. Readers could create their own index and indicate links between documents. All this was, however, purely speculative.

Xanadu and the Hypertext Dream

Although Licklider's ideas were along the same lines, the technological context had changed: the computer age was dawning. He thought of replacing the book with a device that would make the physical transportation of data unnecessary and that could be used to process it. Computer technology was the appropriate solution. Licklider imagined that in the year 2000 the average individual

may make a capital investment in an "intermedium" or "console"—his intellectual Ford or Cadillac—comparable to the investment he makes now in an automobile, or that he will rent one from a public utility that handles information processing as Consolidated Edison handles electric power. In business, government and education, the concept of 'desk' may have changed from passive to active: a desk may be primarily a display-control station in a telecommunication-telecomputation system—and its most vital part may be the cable ("umbilical cord") that connects it, via a wall socket, into the procognitive utility net.[114]

This utopia was partially experimented with in the late 1960s, in Engelbart's Augmented Human Intellect Research Center. In a book entitled *Dream Machines*, a brilliant young computer whiz described Engelbart's contribution to experimentation on information retrieval: "Whatever you want to look up is instantly there, simultaneously interconnected to everything else. It should be connected to source materials, footnotes, comments and so on. . . . All handling of paper is eliminated." He concluded: "In building his mighty system he points a new way for humanity."[115]

This fascination with the Stanford master did not, however, prevent him from also having a critical view. Nelson questioned Engelbart's rigorous hierarchical organization of documents. For at least ten years, he had been thinking about a nonsequential organization of texts that he called hypertext.[116] An author could thus write in a nonlinear way by proposing branches or alternatives. Nelson's main idea was a great hypertext "consisting of everything written about a subject or vaguely relevant to it, tied together by editors in which you may read in all directions you wish to pursue. There can be alternative pathways for people who think different ways." He further added: "The real dream is for everything to be in the hypertext."[117] He called his project Xanadu, with reference, of course, to Coleridge's poem about a magical world where nothing is ever forgotten, and to the house of Orson Welles's movie *Citizen Kane*. The aim was to provide everyone with "a screen in your home from which you can see into the world's hypertext libraries."[118] Nelson and his assistants tried to create a powerful software package that would enable readers to create their own links with extracts or whole texts. The system had to function both ways, so that readers could not only follow the links accompanying the text but also find all the texts with links to the one they were busy reading. The basic idea was, in a sense, to set out clearly all connections among knowledge. Both Nelson's attempts in the 1980s to develop his software were unsuccessful. Gary Wolf concludes an extremely well documented article on this adventure with the following: "Today, with the advent of far more powerful memory devices, Xanadu, the grandest encyclopedic project of our era seemed not only a failure but an actual symptom of madness."[119]

In 1988, when Nelson was launching his second attempt to write the Xanadu software, Vinton Cerf and Robert Kahn, the fathers of the TCP/IP protocol, published a document on the digital library,[120] proposing the creation of a network of interconnected libraries. When users cannot find what they are looking for in the local data base, their requests are routed to distant digital libraries. One of the key elements of the project was the concept of an intelligent agent called a "knowbot." These agents were to locate and retrieve information in a huge, complex, and heterogeneous network of libraries. They could also constitute a sort of cognitive filter that let through only selected information with a certain degree of precision.

The Web
In 1990 a hypertext document system was developed at the European Nuclear Research Center (CERN) in Geneva. The aim of Tim Berners-Lee, the main author of the project, was to meet the documentation

needs of a large research center in which information is fragmented and decentralized, and where teams are constantly changing. He wanted to produce operational software suited to researchers' needs: "The problem of information loss may be particularly acute at CERN, but in this case (as in certain others), CERN is a model in miniature of the rest of the world in a few years' time. CERN now meets some problems that the rest of the world will have to face soon. In ten years there may be many commercial solutions to the problems above, while today we need something to allow us to continue."[121]

This view was expressed in another text by Tim Berners-Lee and Robert Cailliau. Their project consisted neither of intervening on information nor of organizing it hierarchically, but of establishing links between it:

The texts are linked together in a way that one can go from one concept to another to find the information one wants. The network of links is called a web. The web need not be hierarchical, . . . is also not complete, since it is hard to imagine that all the possible links would be put in by authors. Yet a small number of links is usually sufficient for getting from anywhere to anywhere else in a small number of hops. The texts are known as nodes. The process of proceeding from node to node is called navigation. Nodes do not need to be on the same machine: links may point across machine boundaries. Having a world wide web implies some solutions must be found for problems such as different access protocols and different node content formats. . . . Nodes can in principle also contain non-text information such as diagrams, pictures, sound, animation, etc. The term hypermedia is simply the expansion of the hypertext idea to these other media.[122]

To organize this navigation, users needed a browser or navigator enabling them to select information and display it on the screen. This software, that its author called the World Wide Web, was ready in 1991. It included a HyperText Markup Language (HTML) for describing documents and another language called the HyperText Transfer Protocol (HTTP) for managing and transferring them. The documents were placed in servers with a Uniform Resource Locator (URL) address. Soon the World Wide Web software was circulating on the Internet. The international community of nuclear physicists started to use it to share documentation. Hypertext specialists who obtained the information in the "alt-hypertext" newsgroup examined it and created other navigators, the most well-known of which is Mosaic, written by Marc Andreessen at the National Center for Supercomputing Application (NCSA), University of Illinois.

The Republic of Computer Specialists

Over a period of twenty years, from the opening of the Arpanet to the invention of the Web, a very particular process of innovation was under way. Unlike many other technologies, the Internet with its various components was developed almost exclusively in the academic world. This research led directly to operational devices, thus short-circuiting, in a sense, the traditional step of transfer to industry. Such an exceptional process was possible because computer scientists were the first users of their own inventions, and because those inventions were based essentially on computer programs, that is, intellectual work, something academics can provide. For them, the object was not only to steer computer science in a new direction, toward networks, but also to endow themselves with the working tools (message services, cooperative devices, collective documents) that they needed and that the market could not provide.

This shortcut between research and use, in which the two positions merged, was reinforced by the fact that the development of tools and their uses enhanced the productivity of scientific work. As computer scientists linked up computers in a network for exchanging information, the very content of their dialogue concerned the construction of that same network. This type of virtuous circle was possible only because they were outside the ordinary world, the market society where production and consumption are totally separate.

These academics, richly endowed by ARPA and the NSF, were thus able to create a propitious environment for the realization of their project, which they modeled in terms of their own practices and representations of modes of sociability. The operation was carried out by a group of young researchers who saw the university as a peer group. The social organization of the Internet therefore had the following four characteristics:

• *Interaction and cooperation was first and foremost among specialists or people with the same interests.* These specialists did not necessarily meet in their laboratory or university. They were distant colleagues who constituted an "invisible college," published in the same journals, met at the same conferences, and sometimes traveled from laboratory to laboratory. This invisible college, which initially included some industrial labs such as the Bell laboratories or Xerox Park, was to design the Internet along the same lines and thus to meet its own needs. Pioneers such as Licklider[123] were to call this social organization a community of interests; others like Turoff[124] spoke of a network nation.

• *It was a community of equals where the status of each member was based essentially on merit, evaluated by peers.* But unlike the regular university tradition, this evaluation was not only by legitimate authorities (commissions, journals, etc.) but also by ordinary colleagues who tested, commented on, and improved proposals. The debate was therefore wide open and could not be closed by any authoritative argument. Information flowed freely. A BBN-type of management, Arpanet Requests for Comments, and newsgroups were the manifestation of this adhocracy.

• *Cooperation was an essential element, at the core of this scientific activity.* Computer software is something too complex to be created by a single individual; it requires teamwork. This collaboration is more intense when the aim is to network computers deliberately designed to differ. Corbato and Fano[125] had already observed the existence of such cooperation in time-sharing computing, and Richtie,[126] one of the creators of Unix, also noted this principle of cooperative work. Turoff[127] and Lederberg[128] showed the effectiveness of Arpanaut communities. The fast flow of information allowed for a high level of transparency, which in turn facilitated cooperation. Yet as Conway[129] notes, transparency also helped to intensify competition between teams.

• *It was a world apart, separate from the rest of society.* The university campus is a world of its own, a pathway for students between adolescence and the adult world, between school and the professional world. In this place of innovation and experimentation for academics, computer technology reigns. Richard Cyert, Chancellor of Carnegie Mellon University, commented in 1984: "The great university of the future will be that with a great computer system."[130] Backed by IBM, he embarked on the construction of a network of 7,500 terminals.[131]

These academic computer networks and more especially Arpanet seemed to certain participants[132] to be a closed community, separate from the rest of the world. In their history of the Arpanet, John King, Rebecca Grinter, and Jeanne Pickering[133] use the metaphor of a mushroom town called Netville, protected for a long time by the Great Divide. In the mythology of the conquest of the West, it separated the conservative East from the West with its freedom and abundant new opportunities. To conquer new technological opportunities, pioneers in the computer field needed to be protected from the old world by the Great Divide. This boundary was codified in the form of rules reserving use of the network for certain laboratories and subsequently for the academic world. Nsfnet thus developed an "Acceptable Use Policy," which specified that the network was intended exclusively for U.S. research and teaching institutions.[134] By extension, the network was opened to foreign universities (provided they opened their sites to U.S. universities), to private firms' research centers collaborating with the academic world, and to parauniversity institutions. Other commercial uses were not accepted.[135] The republic of computer specialists could thus function, sheltered from the outside world.

In the final analysis, the founding utopias of computer communication not only guided the initial Arpanet project but also constantly interacted with its technical realization. As the technical project took shape and developed, new utopias appeared (the idea of communication and interaction replaced that of distance calculation), feeding on early experiments and orienting future technical options and their uses. This exceptional virtuous circle of the elaboration of utopias, technical work, and the construction of uses was possible because it took place in a relatively closed and uniform community that saw it as a working tool that it both needed and could organize to suit its own practices.

Because of these constant interactions, my study of academic Internet utopias presents both the technical decisions that were made and the first uses of computer communication. This is the last time in this book that we see such a perfect balance among *imaginaire*, technique, and uses. The new social world that we are about to consider, the counterculture, also produced a utopia, that of online communities, embodied in projects. But we see that the gap is often wider between the utopia and its realization, and that the technical debate is less intense, since most innovation concerned experiments in use of the technique.

3

Communities, a Different Internet *Imaginaire*

As the Internet culture developed in the 1970s and 1980s in a relatively closed academic computer science community, a few dropouts on the fringes of the university world were trying to do computing in an autonomous and different way. Steven Levy, who studied these hackers,[1] summed up their ethic in six points:

- access to computers ought to be total and unrestricted
- all information should be free
- it is advisable to be wary of authority and to promote decentralization
- hackers should be judged on their production and not artificial criteria such as qualifications, age, race, or social status
- you can create art and beauty with a computer
- computers can change your life for the better.[2]

The hacker culture clearly had certain points in common with the hippie counterculture and with Arpanauts' representations. It shared the same refusal of centralized and commercial information technology that IBM symbolized at the time. The main difference between the two cultures lay in hackers' far broader view of the use and future of IT. For them it was not only an intellectual tool for academics but also a device to put into everyone's hands, capable of building not only new invisible colleges but also a new society. Steven Levy, among others,[3] considered that most of these hackers were designers of the microcomputer. Others were also interested in computer networks. Three main currents can be distinguished: those who believed in a vaster project, namely, the counterculture and hippie movement; those who sought technical performance above all; and those who put themselves at the service of community projects born in civil society.

New Communities Spawned by the Counterculture

Information Technology for Communities
Lee Felsenstein was a hacker who had dropped out of university and lived on the fringes of mainstream society in Berkeley, California, where his time was divided between political activism and computing. Felsenstein also wrote for an avant-garde publication *The Tribe,* and in 1973 he was the leader of a project called Community Memory. The project consisted in an experimental network with two terminals connected to a computer on a time-shared basis, set up in public places (a university record shop and a popular library). According to one of the theoreticians of the project: "Community Memory is convivial and participatory. [The] system is an actively open ("free") information system, enabling direct communications among its users with no centralized editing or control over the information exchanged. . . . Such a system represents a precise antithesis to the dominant uses both of electronic media, which broadcast centrally-determined messages to mass passive audiences."[4] Felsenstein had developed this communicational and convivial view of computers after reading Ivan Illich's *Tools for Conviviality.*[5]

This wish to create human-machine symbiosis corresponded to a typical approach of the California counterculture at the time, which saw electronics and computers as ecological techniques. The association that had organized the Community Memory project was called "Loving Grace Cybernetics," the title of a hippie poem by Richard Brautigan:

I like to think
(and the sooner the better!)
of a cybernetic meadow
where mammals and computers
live together in mutually
programming harmony
like pure water
touching clear sky
I like to think
(right now, please!)
of a cybernetic forest
filled with pines and electronics

where deer stroll peacefully
past computers
as if they were flowers
with spinning blossoms
    I like to think
(it has to be!)
of a cybernetic ecology
where we are free of our labors
and join back to nature,
returned to our mammal
brothers and sisters,
and all watched over
by machines of loving grace.[6]

This poem combines a number of important features of the hippie culture: the ideas of peace and love, the desire to return to nature and, simultaneously, the passion for certain electronic technologies. The Community Memory experience was part of this cultural scene. It lasted for a little over a year. The computer terminal became a sort of public electronic notice board where a wide diversity of advertisements and information were displayed: from requests for chess partners, babysitters or secondhand records to such collective information on certain aspects of the hippie culture at the time as anti–Vietnam War demonstrations and rock concerts by the Grateful Dead (the most famous California band owing to its ability to thrill audiences during its concerts, which could last up to four or five hours, and its full exploitation of the capacities of electronics: amplification, lighting, etc.). This electronic notice board thus became a means of coordination within counterculture communities.

Felsenstein subsequently tried to revive the Community Memory project while participating in the creation of the first microcomputers. In 1975, in the ephemeral *Journal of Community Communication*, he talked of microcomputers "created and used by people in their daily lives as members of communities."[7] Two years later he conceived of a public terminal as the heart of an information center that would be an "amalgam of branch libraries, game arcades, coffee houses, city parks, and post offices."[8]

Yet Community Memory and Felsenstein's projects should be seen not as the matrix of community network computing, but rather as the sign of a utopia embodied in fledgling techniques in the mid-1970s on the fringes of the university world. This utopia, closely connected to the California counterculture, combined two projects: an individual computer for all—the project of Apple and many others—and a communication network among equals. The former was to develop very quickly in the late 1970s and early 1980s; the latter evolved more slowly, but a series of experiences emerged underground. All of them relied on a new machine: the microcomputer. Most of these innovations were amateur inventions that never attained the legitimacy of Arpanet and Internet.

Using Information Technology to Build a Community

In 1978, a year after Apple commercialized its microcomputer, a San Francisco group led by another nonconformist computer specialist John James, launched a computer conferencing system for amateurs, accessible by phone. The name of the system, CommuniTree, referred both to the ecological tradition of the California counterculture and to the tree-shaped organization of the various conferences proposed. The founders' aim was more ambitious than that of Community Memory, for the idea was less to adapt computing to communities than to build a community through networked computing. The high goals of the project are evident in this slogan launched at the first conference: "We are as gods and might as well get good at it."[9]

This megalomaniacal technospiritualism is a regular feature in the New Age culture. The project's first conference was called "Origins," and it proposed that the participants create their own religion. The initiators made the following declaration: "Origins has no leaders, no official existence, nothing for sale. Because it started in an open computer conference, no one knows who all the creators are."[10] This total freedom of communication characterizing CommuniTree as a whole was inscribed in the software since the system operator was unable to read messages before their diffusion or to delete any, or even to perform the operation automatically via a control device. The software was moreover very difficult to alter since it had not been documented.[11] Hence, the total freedom of expression proposed at the outset could not be changed.

CommuniTree died as a result. When in the early 1980s young computer hackers discovered access to the system and flooded it with obscene and scatological messages, the system managers were unable to stop them. CommuniTree was a prime example of a New Age social utopia realized through network computing. A project of such a radical nature without the means to control its own development was doomed to failure.

The Well, a Lasting Electronic Community

At the origin of The Well we also find two former hippies, Steward Brand and Larry Brilliant. Brand belonged to the group The Merry Pranksters that had traveled across the United States in 1964 in a bus, promoting the use of drugs and putting on psychedelic shows.[12] Brilliant was a member of Hog Farm, a hippie commune in the country. Unlike many other hippie groups, these two communities did not spurn technology and advocate a return to nature. On the contrary, they wanted to combine a natural lifestyle with technologies and thus break away from a reality they saw as conformist. They consequently used LSD, an artificial drug, and multiple tools for electronic manipulation of sound.

Brand worked with Engelbart in the autumn of 1968 when the latter organized a huge demonstration of his computer systems designed to enhance human intelligence. During the same period he launched the *Whole Earth Catalog* for those who wanted to return to the earth or simply live a "more natural" life. Two million copies were sold, and the guide became a sort of counterculture bible. The range it proposed was wide: from traditional tools for practicing organic farming to electroacoustic amplifiers. This association of traditional techniques with high-tech corresponded not to a refusal of modernity but to a will to master technical tools, to produce both one's own music and one's own food.

Very soon the catalog proposed microcomputers. Brand even claims to have been the first to coin the term *personal computer* (PC).[13] In 1975 (the year in which the first microcomputer was sold in kit form) *The Co-evolution Quarterly*, the magazine associated with the catalog, started to feature a section on personal computers. In the editorial Brand wrote: "It is very likely true that little computers are on the way to revolutionizing human behavior. . . . Personal computers are defining a generation the way dope did ten years ago."[14] This comparison was often made by the former hippie, a regular user of drugs.[15] It shows just how essential he considered computers to be in the counterculture. In his opinion, hackers had achieved the goal they had set in the 1960s: taking over the technique to give it other development possibilities. According to him, those "dedicated, innovative computer programmers were the only group he had ever heard of to 'successfully' liberate a technology."[16]

In 1984, the year the Macintosh came out, Brand launched the *Whole Earth Software Catalog,* which proposed the best software for amateur use. In the chapter on network computing, he recounted his experiment in 1983 in the use of EIES teleconferencing: "The project revolutionized my writing, my thinking, my work network, and my business," he wrote.[17]

In the meantime, Brilliant, who had become a medical doctor specialized in epidemiology, had also used teleconferencing.[18] As a sideline he had started a business commercializing computer conferencing software. He suggested that he and Brand launch an experiment together, not with a small group of scientists but with a much larger group of computer hackers. Brilliant provided the hard- and software, Brand the people. The operation, called *The Whole Earth 'Lectronic Link* (The Well), was launched in 1985.

Some of the first participants were familiar with the developments of network computing. Freelance journalist Howard Rheingold, for example, had just published a book entitled *Tools for Thought: The People and Ideas behind the Next Computer Revolution,*[19] in which he presented the work of Licklider, Engelbart, Taylor, Nelson, and others But most of them shared the wish above all to recreate communities in the spirit of the counterculture. In 1987 Rheingold wrote an article in *The Whole Earth Review* (that had replaced *The Co-evolution Quarterly*) entitled "Virtual Communities." He explicitly referred to Licklider's thesis on communities of interest but took it even further. In his opinion virtual communities were better than traditional ones in so far as they enabled people immediately to find others with the same values and interests. By contrast, in real life that search was long and uncertain.[20]

In the following year the same magazine published a column by editor in chief Kevin Kelly, also one of the founding members of The Well, entitled "Tales from Two Communities." Kelly compared The Well to hippie communities and concluded: "The Well has become a way to live in a commune without having to live on one."[21] But this was more than a metaphor since the first managers of The Well[22] had been members of The Farm, one of the most well-known hippie communities that had lasted the longest. They had been chosen for their ability to maintain cohesion in a group that functioned with relatively lax rules. Cliff Figalo, the second manager, commented: "We were conditioned to respond to the Community Imperative—the need to build and maintain relationships between people and to preserve the structure that supported those relationships. . . . It became our thing; a living, breathing collaboration that we could recognize as having real community characteristics."[23]

Although the link with the counterculture commune tradition was obvious,[24] the founders' aim was not to recreate the communes of the 1960s in virtual form but rather to build a new public sphere. Mathew McClure, The Well's first manager, explained: "It was our idea in the beginning that The Well could turn into the electronic equivalent of the French salons during the Enlightenment period."[25] In this virtual public sphere, documents were signed and could not be censored by the editors. One of the main principles clearly established from the outset was "You own your own words," which meant that each person was responsible for what they said, and that everyone could change or even delete their writings and prevent their use by others.

The themes of the conferences varied. Some were general—Brand had offered journalists and intellectuals the possibility of chairing them, with free connection in exchange—while others concerned the reactivation of the counterculture. In 1987, a year that ended with two thousand subscribers, a conference on the Grateful Dead constituted between one-third and one-half of The Well's activity.[26] The group's fans ("Deadheads"), some of whom belonged to a different generation than the hippies, enjoyed the collective atmosphere during the Grateful Dead's long concerts. In 1991 the group was still one of the seven chapters in The Well's index of 180 conferences. Other topics were "Business, Education, Social Political Humanities, Arts Recreation Entertainment, Computers, Technical Communications, and The Well Itself."[27]

Behind this cultural homogeneity lay social homogeneity. In 1987 one of the managers of The Well noted that "The Well's character comes from hackers, writers, artists, Deadheads, knowledge workers, fugitives from the counterculture, educators, programmers, lawyers, musicians and many more"[28]—in short, the intellectual middle classes.

A study undertaken in 1992 informs us on users' expectations and practices. Marc Smith studied conferences in which users expressed themselves on their lives as "Well-Beings." They participated in topics such as "What am I doing here?" "What does The Well do for users?" and "The Well's Mission Statement." In these documents that inform us on users' representations, one word is omnipresent: community. According to one participant, "In electronic communication, we find aspects of community which are sometimes similar to, and sometimes different than, the communities we are all part of."[29] Thus, in this respect participants repeated the discourse of the founders.

Two other notions add clarity to this community life: knowledge trading and communion. The phrase "Does anybody know?" was a regular feature on The Well, a place where expertise on the most varied subjects could be found. As early as 1987 Rheingold had identified this trading of expertise, this social contract of gift and countergift.[30] But The Well was not only an information market; it was also a communion, which "suggests a noninstrumental contact with the group, an emotional bond," as one participant put it. "But can people come to have emotional attachments to one another without ever facing each other? As the history of romantic correspondence shows, the answer is emphatically yes. And this can be seen again in The Well. Well-Beings often turn to one another for more than information that can be parlayed into other forms of capital. Within The Well people turn to each other for support during crises and camaraderie during triumphs."[31]

Was this exchange of feelings, completing the exchange of information, as common as this witness suggests? The rare statistical data cited show that at the least it concerned unequal interaction (as we have seen with regard to Usenet). Smith calculated that in 1992, 1 percent of the participants, that is, seventy people, produced half of the messages,[32] while Rheingold estimated that during the same period 16 percent of Well-Beings provided 80 percent of the texts.[33]

Would it be accurate to say that the project evolved from communicational interaction to an online show? This is what Katie Hafner suggests in her account of the saga of The Well. She cites the tumultuous romantic affairs of Mandel and Nana witnessed by Well-Beings. Meeting, breakup, then marriage, and eventually Mandel's death were all events that took place online or were commented on almost instantaneously. As Hafner says, this story became a sort of soap opera and Well-Beings, like TV viewers, were familiar with the characters and the intrigue.[34]

The Amateur Network

Parallel to these electronic community projects, hobbyists pursued their own essentially technical goal: communicating by computer. In 1978, a few months before CommuniTree, Ward Christensen, a member of a Chicago computer club, developed a program for computer communication via the telephone network. The Computer Hobbyist Bulletin Board System, created with Randy Suess, was the first electronic version of the bulletin board system.

In November the two innovators published an article in *Byte*, the reference magazine for computing, in which they presented their system as a device "for message communication among experimenters."[35] Their program, of which they gave a technical description so that other hobbyists could create their own BBS, circulated widely on the network. They also envisaged linking up these experiments one day: "These bulletin board systems could then become *nodes*[36] in a communication network of automated message and program switching."[37]

A Decentralized Cooperative Network: Fidonet

By 1983 a few hundred BBS existed. San Francisco hacker Tom Jennings had created one called Fido. To be able to communicate with another computer scientist in Baltimore who also had a BBS, he conceived of a program to link the two. In a sense, this was a realization of Christensen's and Suess's intuition. Jennings called this future network Fidonet. As he noted shortly afterward, his aim had been above all technical, "to see if it could be done, merely for the fun of it, like ham radio. It quickly became useful; instead of trying to call each others' boards up to leave messages, or expensive voice phone calls, Fidonet messages became more or less routine."[38] The technical device was similar to that of Usenet. The various nodes in the network, the BBS, called one another via the telephone network to deliver messages from other servers. The main difference from Usenet was that these were no longer powerful computers running on Unix, but microcomputers. The network's success was almost immediate. In January 1985, just fourteen months after opening, it already had 160 BBS linked up. The casual coordination of the early stages was no longer possible though; routine calls had to be scheduled at night and the network had to be structured so that each node could call the closest one.

It was unquestionably this technical performance that motivated the founders most. Jennings proudly stated that Usenet was less complex and that only Arpanet had some of the same characteristics. Despite this success, the objectives were the same: "it is a noncommercial network of computer hobbiests ('hackers,' in the older, original meaning) who want to play with and find uses for packet switch networking . . . Fidonet is totally supported by its users and system operators. . . . Each sysop runs their system in any way they please, for any reason they want."[39] Initially, Fidonet could handle only a message service, but in 1986 a newsgroup called "echomail" was created as well.

The Fidonet architecture was based on a principle of maximum decentralization. "Its design," wrote Jennings, "was explicitly based upon anarchist social principles."[40] Each node in the network was self-sufficient and could communicate in isolation with all the other nodes since its modem had all their telephone numbers in its memory. This type of functioning was naturally expensive, and in reality the nodes used the relay procedure previously described. Yet such decentralization, potentially stronger than that of Usenet or Internet, was presented as one of the characteristics of the network. "Fidonauts'" freedom was bounded only by a grand principle: "do not be excessively annoying and do not become excessively annoyed." Clearly, a project that was defined above all in terms of its technical objective was also a social project. The counterculture and anarchist utopia was thus present in Fidonet as well.

Yet these two network approaches were often defended by different individuals who at times were violently opposed. In 1986 Fidonet participants created the International Fidonet Association to promote the network and organize a newsletter. Evidently, the leaders of the association had limited technical skills and saw the network first and foremost as a social and political project. Gradually they tried to turn the association into an instrument to control the network, and in 1989, after an online referendum, they were permanently expelled.[41]

In a sociological study in 1992, Carol Anne Dodd noted that users had two main approaches to the new medium. Some saw it primarily as a means of communication enabling people to exchange ideas and information freely, while others wanted above all to develop a fast, efficient data transmission system. Those that she called the technoids "believe that technical performance outweighs whether anyone actually enters messages or not."[42] The contradictions of this project were summed up by Jennings when he simultaneously emphasized the libertarian aspect of the system and presented himself as apolitical. He even received a prize for the quality of the Fidonet software, sold his programming skills, and eventually started his own business as an Internet service provider.[43]

Network and Community Development

The idea that neighboring communities could express themselves through new media had already appeared in the early 1970s with the birth of video and public access to cable networks. In 1971 Michael Shamberg commented on the arrival of these new media: "Thus, people can control information about themselves rather than surrender that power to outsiders." He spoke of "a grassroots network of indigenous media activity. In place of a mass consciousness of millions of people all plugged-in to the same "show" is a more flexible collective mind with the option of a high variety of available viewpoints."[44] The People's Video Theatre and the Alternative Media Center were projects created to enable communities, especially the most underprivileged, to express themselves. For John Reilly, Global Village leader, "The best use of video is in person-to-person relations. . . . It's a tool for mediation between individuals."[45] But other video producers considered that these new media should be used to launch local development projects, for video could serve to express needs and mobilize future participants.[46] As for "cable television [it] can make it possible for your community organization to conduct a meeting of all people in your neighborhood, without any of them having to leave their homes."[47]

Free-Net, Public Information Technology that Defends Local Identities
Similar projects were born fifteen years later in the computer network domain. Unlike the cable where community projects developed twenty years after the new networks were first commercialized, these new computer networks were put on the market only after a phase of community computing. In 1984 Tom Grundler, education science lecturer at Case Western Reserve University in Cleveland, opened a bulletin board called "St. Silicon's Hospital and Information Dispensary" to provide medical information to the general public. In order to develop health education at a local level, doctors provided answers within twenty-four hours to questions put to them anonymously on the BBS.[48] Two years later the initial project was extended to other areas of information, namely, law, education, and local administration.

That BBS became the Cleveland Free-Net. In 1989 Grundler and his colleagues launched the National Public Telecomputing Network (NPTN) to promote the creation of community bulletin boards. The reference document of the NPTN, sometimes presented as the "bible of the community networking movement," defined community computing as follows: "The system is literally run by the community itself. Almost everything that appears on one of these machines is there because there are individuals or organizations in the community who are prepared to contribute their time, effort, and expertise to place it there and operate it over time."[49] By 1992, 250 volunteers were regularly updating the data for 40,000 registered users who asked a total of 10,000 questions daily.[50]

This information produced by the community for the community not only had to be free but also had to be selected according to the wishes of the transmitters and not the receivers. Hence, the rationale was quite the opposite of a commercial system where information must above all be adapted to the customer, or even of The Well's system where information requests were linked to supply. As Grundler notes, "Free-Net allows people unparalleled access to some of the best services and resources our computerized Information Age has to offer; and they do it in a way which makes them free to the user—in much the same way that our public library system, for example, has been free to its patrons for over 100 years."[51]

The rationale here is not communication but education. The theme of community computing as a new public library appeared often. This was partly a gamble on modernity (in the computer age, public information is found on BBS), and partly an emphasis on the free-of-charge nature of the Free-Nets—as indispensable and legitimate as that of libraries. Moreover, this example of libraries shows that the noncommercial sector was not really competing with the commercial sector and that, on the contrary, it cultivated a taste for books and computing. In short, it trained tomorrow's consumers.

This idea that today's traditional library, like tomorrow's virtual one, are instruments of community identity was also developed in an article published at the same time by a Stanford librarian and the head of the Xerox Park computer laboratory: "A library," they said, "is not just an information source, it is also a place to go after school, . . . We believe that the networked library should strive to provide the following functions for community identity: distinctive 'places,' geographically local networked meeting rooms, and a physical community presence." [52]

It was precisely this rehumanization of urban life that community BBS allowed. A user commented: "The Free-Net has put a human face on an otherwise impersonal city. I now feel that my home is directly connected to thousands of friends through my modem." [53] This importance of the local is also one of the main features of Grundler's utopia. In a programmatic paper written in 1994, he explained: "America's progress toward an equitable Information Age will *not* be measured by the number of people we can make *dependent* upon the Internet. Rather, it is the reverse. It will be measured by the number of *local* systems we can build, using *local* resources, to meet *local* needs." [54] This attachment to the local, which clearly distinguishes Free-Net from the Internet universal communication project, can be found in the metaphor of the electronic city used for the organization of the Cleveland Free-Net. The different services are called: administration building, post office, public square, courthouse, schoolhouse, and so forth.

Big Sky Telegraph, a Regional Cooperative

In the United States the concept of community has its origins not in the urban groups involved in Free-Net projects, but in the rural villages that were a basic feature of the colonization of America. It is therefore hardly surprising to find computer communication experiments in the rural world. In 1980 Dave Hughes created a bulletin board called the "Old Colorado City Electronic Cottage." This former U.S. army colonel described himself as follows: "I am a happily married middle-aged family man who has seen enough of Big Government, Big Wars, Big Industry, Big Political Causes—either of the left or right—to now prefer to operate a small business out of a small house, in a small neighborhood, working with small organizations, using a small computer to make it all possible."[55] Yet this "small is beautiful" enthusiast was not part of the counterculture; it was with ordinary people that he wanted to build a local communication project. In this sense he fitted into the old American tradition, often called Jeffersonian, that considers that political action is situated above all at the local, rural community level. Unlike Free-Net, the idea behind his bulletin board was not to help the disadvantaged. In the 1980s Hughes participated in several computer-based community development projects, all designed for the rural middle classes.[56] In Colorado Springs he used his BBS to orchestrate a public opinion campaign against the municipality's plan to increase taxes on home industries.

In 1987 Hughes supported a computer-aided conference project launched by Frank Odasz in Montana to develop mutual aid between isolated teachers in this mountainous area. Since schools owned computers that in many cases had not been used, Hughes and Odasz conceived of expanding the project and, through computer links between schools, launching a rural development project. As Hughes said: "In many small towns in America, the concept of 'community' is so strong that nothing is 'just' school, or government, or business, or private group."[57] It was on this new basis that a project called Big Sky Telegraph was launched.

Some years later Frank Odasz described this school-community articulation: "The community outreach potential for schools has many advantages, such as involving community expertise in making K–12 education [elementary and secondary schools] immediately relevant to real-world community needs. Email allows 24-hour contact between students and the community, opening doors to many new levels of interaction. . . . Local experts can assist the general public in accessing information and services through the convenience of email. Those government services most important for a given community can be tailored through customized online menus for enhanced ease of access by the public." In the final analysis, "BBSs help integrate a community."[58] Independent of schools, several cooperative projects also used the computer network (water management, tourism, social services, etc.). Although ranch owners used the system very little, women's groups adopted it on a big scale. Big Sky Telegraph thus afforded opportunities that only certain groups were able to take advantage of.

An Experiment in Local Democracy: PEN

Computer communication has sometimes also been developed by municipal authorities and has thus helped to revitalize the local social fabric which, according to certain observers, is breaking down in our contemporary world. The town of Santa Monica, California, which had already launched an email experiment in 1984 among municipal staff, opened the Public Electronic Network (PEN) in 1989. The system, accessible to all citizens equipped with a microcomputer (twenty terminals were also installed in public places), was designed to

• provide access to public information;
• make city services more accessible to the public;
• provide an alternative form of communication for residents;
• provide electronic forums to enhance the sense of community in Santa Monica; and
• facilitate knowledge of computers and new communication technology by all city residents.[59]

Kevin McKeown, chair of the PEN Users group, compared the system to a traditional New England town meeting, except that PEN was ongoing: "You put something provocative on PEN, and you get responses. And then other people chime in and pretty soon you've got a good debate going."[60] In fact, the public discussion seemed to crystallize around topics introduced by a few dynamic groups, primarily around protection of the marine environment and dialogue with homeless people. This case is particularly interesting, for it illustrates the prevailing idea that the Internet allows communication with people in different localities and, above all—as we are about to see—puts all inter-locutors on the same footing since they communicate behind a mask.

A homeless man who participated with sociologist Everett Rogers in an evaluation report wrote: "No one, on PEN, knew that I was homeless until I told them. After I told them, I was still treated like a human being. To me, the most remarkable thing about PEN community is that a city council member and a pauper can coexist, albeit not always in perfect harmony, but on an equal basis. . . . I have been helped, rebuffed, scorned, criticized, considered, and, in most cases, respected as a human. PEN is a great equalizer. . . . We are not one happy family; like most fam-ilies, we squabble. On any topic, no one can accuse PENers of agreeing fully. But we *are* communicating, and that is a start."[61]

Although the PEN was a far cry from the consensual community envisaged by some, this type of public debate was hardly commonplace. Out of a total of 85,000 residents, 5,000 joined the PEN but only 500 to 600 logged on at least once a month. In fact, only a small core of heavy users were really active.

However, McKeown commented: "I see PEN as a way to change the whole political process, the whole exchange of information with voters, the whole way that we interact with our city government."[62] It seems that this project turned out to be more of an opportunity for community debate than for political confrontation. The community dimension there-fore seems to have been a strong element in the project, as in others. With Free-Net, local groups used the possibilities of computer communi-cation to create a resource center accessible to all and to structure collec-tive debate; the BBS strengthened existing community life and was organized by intermediaries. Big Sky Telegraph set out to develop new community projects bringing together people living in different places in the same region, and the community managed the system. With the PEN, by contrast, it was the municipality that managed and funded the proj-ect. But this open electronic space served to discuss problems concerning particular social groups which did not all have a specific structure, so that the organization of public debate would ordinarily have been espe-cially difficult. Ken Philips, the project leader, considered a posteriori that "it's important to recruit opinion leaders to set the tone."[63] In all cases, it was local communities that expressed themselves and sometimes prepared actions via the BBS.

The issue of political debate is different; individual community interests evaporate as a more general debate emerges. In fact, computer communication was launched much later in this arena. In 1994, during the election campaign for the governor's and senator's positions, an attempt at public debate was made, apparently for the first time with the support of a Free-Net network. MN-Politics was a forum "for the sharing of information on and discussion of Minnesota politics and public policy."[64] According to the project leaders, "This effort may demonstrate how electronic communication can be a positive contribution as well as a challenge in our democracy."[65]

The Electronic Social Link

The pioneer electronic communities presented in this chapter are based on different conceptions of the links constituting them. Three different features characterize the social link of cybercommunities: geographical proximity, institutional affiliation, and degree of mutual knowledge. Positions on each of these points often differ.

Geographical Proximity

All these communities appeared to have a local identity—a founding element of local development projects. In the case of The Well and hobbyists' BBS, the local character was defined primarily by technical constraints. All these communities used telephone networks which, in the United States, applied a flat rate to local calls. This technicoeconomic factor severely limited use of the system by people far away. The Well was furthermore the vehicle of a cultural current that was strongly rooted in the San Francisco Bay area. In the case of the PEN, the fact of living or working in Santa Monica was a condition for participating in the electronic community. But although this local identity, asserted to a greater or lesser extent, was opposed a priori to the Internet universal model, it did not prevent these systems from subsequently trying to link to other BBS and thus from becoming stakeholders in the network of networks.

During 1983 amateur BBSs had Fidonet, a national network enabling them to link to one another. Computer expertise was not always available at that level, however, and had to be sought elsewhere. Amateurs also wished to develop technical devices comparable to those of Arpanet or Usenet. Although they managed to build up a very wide network with over fifty thousand nodes in 1996,[66] Fidonet came nowhere near linking up all existing BBSs—unlike university networks. Depending on the source, an estimated 25 to 40 percent of local servers were connected.[67]

Computer networking enthusiasts soon linked up to networks outside the United States. Fidonet thus became truly international. In 1992 countries outside North America accounted for 40 percent of the nodes.

Community BBS were more wary of anything outside their local context. Whereas Free-Nets established a national organization (the NPTN), they did not create a national computer network. Grundler, chairman of the organization, conceived of a network in the broadcasting sense of the word, to download a particular type of information onto the BBS that requested it. Connection to Usenet, when available, was likewise incomplete. The manager chose the newsgroups to which he or she allowed access.[68] In a model in which information was more important than communication, local editors had the authority to select the information or debates that seemed relevant in the community.

In other electronic communities it was first through Usenet that connection was made with the outside world. This was the case of The Well and Fidonet in the years 1988–1989. A few years later they linked up to the Internet (The Well in 1992 and Big Sky Telegraph in 1993). As time went on, connection to outside networks, which in the early 1980s was simply an additional element of local electronic communication, seemed to become increasingly important. The authors of a report written in 1994 noted: "We strongly believe that the desire to gain local access to the Internet has been one of the driving forces behind the growing interest and involvement with community networking."[69] Should we conclude that the appeal of the local declined, or that the image of computer networks changed when the model of global communication that came from the academic world replaced local perspectives? The latter assumption is the most likely, for despite the attraction of universal communication, use of computer networks remained essentially local.

Institutional Affiliation and Degree of Mutual Knowledge

Unlike pioneer experiences such as CommuniTree, BBS were rarely completely open systems. Ordinarily users could not join freely. In many cases they first had to pay a subscription fee, albeit small, or become a registered member of the community, as in the case of free systems such as Free-Net and PEN. This electronic club was either related to existing associations (Free-Net) or constituted an entirely new institution. Institutional identity was usually manifested in a particular name for its members (e.g., Well-Beings, in the case of The Well). The group furthermore had a cultural identity. In BBS writing was the only form of interaction between individuals, and that interaction was possible only if members shared a common vocabulary, forms of speech, and, more generally, culture. Vocabulary and specific expressions were strong identity markers.

Community members' mutual knowledge varied widely. It depended on the size of the group, the regularity of participation in the forum, and the existence of community life outside the computer network. Two emblematic cases of the latter point were the Big Sky Telegraph, in which the network was the vehicle of collective projects uniting teachers in a mountainous region, and The Well, which regularly organized face-to-face meetings. The forum on children's education organized a spring picnic in a San Francisco park, which became a sort of annual party of The Well. In 1986 monthly meetings were also organized. These seem to have played a large part in structuring interaction. Katie Hafner cites a person who participated from Texas and whose "posts were more or less ignored until he went out of his way to travel to the Bay Area for a Well party. It was the fact of face-to-face contact, not so much the quality of it, that made the difference."[70]

The Community Utopia

The Electronic Community

Despite the differences that appeared among the BBS presented in this chapter, a new computer network model appeared. Alongside the university model, a second utopian project developed in the 1980s: the electronic community. This project was initiated by three social movements that appeared independently. The first consisted of amateurs who wanted to create a system similar to the one that academics had set up. The second was spawned by the California counterculture and saw computer networks as the association of a community utopia with an ecological (soft and nonpolluting) technique. These two currents had one thing in common: the part played by hackers, brilliant hobbyists who often had connections with the counterculture. The community development movement was the third current. In this case, computer networks were seen as a means to organize local awareness and structuring, as radio had been in the 1920s and later cable television and video in the 1970s. At times this movement was linked to the counterculture in one of its initial dimensions, political and social activism, but it also had strong ties with the academic world and most Free-Nets used university computer infrastructures.

Despite the diversity and heterogeneity of its origins, this electronic community differed in several respects from the invisible university college studied in the preceding chapter. First, the real or imagined local component remained essential—unlike the university network that by definition had freed itself from physical space. The social link was also different. Any academic was a potential member of the Internet provided his or her university and office were online. This was less a matter of a club spirit, as in electronic communities, than a consequence of professional status. In the invisible college the degree of familiarity was relatively high, for "dear colleagues" regularly met at conferences or seminars and exchanged their articles, and Arpanet or Nsfnet reinforced this contact. Yet their interaction remained essentially linked to their scientific activity.

With Usenet the geography of invisible colleges changed profoundly. The groups' dimensions increased while their boundaries faded and sometimes even disappeared. This was an anonymous world, far from the idea of a community so dear to most BBS. The last point distinguishing the university from BBS was the fact that the former played a key part in technological development. Its members were both designers and users. In the world of electronic communities, by contrast, the division of work was much more distinct: while a few hobbyists devoted themselves to the technology, most users were content to communicate via the tools developed by others.

The Microcomputing World

The difference between academics and BBS users also appeared in the fact that they belonged to different technical worlds. Most of the former used powerful terminals running on Unix, situated only on university campuses, and had real computing skills. The latter, on the other hand, used microcomputers at home. The computer was less a programming tool than a means for processing and storing data. Users needed standard software packages to perform these tasks. They used their computer for intellectual work rather than scientific research. Although the microcomputer of the 1980s had not yet spread to the public at large, a large proportion of the people who owned one were not computer specialists. Their use of microcomputers made them pioneers but it was not their computing skills that united them; it was a desire to communicate with a new tool, even if they were able to input data into a server (Free-Net) or host forums (The Well).

From Utopia to Community Ideology

Last, the community utopia differed from the invisible college utopia insofar as the initial dream was further from its realization. The local aspect gradually faded away behind a universal aspect, and the nature of communication, of egalitarian interaction at the origin of communities, hardly seemed to correspond to real practices. At PEN or Big Sky Telegraph, for example, only a small minority actually participated. In the case of The Well, where the community was not linked to a geographic territory, very few people expressed themselves and the vast majority simply observed the debate (read messages)—as in most online communities. Most users seemed to use computer networks, the interactive medium par excellence, in the same way that they used the traditional mass media. The great divide between broadcasters and receivers seemed to persist, despite technological change. Whereas the initial utopia embodied in CommuniTree, in particular, foresaw totally free, unrestricted dialogue, those experiments that actually lasted, such as The Well or PEN, soon saw the emergence of actors organizing the discussion. The leaders of forums, responsible for launching and moderating debate, thus played a key part in the community. These individuals who in the old media are called mediators or editors also had an essential role in BBS in bringing together transmitters and receivers, authors or artists, and the public.

But no change in the community *imaginaire* resulted from this evolution of communities' online practices in relation to the initial utopia. The idea of a virtual group in which everyone expresses themselves equally still dominates. The utopia has thus become an ideology partly masking the reality but also mobilizing actors. This ideology is particularly powerful insofar as it is embedded in a long American tradition in which society has always emphasized the notion of community. Tocqueville, in his day, already noted this point. During the twentieth century several new media—radio at first and, more recently, cable television—presented themselves above all as the media of communities.[71]

4

From Internet Myth to Cyber-*Imaginaire*

In the early 1980s the founding experiments stabilized and academic and community utopias were fleshed out. We can therefore consider that two sociotechnical frames were set, that of the academic Net and that of the community Net. From then on use of the Internet soared. In late 1989 there were about 180,000 host machines,[1] and by the end of 1992 there were 1.3 million.[2] This growth is explained by the development of academics' use of the Internet and by the fact that many BBSs linked up to it.

In 1993 the Internet was put on the media agenda for the first time and hundreds of articles were published on the subject.[3] This may appear to have been an essentially quantitative evolution, for whereas discourse on the Internet had previously been diffused in limited circles (computing, counterculture, etc.), by more or less private media, from 1992 to 1993 it became a regular feature in the national media. It was the beginning of a classic phase in the development of a technology, that of mass diffusion following laboratory research and early trials. From this viewpoint—a traditional perspective in the sociology of techniques[4]—new discourse on techniques is seen as simply aiding diffusion and as bearing no relation to the initial designers' debates. But, on the contrary, what the *imaginaire* proposed to users was largely inspired by the designers' utopias, despite the fact that it underwent a number of changes.[5]

Virtual Communities, Founding Myth

At the beginning of 1993 *Time* magazine published a feature called "Cyberpunk." After pointing out the link between cyberculture and the counterculture, the article discussed computer viruses, virtual reality,

rave parties, drugs (ecstasy), and The Well, the most well-known California BBS.[6] In particular, it cited Howard Rheingold, pioneer journalist in the electronic community: "We're replacing the old drugstore soda
fountain and town square, where community used to happen in the
physical world."[7] In contrast to those traditional communities, Rheingold spoke of the "virtual community"—the title of his book published
at the end of the year.

In September, when the information highway project—debated extensively during the previous year's presidential election campaign—was in
a bad way, *Newsweek* published a feature on online life.[8] One of the
experiences presented was The Well. Rheingold signed an article, an
extract from his forthcoming book, in which he emphasized the fact that
virtual communities were not utopias since they had actually been created. The book, *The Virtual Community*, was a best seller,[9] selected by
Business Week as one of the books of the year. It was the first volume on
the Internet that was neither a technical nor practical manual. The
author discussed The Well and his own experience as a newsgroup user
and host at length. He also presented other electronic communities such
as Arpanet. Through his account he constructed a representation of the
Internet that combined characteristics of electronic communities and
invisible colleges. Virtual communities were described as bringing
together people from all corners of the globe, many of whom remained
attached to their locality. These individuals developed conversations that
were as intellectually and emotionally rich as those in real life, in a world
of balanced interaction between equals. The Internet was presented as
helping to recreate a social link and to breathe life into public debate
and, more generally, into democratic life.

Rheingold's book thus proposed one of the founding myths of the
Internet. The author took the sociotechnical frame of the electronic community and invisible college and placed it in a different sphere, that of
ordinary sociability. He then presented that as the reference model of the
Internet, although the change of social sphere modified the situation fundamentally, for the mode of functioning of counterculture or university
communities was obviously not that of society at large. As a result, Internet *imaginaries* evolved rapidly. Computer communication was no
longer a matter of experimentation, part of a technical project. It aimed

not to mobilize a small group of academics, but to offer American society the large-scale realization of new communicational relations that until then had been experienced only within small groups. This change is perfectly characteristic of a myth.

It is hardly surprising, therefore, that the media used Rheingold as a reference to talk of a universal Internet, and that they proclaimed him the "first citizen of the Internet."[10] It is similarly understandable that all those who wanted to launch out into the Internet business studied The Well which they considered as the prime example of a virtual community, "hoping to divine the magic formula that made it so special, so captivating, so unique" when in fact it was little more than a social experiment.[11]

Rheingold's *imaginaire* also introduced a new division of work. We have seen that one of the original features of the Arpanet was that the same actors conceived of, designed, and used the technique. These three activities were thus constantly entangled. By contrast, in the community Internet technical conception was partly severed from the rest, while users constructed new uses and a discourse to match. After 1993, this division of work was accentuated. Designers left university or groups of hobbyists to join existing companies or found their own startups. At the same time, users lost some of their autonomy, while utopian discourse became more autonomous as professionals took over. The production of an *imaginaire* thus developed an aura and was spread far more effectively than before. There was a clear shift from the *imaginaire* of computer scientists and community groups to one of the masses. In particular, the digital intelligentsia was to produce the *imaginaire* of a universal Internet with the basic characteristics of the invisible college and electronic communities. Licklider's idea of a community of interest was adopted by Rheingold.

The fact that this *imaginaire* was based on the characteristics of the initial use of the Internet nevertheless prevented digital intellectuals from building utopias removed from technological reality. They were to act as mediators between designers and users. Like any good mediator, they not only served as a link but also participated intensely in the definition of the new sociotechnical frame and stabilization of the new medium. More generally, they were to launch and structure public debate on the Internet and other digital technologies.

Internet for All

The Beginnings of Popularization

The first literature specifically on the Internet for the lay public consisted of handbooks for beginners, first found in bookshops in 1992. These books, written by computer specialists with extensive experience in the new medium, but intended for the general public, offered a wealth of practical information on how to access and surf the Web. But they also provided precise representations of this new technique.

Zen and the Art of the Internet opens with the following statement: "We are truly in an information society." The author later describes the future Internaut: "You have at your fingertips the ability to talk in 'real-time' with someone in Japan, send a 2,000-word short story to a group of people who will critique it for the sheer pleasure of doing so."[12] Ed Krol expanded on that description: "Once you're connected to the Internet, you have instant access to an almost indescribable wealth of information. . . . Through electronic mail and bulletin board, you can use a different kind of resource: a worldwide supply of knowledgeable people, some of whom are certain to share your interests, no matter how obscure. It's easy to find a discussion group on almost any topic. . . . While free advice is often worth what you pay for it, there are also lots of well-informed experts who are more than willing to be helpful."[13] He thus conveyed the idea of a sharing of information that prevailed in The Well. Moreover, the title of Krol's book (*The Whole Internet Users Guide and Catalog*) was an explicit reference to the *Whole Earth Catalog* and to counterculture.[14]

These guidebooks catered to a public of lay academics (i.e., not computer specialists) and professional users. But Krol foresaw an evolution: "About ten years ago," he wrote, "personal computers brought computing from the realm of technical gurus to the general public. . . . The Internet is currently making the same transition"[15]—and his guide had a wide readership, with over 750,000 copies sold. *The Internet Companion*, published in late 1992, was also intended for a larger public constituting "the network community." This community was defined as follows: "The Internet has always been and will always be a key part of the research and development community, but the increase in access and the network's potential for becoming the basis for worldwide communication between people in all walks of life cannot be ignored by the rest of us."[16] To show how this extension of the Internaut community was going to affect everyone, the authors warned their readers in the introduction: "If you want to stay current in the nineties, and even into the next century, you need to learn about the Internet." In the following year this broader diffusion was noted by the author of *Internet Starter Kit for Macintosh*: "People are connecting to the Internet because the Internet is becoming more than just an elite club of technoweenies, it has become a virtual community in and of itself. . . . The Internet continues to thrive because of the volunteer labor pumped into it; but also important in its growth is the fact that it provides as much information as an individual can handle, and in this day and age, information is power."[17] This electronic community, which was attracting an ever-larger public, needed a guide, as Al Gore—then campaigning fervently for information highways—pointed out in the preface to *The Internet Companion*: "For too many people the Internet has been uncharted territory, and as a result they have hesitated to explore the vast potential of networking. I trust this book will change that."[18]

Naturally, the authors of these manuals wanted to set the example. Most of them used the Internet as a tool in their editorial work. The authors of *The Internet Companion* noted in their foreword that "despite the fact that the authors have never met face-to-face and live almost 2,000 miles apart, we were able to write this book in less than eight weeks by exchanging ideas and drafts through the Internet. If *we* can do that, just think what *you* can accomplish!"[19] Likewise, the author of *The Whole Internet User's Guide* met his editor on the Internet and the manuscript and various stages of correction were transmitted by email.

All these manuals proposed fairly coherent representations of the Internet as a tool for academic work that could be proposed to a broader public for searching for information, producing documents, and working with people throughout the world. In this way users could participate in virtual communities, as clearly shown by Mitch Kapor in the preface to another guide available on the Internet before being published as a book: "Freed from physical limitations, these people are developing new types of cohesive and effective communities—ones which are defined more by common interest and purpose than by an accident of geography, ones in which what really counts is what you say and think and feel, not how you look or talk or how old you are. The oldest of these communities is that of scientists, which actually predates computers. . . . I look forward to a day in which everybody, not just scientists, can enjoy similar benefits of a global community."[20] We find here all the components of the Internet myth as described by Rheingold.

In the autumn of 1993 the national media, which had spread the virtual communities myth, started to see the Internet as a means of mass communication. "Is Middle America ready for the Internet?" asked *Business Week*,[21] while *Time* noted that "suddenly the Internet is the place to be."[22] In the spring of 1994 *Business Week* went further: "Hardly a day goes by when there isn't some story in the paper or on the tube hyping the Internet."[23] These journalists were partly surprised by this success, for the Internet culture seemed distant from that of the public at large. *Business Week* cited the president of the online service Prodigy who calls the Internet "a Wild West show that will never become the backbone of a national data superhighway unless it's usable by mere mortals."[24] *Time* presented the Internet as "an anarchistic electronic freeway,"[25] and in another issue the same journalist, Philip Elmer-Dewitt, cited a consultant for whom "if there is a soul of the Internet, it is in that community [of hackers]."[26] This argument was in line with the feature that Elmer-Dewitt had already published the previous year on the cyberpunk. It can be seen as a clear illustration of the ambiguous attitude of *Time* toward the counterculture. The magazine presented it as a key element in the evolution of American society; it granted it a lot of space[27] and became a sort of mouthpiece for this social movement. Yet, at the same time, it denounced the movement's antiauthority and anarchic behavior. *Time* and the other news magazines consequently changed the way they presented the Internet. After the period of promotion of Rheingold's electronic communities came the denunciation of anarchic behaviors. Many articles presented the Internet as a medium for pirating and pornography. My study reveals that these two topics constituted roughly half of all articles on the Internet in *Time* and *Newsweek*, and about one-eighth of those of *Business Week* in 1993 and 1994.[28]

But the news magazines also fulfilled an educational role by explaining how to use the new medium: "[The] Internet seems to be everywhere, but frankly, you're still puzzled about what it means to you," wrote *Business Week*.[29] A few months later Katie Hafner wrote an article in *Newsweek* entitled "Making Sense of the Internet," with the subtitle "You keep hearing about cyberspace. But what is it, exactly? What's the best way to try it out? And do you really need to care?"[30] For people who did not have the possibility of logging onto the Internet at work, articles advised them to subscribe to the online services that were to become the main access providers, and thus to get a new lease on life.

These services developed during the 1980s along the same lines as the Minitel, although they used a microcomputer rather than a dedicated terminal. As in the case of videotext, each of the access providers (Prodigy, CompuServe, AOL, etc.) offered its own information services. Prodigy designed its service as an interactive medium largely financed through advertising. CompuServe and AOL also offered message services and newsgroups that were limited to their subscribers. These access providers found relatively few customers (a little over 2.5 million subscribers in 1992), and they were ridiculed by the apostles of the Internet who accused them of failing to perceive the demand for bidirectional, universal communication.[31] On discovering the success of the Internet in 1992–1993, they were the first to propose access for the general public. Subscriber numbers shot up to five million in 1994.[32] The new Internet utopia had become a reality.

But the advent of the new Internauts often generated conflict. *Internet World*, from 1992 to 1994 the only magazine on the Internet for the general public, published a story in November 1994 entitled "Aliens among Us: A horde of new users from America Online, Compuserve, Genie and Prodigy is coming onto the Internet."[33] This magazine, which published popularized and thought-provoking articles, also wanted to be the mouthpiece of real Internauts. In the same issue it published an article denouncing the biased image that the media gave the Internet: "Judging by what you read in the press, you'd think the Internet was primarily a morass of newsgroup in-fighting, purpoiled programs and pictures, retro ex-hippie anti-establishment types and cyber-cowboys and gunslingers."[34]

The Internet general public, presented ambivalently by the commercial media, gradually changed. In 1994 *Net Guide* published a description of potential uses of the Internet under the heading "Your Map to the Services, Information and Entertainment on the Electronic Highway," highlighting recreational uses more than any of the guides published in previous years had done: "You can start relationships, fire off insults, publish your own writings. You can get help on your screenplay. You can get updates on the TV soaps you've missed. You can play games. . . . You can search through libraries around the world . . . You can lose yourself in a new medium and a new world."[35] The guide also answers the question "Do I really need it?" with "You'll be part of an active, expanding community of people exploring . . . the information frontier."[36] Once again, we see the same discourse as that of The Well: by participating in this pioneering experience, one tries out a new form of community. Yet a new orientation of Internet was also emerging, owing primarily to the success of the Web and the diffusion of Mosaic: a medium for consultation. The advertising banner "Netguide is the TV guide to Cyberspace" is clearly indicative of this development.

Netiquette
As previously indicated, the arrival of new Internauts in the forums and, more particularly, on Usenet, often caused conflict due to inappropriate contributions. Yet the wish to formalize the rules of electronic communications had been expressed on the Internet early on. In 1985, two computer scientists who were thoroughly familiar with electronic mail wrote a report at the request of the National Science Foundation on the ethics and etiquette of electronic mail. The question of etiquette seemed particularly important to them, "because certain standard social norms must be reinterpreted and extended to cover this quite novel medium."[37] These ideas were very soon codified and rules of electronic savoir-vivre circulated on Usenet. General principles of any social interaction (identifying oneself, thinking of one's interlocutor, contributing new ideas, etc.) were found alongside rules pertaining to the written media (read before answering, don't answer in the grip of emotion, etc.) or to electronic media (choose the right newsgroup, control the feeling of ubiquity, think that messages are archived, etc.), and, more precisely, to the format of

messages (give a title, be brief, etc.).[38] "Net etiquette" was to become netiquette for short. Articles dealing specifically with this question and intended for new users were published primarily in electronic form. In a biblical tradition, some proposed "the ten commandments for computer ethics."[39]

This netiquette gradually became a code of chivalry that real Internauts respected and got others to respect. As indicated in *Zen and the Art of the Internet*, "There are many traditions with Usenet, not the least of which is dubbed netiquette."[40] Virginia Shea, who devoted a book to this question, tried to define the term: "Etymologically, it comes from the French word for 'ticket.' If you know the etiquette for a particular group or society, you have a ticket for entry into it." She also noted that the aim of her book was "to give you a 'ticket' to the cyberspace. 'Netiquette' is the etiquette of cyberspace."[41]

Ed Krol used another metaphor for Internet etiquette: "frontier justice." "When the West was young," he wrote, "there was a set of laws for the United States, but they were applied differently west of the Mississippi river. Well, the network is on the frontier of technology, so frontier justice applies here, too."[42] For these new pioneers, there were two fundamental ethical principles, individualism and the protection of the network. "Individualism is a two-edged sword. It makes the network a nice place for finding diverse information and people, but it may tax your liberality. People have many differing opinions about acceptable behavior."[43] But as soon as the practices of certain users disrupted the normal functioning of a part of the network, pressure of varying intensity was exerted on them. Among such deviant behaviors, Krol noted "hateful, harassing or other antisocial behavior, intentional damage or interference with others, and publicly accessible obscene files." Internauts thus practiced self-discipline, for they believed that "if these problems aren't resolved within the network community, but are thrown into newspapers and Congress, everyone loses."[44]

To become an Internaut it was therefore necessary to abide by the rules of savoir-vivre or certain linguistic forms[45] used by the oldest members of the community, academics, and researchers. One thus took a "ticket" to join the community or at least to develop practices similar to theirs. Netiquette was designed to promote harmonious debate, moderate controversy, and the search for consensus and, on the other hand, to exclude violent debate, which was anathema (sending "flames"). This was a traditional code of conduct in the academic community, considered necessary for the functioning of invisible colleges. By proposing these rules as valid for any electronic social interaction, new Internauts' identification with the academic model was reinforced. Netiquette was often mentioned in forums to call to order recalcitrant users and enhance the feeling of belonging to the Internet, which is what made it different from other codes of conduct such as those drawn up for written correspondence or, more recently, mobile telephone use.[46] It participated in the symbolic creation of the electronic community and as such was another element in the construction of the Internet myth.

Advice and Illusion

The different guides presenting the Internet thus argued that the model of sociability developed in the academic world around and through the Internet could be transposed to the ordinary world. They believed that the principles of egalitarian interaction and free circulation of information in the framework of a cooperative network managed by its users—who constituted the heart of the academic Internet sociotechnical frame—would spread with the new technology. In their opinion, there was a kind of Internet nature, and they saw no reason for that to change in different social spheres of use.

This type of discourse was crucial for the future of the Internet. It proposed a frame of interpretation and action for computer communication that was especially powerful insofar as it described communication practices that already existed in the academic world and could be adopted. By becoming a new Internaut, one did not simply become a user of networked computing, communication tools, or data searches; one also penetrated another social world in which relations between individuals were based on equality and cooperation, and information was free.

This discourse was certainly partly deceptive, for society is not a cybercampus. Far greater inequalities in competency than in the academic world were to emerge and the principle of gratuity was to disappear. There was thus a strong mythical component in these views which were at the origin of the Internet ideology that appealed to people, mobilized them, and masked the real functioning of the new technology. But the initial model was also to last. Forums were created for the public at large, diverse users consulted information collated by academics, and ordinary individuals created sites with content that was sometimes immensely valuable. The initial utopia thus lasted in a different form.

Digerati and the Cyberelite

Wired: *The Cybermagazine*

Alongside books introducing readers to the Internet and early articles on it in the general press, another type of literature appeared that developed a far broader *imaginaire* concerning the entire computing world. In January 1993, when the public at large was timidly starting to link to the Internet and information highways were at the center of the political agenda, a new magazine was launched in San Francisco: *Wired*. Like their first sponsor, Nicholas Negroponte (director of MIT's Media Lab), the founders, Louis Rossetto (managing editor) and Jane Metcalfe (president), were persuaded that computer technologies were going to trigger a real revolution. Apart from the universal Internet that some were promoting, computing was infiltrating all human activities, professional and personal, intellectual and artistic alike. To the question asked in the editorial entitled "Why *Wired*?" Rossetto answered: "Because the Digital Revolution is whipping through our lives like a Bengali typhoon . . . and because the computer 'press' is too busy churning out the latest PCInfo-ComputingCorporateWorld iteration . . . to discuss the meaning or context of social changes so profound their only parallel is probably the discovery of fire. . . . *Wired* is about the most powerful people on the planet today—the Digital Generation."

The tone was set: *Wired* was to be the standard-bearer of the new computer culture. As Metcalfe later said: "What we are really talking about is a fundamental shift in society that is being led by technology but is infiltrating every aspect of society."[47] Not only was this new magazine the tribune for new ideas on the computer revolution, it also had a new layout that was a milestone in the history of press magazines. Articles were presented in the same way as advertisements, with slogans over photos or huge graphic illustrations. Photos were often manipulated and represented anything from landscapes or people to printed circuits or computer terminals. The picture rarely had an illustrative function; it was in constant interaction with the text, sometimes even making it difficult to read. This layout was similar to that found shortly afterward on Web sites or CD-ROMs. It was even judged sufficiently innovative to be exhibited in the San Francisco Museum of Modern Art. *Wired* was more like *Rolling Stone* than like an intellectual journal, and this resemblance was not only formal. It was also a standpoint deliberately adopted in the cultural field. *Newsweek*, which announced the launch of the magazine, noted that Rossetto's aim was to create the *Rolling Stone* of the computer generation.[48] Two years later, Paul Keegan noted: "Like *Rolling Stone* in the '60s, it has become the totem of a major cultural movement."[49] The publication was also largely inspired by the cyberpunk magazine *Mondo 2000*, both in its presentation and in its choice of contributors.[50] *Mondo 2000*, founded in 1989, initially on an irregular basis but then as a quarterly in 1992, was the first magazine that managed to mix artistic circles and computer freaks. This carefully illustrated publication on glossy paper combined some of the weird, sometimes confused currents of thinking that California had spawned in the 1980s. One type of rhetoric that associated the New Age revolution with derision appeared in articles that both appealed to and disgusted readers. Editor in chief R. U. Sirius wanted to create "a commercial success by shocking in a pleasant way, by being subversive through the media, not because you believe you can 'change the system,' but because there's nothing more exciting than tickling America or prodding it where it hurts."[51] This provided *Wired* with ideas for a brilliant and fashionable magazine.

In March 1996 *Wired* invented the neologism "netizen" (citizen of the Internet) and created a section under that heading. The magazine thus hoped to act as netizens' mouthpiece. In an article it criticized the *New York Times*, for example, for presenting the Internet as a vehicle for free and uncontrolled talk, computer piracy, and an advocate of drugs.[52]

One of the appealing aspects of the magazine related to the fact that Rossetto managed to attract a group of intellectuals and journalists who came to be known as the cyberelite. Kevin Kelly, former editor in chief of the *World Earth Review*, occupied the same position at *Wired*. Steward

Brand, founder of the *World Earth Review* and The Well, and Howard Rheingold were also on the editorial committee. Many editors were members of The Well.

We also find journalists from other backgrounds, like Steven Levy, editorialist with *Newsweek*, Joshua Quittner, journalist for *Time*, John Markoff, correspondent for the *New York Times* in Silicon Valley, and R. U. Sirius, editor in chief of *Mondo 2000*. Two science fiction novelists, William Gibson—the first person to use the term "cyberspace," in his novel *Neuromancer*—and Bruce Sterling also participated in the undertaking, as did creators using new technologies, such as Jaron Lanier and Brenda Laurel. Last, consultants, specialists in forecasting, like Esther Dyson and Paul Saffo, were also there. In fact, forecasting had a place of honor in the magazine. For example, the fifth issue featured a long interview with Alvin Toffler whose thinking directly inspired Rossetto: "It's a new economy, a new counterculture and beyond politics. In ten or twenty years, the world will be completely transformed. Everything we know will be different . . . I think Alvin Toffler's basically right: we're in a phase change of civilizations here."[53] Rossetto's esteem for the futurologist seems to have been mutual, for Toffler commented: "I think the readers of *Wired* are a unique resource for the country."[54] And indeed, as Keegan noted: "The genius of *Wired* is that it makes the Digital Revolution a self-fulfilling prophecy, both illuminating this new subculture and promoting it—thus creating new demand for digital tools, digital toys, digital attitudes."[55]

Rosetto and Metcalfe had a lot of difficulty finding capital to launch their magazine. Many publishers thought the market was too limited. As one of them said: "If you get out of Silicon Valley there are not a lot of places where you find that psychographic group."[56] But contrary to all expectations, *Wired* immediately had a vast readership: 110,000 digerati (digital generation) after one year in existence,[57] 230,000 after two years,[58] and 450,000 after four,[59] that is, nearly half the readership of the first popularized technical magazines such as *PC World*. These readers were people with a passion for the Internet and other digital media. We find among them many professionals of these new technologies: computer scientists, multimedia designers, artists, and so forth.[60]

Forecasting Club and Association to Defend Computer Freedoms

The cyber-*imaginaire* appeared not only in the media but also in think tanks. In 1988 Brand, along with futurologists who had worked for Shell and graduates from Stanford Research Institute, formed a forecaster's club that they called the Global Business Network (GBN). This institute sold services to firms and administrations. As one of its clients commented: "The network is a curious blend of scientists, musicians, artists, economists, anthropologists, and information technology gym rats who form a mosaic by which us capitalists can view our business environment and even our company."[61] The GBN was thus to act as an interface between the business world and heterodox future scenarios in which information technologies and ecology were to be of prime importance. Apart from a small core of permanent members, the institute used a network of experts, including academics (economists Michael Porter, Thomas Malone, and Brian Arthur; sociologist Sherry Turkle; cognitician Francisco Varela), musicians (Peter Gabriel and John Cage), science fiction authors (William Gibson and Bruce Sterling), journalists, consultants, and others. It used The Well to organize a private teleconference among its experts and to host its presentation on what would later be called a web site. *Wired* developed close ties with the GBN, and the magazine's forecasts owe a lot to the institute. About ten members of GBN were on the magazine's editorial committee. Four of them were on the cover pages of the first seventeen issues.

While the GBN developed forecasting on the information society and provided a link with thinking in the business world, another, more political, line of thought was established with the Electronic Frontier Foundation. At the origin of this association lay an event that marked the computer specialist community. In 1990 the FBI launched an inquiry that implicated a large number of hackers suspected of pirating software. John Perry Barlow, former hippie (lyric writer for the Grateful Dead) and computer journalist, Mitchell Kapor, cofounder of the computer company Lotus (later sold), and John Gilmore, another hacker who had got rich from computing,[62] decided to found an association to defend freedom in cyberspace. The Electronic Frontier Foundation (EFF) was "established to help civilize the electronic frontier; to make it truly useful and beneficial not just to a technical elite, but to everyone; and to do this in a way which is in keeping with our society's highest traditions of the free and open flow of information and communication."[63] More precisely, it defended individual cases and its Washington office lobbied the government and Congress. Kapor, an habitué of The Well, naturally opened a conference on the foundation in the California BBS. The founders moreover considered The Well to be "the home of the Electronic Frontier Foundation."[64] The EFF was also complementary to *Wired*. It provided the magazine with one of its main topics, and *Wired*, in turn, constituted an excellent tribune for the association. Two of the three founders, half the board of directors and the legal adviser (Mike Godwin) wrote in the magazine. Jane Metcalfe was also elected to the board.

Thus, The Well, the Global Business Network, the Electric Frontier Foundation, and *Wired* all had a lot in common. By clicking on the name of one of the actors of these institutions, one often found oneself in another institution, in the hypertext of the cyberimagination. Referrals were constant as each institution supported the others. GBN contributed its forecasting and its contacts with big business, EFF its political project and struggle to defend the freedom of Internauts, *Wired* its ability to format and adhere to the cyberpunk culture. Steward Brand, one of the main links among these institutions, summarized the relations of all these projects with the counterculture when he noted: "One advantage of working with survivors of the '60s is, we've had an experience in creating utopias. We've had our noses rubbed in our fondest fantasies."[65]

The Cyberelite Takes Charge of the Internet *Imaginaire*

The editors of *Wired* and members of the Electronic Frontier Foundation or the Global Business Networks were not only like the editors of popularized manuals, the agents of the diffusion of Internet. They saw themselves above all as an elite, as the avant-garde of the information society. As Steward Brand said: "Elites are idea and execution factories. Elites make things happen; they drive culture, civilization."[66]

Different lists of the people who would count in the future information society were published in the press.[67] Journalist and literary agent John Brockman published a digerati "Who's Who" in 1996. The forty or so people selected included computer scientists, entrepreneurs, and intellectuals, among others (of whom about ten were editors of *Wired*).

The intelligentsia who wrote in *Wired*, militated with the EFF, or offered advice in the GBN included many academics, artists (novelists, musicians, visual artists), computer scientists, and journalists who also worked for other newspapers. Thus, even though most of them were not innovators, they had links to this environment. On the whole they were specialists of discourse who produced the information society *imaginaire* in the mid-1980s. This was not only the *imaginaire* of a technical project or information highways or the Internet, as in the case of the discourse studied in preceding chapters, but that of a new society whose relationships with individuals, the state, and the market were changing. The digerati's discourse presented us with new forms of politics and economics, and a new definition of the self that emerged with the digital revolution.

These themes were diffused not only in *Wired* and via other specialized online or hardcopy mediums. In 1995 the national media popularized the differing points of view and thus diffused the Internet *imaginaire*. *Newsweek*, for instance, made 1995 Internet Year and opened its year-end issue with the following phrase spread across four pages: "This changes . . . everything." The editorial described the Internet as "the medium that will change the way we communicate, shop, publish and (so the cybersmut cops warned) be damned."[68]

II

A Virtual Society *Imaginaire*

5

Dawn of a New Communication Age

The technological *imaginaire* explored until now was associated with technical projects. Information highway, university Internet, and online community utopias were produced by politicians or industrialists in the first instance, computer scientists in the second, and hackers, social experimenters and innovative users in the third. Their discourses spawned the Internet myth that was then popularized for the general public.

The cyber-*imaginaire* presented in this second part of the book is, by contrast, far broader in scope. Linked to no specific project and intended for no particular public, it is a complete imaginary construction encompassing all aspects of the new digital society: individual life, relations between body and mind, micro- and macrosocial management of society, and production and distribution of wealth. Although all these components of the cyber-*imaginaire* were never combined in a single discourse, a synthesis would reveal something similar to the great utopias of the seventeenth and eighteenth centuries in which the functioning of a different world was described.

Of course, such a synthetic account would have little meaning, for whereas traditional utopias are literary works with a single author, the cyber-*imaginaire* examined here corresponds to the representations of a whole section of U.S. society today. The utopias concerned are not set in another time or space; on the contrary, they are about the evolution/transformation of today's world. That is why I first examine the new visions currently emerging, and then in the following chapters successively consider the different facets of the cyber-*imaginaire* concerning individuals' lives, political life, and economic activity.

The utopias of the information society analyzed in this chapter were mostly produced by intellectuals whose job is to think about tomorrow's world; intellectuals who are neither computer scientists nor politicians but thinkers about the future.

The Gurus of *Wired*

Of the many specialists on the future who reflected on the information society I will present only those whose thinking appeared in *Wired* in the form of interviews, original documents, or comments (in the case of those who are no longer alive). I first selected those who had written a lead story in *Wired*. They account for about one-third of the cover story articles of the first thirty-six issues.[1] I then added three influential authors who had written important articles not featured as cover stories.

These authors corresponded to three different intellectual currents: visionaries (McLuhan and Teilhard de Chardin[2]), futurologists (Alvin Toffler, George Gilder, Nicholas Negroponte, and Peter Drucker[3]), and science fiction authors (Bruce Sterling, William Gibson, and Neal Stephenson). With the exception of Teilhard de Chardin, they were not only writers but also consultants or journalists; intellectuals engaged in high-tech modernity, they maintained regular contact with corporate life. In this current thinking of digital technology, *the* technological revolution of today, was seen as the basis of an essential transformation of our civilization. To support their ideas, these intellectuals also presented descriptions of the past, not as historians but to afford themselves elements of comparison and insight into contemporary changes.

The same optimistic vision of technological progress was shared by most of them. Discordant voices were rare in the magazines that I studied. A book published in 1995 by astronomer and computer scientist Clifford Stoll, denouncing the uselessness of computer communication networks in daily life, was nevertheless a major success.[4] *Business Week* chose it as one of the books of the year. *Wired* also devoted several articles to the antitechnology movements,[5] although these points of view were presented as totally marginal. The editors clearly considered them to be nothing more than an amusing incongruity.

As regards the editorial line of this magazine, I wish to point out that my intention here is not to present all currents of thinking in the United States or even, more modestly, those which influenced *Wired*. As shown in another book,[6] the explanatory powers of intellectual genealogies is very limited. It is not the "intellectual ancestors" who determine the choices of their descendents, but the latter who choose particular authors from available resources. My question here is not who influenced *Wired*, but what resources were mobilized by the magazine to construct its cyber-*imaginaire*. By selecting certain authors rather than others, month after month, and sometimes giving them space again and again, the publication wanted to give its readers a particular idea of the digital world. In this way it built an *imaginaire*. Thus, it was not McLuhan or Toffler who influenced *Wired*, but *Wired* who chose McLuhan as a source of inspiration and drew on Toffler's or Bruce Sterling's ideas.

The Visionaries

McLuhan, the Patron Saint

The *Wired* editorial committee granted McLuhan the very particular status of "patron saint." The Canadian academic had died in 1980 and was consequently unable to contribute to the magazine. The citations opening the first two issues were from *The Medium Is the Message*, and McLuhan's photo appeared on the flag along with the sentence of the month since the last issue of 1993. It seems that the editorial committee believed McLuhan to be "one of the great prophets of our time," in the words of essayist Camille Paglia, who was interviewed in the magazine's first issue.[7] Initially a specialist in literature, McLuhan was one of the first intellectuals to conceive of culture in terms of mass media. He was the intellectual of pop culture.

Wired maintained close ties to its patron saint, and in 1996 the online magazine published a posthumous interview carried out via email with McLuhan. Although this was a hoax, we are told that the author of these messages appeared, through many tiny details, to know the master well. The reader was finally able to see what McLuhan thought about all the new digital technologies.[8] Gary Wolf wrote another story in the same issue, entitled "The Wisdom of Saint Marshall, the Holy Fool. In the tumult of the digital revolution, McLuhan is relevant anew." He believed that the Toronto prophet's success could be ascribed essentially to his aphorisms[9] that appeared all the more brilliant since no one could understand them: "His slogans are like lines of poems or phrases from songs capable of carrying powerful and ambiguous messages into new environments."[10]

Reference to McLuhan therefore appeared somewhat limited intellectually, like the sign of a thought that analyzes modernity through communication techniques, with no a priori. In the Canadian writer, the *Wired* team found a form of thinking based on collage, perfectly suited to the electronic world. But McLuhan also appeared as an example, the representative of a literary culture that had agreed to leap into the new culture and influence it. For example, in 1969 he said: "If literate Western man were really interested in preserving the most creative aspects of his civilization, he would not cower in his ivory tower bemoaning change but would plunge himself into the vortex of electric technology and by understanding it, dictate his new environment, turn ivory tower into control tower."[11]

In the master's thinking, the digerati found a powerful idea of a link between technological revolution and revolution of a civilization. Just as the Marconi galaxy bore no relation to the Gutenberg galaxy, so the digital world was fundamentally different from the analogical one. The citation opening the first issue of the California magazine summed up this perspective very well: "The medium or process of our time—electric technology—is reshaping and restructuring patterns of social interdependence and every aspect of our personal life. It is forcing us to reconsider and reevaluate practically every thought, every action, and every institution formerly taken for granted. Everything is changing . . . you, your government, your relation to 'the others.' And they've changed your education, your family, your neighborhood, your job."[12] In short, "new technology breeds a new man."[13] Such determinism was explained by the fact that intellectual technologies are related to our senses, and that the appearance of a new technology shifts the balance between the two: "The extension of any one sense alters the way we think and act, the way we perceive the world. When these ratios change, men change."[14] But the digerati often retained only a very faded vision of McLuhan's thinking. Computer scientist, musician, and virtual reality specialist Jaron Lanier commented: "I studied McLuhan and the other critics of the media and came to the idea that to have a better world in the future you would have to invent a new media with an eye toward aesthetics and beauty and community."[15]

Teilhard de Chardin: Great Minds Think Alike

Another Catholic thinker, Pierre Teilhard de Chardin, was often cited by *Wired* and cyberintellectuals. This French Jesuit and paleontologist died in 1955. He had tried to synthesize physical and biological phenomena, affirming that they were part of an evolution of the universe leading up to union and fusion with God. There was something similar about Teilhard de Chardin's and McLuhan's thinking, since the latter was said to have conceived of his notion of a global village by reading Teilhard de Chardin.[16] Both were on the fringes of the intellectual world, and although both enjoyed wide renown, they often had conflictual relations with their original institutions, the university and the church, respectively.

One of the *Wired* journalists believed that "Teilhard saw the Net coming more than half a century before it arrived."[17] In her opinion, the process of integration of the universe that Teilhard de Chardin saw happening, with the emergence of an informational membrane enveloping our planet and unifying the human mind (the "noosphere"), was a perfect description of the Internet. John Perry Barlow, founder of the Electronic Frontier Foundation, was also fascinated by Teilhard de Chardin's omega point, the situation closing the evolutionary process of the universe: "The idea of connecting every mind to every other mind in full-duplex broadband is one which, for a hippie mystic like me, has clear theological implications."[18] In an interview, he said "I think about Teilhard de Chardin a lot. . . . [He] used to talk about something called the noosphere which was the combined field of all human consciousness, and how that became stronger and stronger as civilization progressed and how what God wanted was to have someone to talk to on its own level, and that was what humanity was in the process of creating. That comes as close as I can to describing what I think is going on."[19] Although

Barlow agrees that in many respects his culture is very different from that of the Jesuit intellectual, he nevertheless sees it as a mobilizing vision.

The Teilhardian theme also appeared in the writings of R. U. Sirius, editor in chief of *Mondo 2000*, who stated: "We're going through a process of information linkup toward the building of a global nervous system, a global brain."[20] Kevin Kelly, editor in chief of *Wired*, who had been steeped in the New Age culture, described his first plunge into the Internet as a "religious experience." He also saw a link between computing and creation of the universe: "The reason why the hippies and people like myself got interested in [computers] is that they are model worlds, small universes. They are ways to recreate civilization."[21]

Louis Rossetto also saw the Teilhardian noosphere as a metaphor that was relevant to the Internet: "The more minds that connect, the more powerful this consciousness will be. For me, this is the real digital revolution—not computers, not networks, but brains connecting to brains."[22] He also cited McLuhan: "The computer thus holds out the promise of a technologically engendered state of universal understanding and unity, a state of absorption in the logos that could knit mankind into one family and create a perpetuity of collective harmony and peace. This is the real use of the computer . . . to speed the process of discovery and orchestrate terrestrial—and eventually galactic—environments and energies. Psychic communal integration, made possible at last by the electronic media, could create the universality of consciousness. . . . In a Christian sense, this is merely a new interpretation of the mystical body of Christ; and Christ, after all, is the ultimate extension of man."[23]

Teilhard de Chardin's work thus provided cyberintellectuals with a mix of New Age spirituality and strong images to describe the digital communication goal. In a universal and mystical vision they replaced the idea already developed by Turoff (see chapter 2) that computer networks can be used to construct a "collective intelligence." Where Teilhardian evolutionism saw the course of the spiritual[24] in the universe, digital intellectuals saw the bases of a faith in the future.[25]

In the final analysis, the digerati, in the counterculture tradition, found in Teilhard de Chardin and McLuhan a teleological vision of the development of computing—the basic foundations of a new utopia.

The Futurologists

McLuhan and Teilhard de Chardin defined the perspective; they helped digital pioneers get going. "There is a long road ahead, and the stars are only way stations, but we have begun the journey,"[26] said McLuhan in his conclusion to an interview. But the two prophets provided few details on the new era or the functioning of society in the digital age. Futurologists offered this type of reflection but without predictions on the future. On the contrary, wrote Peter Schwartz, cofounder of GBN, "they make their fortune by interpreting the present in a new way—a way that makes more sense and seems more conventional the farther into the future one goes."[27]

Alvin Toffler and Future Shock

In 1980, the year of McLuhan's death and twenty-five years after that of Teilhard de Chardin, Alvin Toffler, the most renowned U.S. futurologist, published *The Third Wave*.[28] In this book Toffler contrasted agricultural and industrial civilizations with a new wave that was swamping everything: information. Ten years later he summed up his theory for *Wired*: "We call it a civilization because it's not just the technology that's changing. The entire culture is in upheaval. All the social institutions designed for the second wave—for a mass production, mass media, mass society— are in crisis. The health system, the family system, the education system, the transportation system, various ecological systems—along with our value and epistemological systems. All of them."[29] It was to stress the extent to which this change concerned all aspects of our society that he called it the third wave and not the computer or digital age. His book, which listed the many aspects of this revolution, had a considerable audience. It was frequently cited by essayists of the information society and by various innovators. Juan Atkins, one of the founders of techno music, was reportedly inspired by Toffler's term "techno-rebel" in *The Third Wave* when giving this new music its name.[30] Likewise, the founder of AOL was said to have discovered online services when reading *The Third Wave*.[31]

Just as McLuhan's thinking was based on a contrast between the electronic media and Gutenberg's books, so Toffler simultaneously conceived of the second and third waves as two contrasting visions of our society.

Utopian thinking seemed particularly relevant when based on a simplified vision of the past. Chapters describing the second wave gave an idea of the third, a contrast. The former was the age of the machine, uniformity, division of labor, a break between the domestic and professional spheres, and representative democracy. The latter, which puts information at the center of its system, is the era of diversity, reorganization of work, telework, and new forms of direct democracy.

Since Toffler addressed multiple aspects of the information society, I have chosen to consider only the following three in more detail: the new generation of information and communication tools; the new organization of production; and new forms of democracy. In each of these sections I also present other, often similar, analyses by different futurologists who published in or were interviewed by *Wired*: George Gilder, Nicholas Negroponte and Peter Drucker.

Computer Technology Replaces the Mass Media

Like McLuhan, Toffler considered information and communication technologies—what he called the "infosphere"—as essential components of our society. With the emergence of the third wave, he predicted that the place occupied by the mass media would shrink: "The demassification of the media demassifies our minds as well. . . . This, in part explains why opinions on everything . . . are becoming less uniform. Consensus shatters."[32] He foresaw that a new intellectual machine, the computer, would spread quickly. These machines would be linked to networks like The Source, the first commercial network to have proposed a computer-aided conference derived from Hiltz and Turoff's system (cf. chapter 2). Users would be able to exchange messages and participate in "electronic communities." But the third wave "also provided powerful facilities, for the first time in history, for machine-to-machine communication and, even more astonishing, for conversation between humans and the intelligent environment around them."[33] Toffler thus popularized the theories of pioneers in new computer techniques of the 1970s (including Engelbart, Licklider, and Hiltz) and the first achievements in microcomputers and computer networks. In a broad perspective he associated the advent of new audiovisual media (VCR, cable, interactive TV, etc.) with computer technology.

Other authors who also diagnosed a turning point in communication technologies emphasized a sharper contrast between the preceding two sectors of communication that were to spawn the information super-highway project and the Internet. Ten years after *The Third Wave*, George Gilder, a conservative right-wing intellectual close to *Wired*[34] (whose book *Wealth and Poverty*, published in the early 1980s, was seen to be the bible of the Reagan revolution) published "Life After Television."[35] He predicted that the telephone and television industries would not survive the century because they were technologically obsolete, over-taken by digital technology, and had failed to see that modern users wanted to interact with the image. Computer nets, by contrast, "afford peer-to-peer interactivity rather than top-down broadcasts. Rather than a few channels, computer networks offer as many potential connections as there are machines linked to the web."[36] This thesis also appeared in another form, in one of the first issues of *Wired*. The main media were presented as a species on the way to extinction. Michael Crighton, a pop-ular author on novels on large saurians, explained his interest in "another dinosaur, one that may be on the road to extinction. I am refer-ring to the American media. And I use the term extinction literally." He warned that "the mass media will be gone within ten years. Vanished, without a trace."[37]

For Gilder, who considered that American society was facing a major crisis in its cultural institutions (the family, religion, and the arts), televi-sion seemed to be the basic cause of this disintegration of family and edu-cational values and disciplines. Like many other thinkers of the digital society, he profoundly despised television, which in his view was a cen-tralized medium imposing the same mediocre and uniform culture on its audiences. By contrast, what he called the "telecomputer" or "teleputer" allowed egalitarian communication between peers. New cultural prod-ucts would be intended for specific publics who could watch them when and where they chose. Production and distribution costs would drop substantially since there would no longer be intermediaries. "In the next decade," he wrote, "thousands of screenwriters will be able to make and distribute their own films."[38] Computer and multimedia production would become as diverse as books. In short, Gilder believed that "a new age of individualism is coming and it will bring an eruption of culture unprecedented in human history."[39] The break between the television era and the telecomputer era was so strong that Gilder hardly believed in this convergence between broadcasting and computing forecast by many futurologists. In his opinion, "the computer industry is converging with the television industry in the same sense that the automobile converged with the horse."[40]

Nicholas Negroponte, computer scientist, director of the Media Lab at MIT, and editorialist for *Wired*, whom the magazine presented as "the most wired man we know (and that's saying something)," explained that since the early 1990s television manufacturers had been putting more and more computer technology into their appliances, while computer manufacturers were putting more and more video into theirs: "When these two industrial trends converge, there will be no distinction between the two. . . . It doesn't matter whether you call the receiver a TV or a PC."[41] The only difference is the position of reception: a TV is watched from a couch. For the rest, the user will move from one situation (that of television) where the broadcaster chooses the information it sends to the receiver, to another (that of the Internet) where the user chooses what she/he wants.

A New Organization of Production

The principle of demassification that Toffler describes in the infosphere is also evident in the world of production: "The mass market has spilt into ever-multiplying, ever-changing sets of minimarkets that demand a continually expanding range of options, models."[42] To satisfy widely diverse markets, the production process has had to be completely reorganized.

Diversification of consumers' demand and producers' supply also alters the boundary between production and consumption. The personalization of products necessitates a real effort by consumers to define their demand. Moreover, users of many services are called on more and more frequently to perform tasks that were formerly done by salespersons. Manpower costs are thus externalized. The consumer carries out part of production activities. Toffler called this new economic agent a "prosumer." He foresaw the end of indefinite development of the market characterizing the second wave, and a sharp increase in domestic self-production.

Peter Drucker, one of the most famous U.S. management experts, gave more details than Toffler on the new mode of functioning of firms. The man who was presented as *Wired*'s official oracle[43] claimed that knowledge is the key production factor in today's economy. The new firm structured around management is also organized very differently. "In its central management, the information-based organization needs few, if any, specialists."[44] To show that the future belongs to small operating units, Drucker used a musical metaphor: formerly the organization resembled an opera; in other words, it was big, with extensive division of labor and rigid coordination achieved through partitioning. By contrast, the new organization should draw its inspiration from the small jazz band, where coordination is based essentially on mutual adjustment.[45] According to futurologist John Naisbitt, these small organizations were becoming players in the global economy, owing to the power of telecommunications. As *Wired* so aptly put it, Naisbitt explained "why small is not only beautiful, but powerful."[46] This idea that we were entering into an economy in which the actors are far more autonomous than in the past was expressed far more provokingly by the person who claimed to be McLuhan's successor, the Canadian Derrick de Kerckhove: "On the Web, Karl Marx's dream has been realized: the tools and the means of production are in the hands of workers."[47]

Thus, with partly different approaches, Toffler, Drucker, and Naisbitt all saw information as the origin of a new organization of work.

A New Democracy
According to Toffler, the nation-state that was the keystone of the industrial era is in the process of disintegration. We are witnessing a top-down transfer of political power, benefiting local regions, and a bottom-up transfer, benefiting transnational organizations.[48] Negroponte put forward the same thesis: "The state will shrink and expand at the same time. It will get smaller in order to be more local, with proximity and place playing a strong role. It will get larger in the sense of being global. I don't have a recipe for managing such a world, but its laws will have to be more global. Cyberlaw is global."[49] Gilder believed that microelectronics would destroy not only totalitarian regimes but also all hierarchies. He saw a new social system emerging in which "each individual rules his own domain."[50]

But apart from shifting the boundaries of public institutions and creating a more egalitarian world, it was the democratic system itself that had to be transformed. For Toffler, "society is becoming more demassified, more heterogeneous, and it is therefore harder and harder to arrive at a majority on an issue. And when you do, it's frequently just an artifact of the voting system rather than an expression of the organic beliefs of the population. So we believe that there are very deep difficulties for mass democracy in the era of diversity, which is being propelled by the computer revolution."[51] He therefore recommended replacing representative democracy by other forms allowed by the new electronic technologies, and suggested that it may be necessary to combine direct democracy with representative devices. Basically, it was the U.S. Constitution that had to be amended.

Toffler's *imaginaire* was clearly ambitious; it concerned all aspects of the information society. Its author considered that he had built not a utopia but what he called a "practopia." "Unlike a utopia, a practopia is not free of disease. . . . It is not static or frozen in unreal perfection. Nor is it not reversionary, modeling itself on some imagined ideal of the past. . . . In short, a practopia offers a positive, even a revolutionary alternative, yet lies within the range of the realistically attainable."[52] Toffler therefore claimed to provide elements for new social projects. With such a high goal it is understandable that he had many readers, and that his writings were a sort of toolbox for those who wanted to imagine the information society.

Negroponte's Forecasting Technique

Even though Toffler conceived of a new society based on a number of elements that he considered as vehicles of change, and even though new technologies unquestionably played a key role in the organization of the third wave, this author never provided a unified vision of technological evolution. Among the gurus at *Wired* it was rather Negroponte who proposed such a vision. His chronicles in the magazine addressed various aspects of the technological debate. In early 1995 he renewed his reflections in his book *Being Digital*[53] that turned out to be a best seller.

Negroponte saw digital technology as a new paradigm that triggered profound upheaval in the electronic world and even profounder upheaval in the information and communication worlds. Atoms were replaced by bits, so that information no longer needed to circulate along with its medium (the book, the record, or the videotape); it circulated in the form of digital data that could be transmitted by networks. As far as transmission was concerned, Negroponte argued for an inversion of networks. Instead of being transmitted by wire, as in the 1990s, telephony was to use radio waves, while radio and television were to be transmitted by cable. Since waves were a scarce resource, they needed to be reserved for mobile terminals.[54] In the new digital paradigm, Negroponte diagnosed a third major trend stemming from the intelligence of digital terminals. Computers were no longer machines that simply captured signals, like telephones or televisions; they were tools that could process those signals. It was thus possible to compress and decompress rich signals such as animated images. Owing to these intelligent terminals, television could be transmitted via telephone copper wires. There was consequently no more need to wait for the construction of fiber-optic networks to transmit multimedia programs.

These broad principles underlying technological change enabled Negroponte to foresee the development of information industries. First, hardware, such as the press or video rental, were destined to disappear. In the future journalists would sell their articles directly on line, while libraries would be electronic, and Blockbuster, the huge U.S. video rental firm, would have to switch to a new line of business.[55]

Analog transmission systems were also destined to disappear. Negroponte considered the fax to be "a step backward, because it does not contain 'structured data' but rather an image of text that is no more computer-readable. . . . Even though the fax is delivered as bits before it is rendered as an image on paper, those bits have no symbolic value."[56] An electronic text sent by email uses four times fewer bits, and allows electronic archiving and the possibility of reworking the text. Likewise, all analog high-definition television systems were, in his opinion, futureless. Negroponte considered that high-definition TV, even digital, was pointless.

"What is needed is innovation in programming, new kinds of delivery, and personalization of content. All of this can be derived from being digital,"[57] he argued. Since digital technology enabled televiewers to consume prerecorded images, they could choose the program they wanted and watch it whenever they liked. The program could be downloaded and stored by the television/computer. Thus, with digital technology, "prime time is my time." This type of reasoning was a regular feature of Negroponte's thinking. He associated certain potentialities of technology with his own usage options and inferred that his view of usage was the only one because it was determined by technical change. The technological visionary therefore soon became a social visionary. Lacking arguments on the evolution of uses, he used technological arguments to justify a preference—personal rather than programmed television—that was above all one of a cyberelite, but that appeared to be a feature of the new digital world.

In parallel with his discourse on the digital technology revolution, Negroponte made the following remark that explains to some extent his shift between technical and social forecasting: "The future of the computer and communications industries will be driven by applications, not by scientific breakthroughs like the transistor, microprocessor or optical fiber."[58] This statement by an engineer is in fact less paradoxical than it seems. Negroponte was not strictly speaking a technologist. The Media Lab that he ran at MIT was a place where new applications, rather than basic technologies, were developed. Negroponte's vision presented in *Wired* was a sociotechnical one, for digital technology related as much to the manipulation of bits as to new communicational perspectives. According to him, "being digital in its literal sense refers to computer-readable ones and zeroes, but at the more global level it has to do with where you find your information and entertainment. It has to do with the computer presence in your life. Being digital is about lifestyle and attitude and usage of this computer presence moment to moment. Being digital is an egalitarian phenomenon. It makes people more accessible and allows the small, lonely voice to be heard in this otherwise large, empty space. It flattens organizations."[59]

Consider two of the sociotechnical projects presented by the Media Lab guru, which clearly illustrate the globality of this view of digital technology. The first, "digital butler," was based on the observation previously mentioned that it is not a question of multiplying the bandwidth, of supplying more and more information, but, on the contrary, of selecting the most relevant information. Intelligent agents capable of serving as an interface between users' needs and available information correspond to this demand. In concrete terms, they may be computer applications that scan data bases and select information.[60] But we can also conceive that "your telephone won't ring indiscriminately; it will receive, sort, and perhaps respond to your incoming calls like a well-trained English butler."[61] Was this the dream of the cyberelite or the democratization of majordomos? Either way, this project fits into the previously mentioned perspective, of the disappearance of mass media: users would consult only information of interest to them since they would be able to select it either via intelligent agents or through media intended for closed groups. In any case, creators would be able to reach their public by short-circuiting publishers and distributors.

According to Negroponte, information would also bring about radical change in the educational field: "All of a sudden, learning by doing has become the standard rather than the exception. Since computer simulation of just about anything is now possible, one need not learn about a frog by dissecting it. Instead, children can be asked to design frogs, to build an animal with froglike behavior, to modify that behavior, to simulate the muscles, to play with the frog."[62] It would be possible to perform experiments or play games with a virtual copy. The principles of active education could thus be applied.

Negroponte developed a prospective discourse complementary to the discourse studied in the preceding pages. In the ever-present alchemy between techniques and society, the share of techniques was simply larger.

Science Fiction Writers

The Cyberpunk Current

Futurologists devoted themselves to thinking about the future; science fiction writers preferred to dream about it. A number of them wrote for *Wired*. The most regular contributors were Bruce Sterling and William Gibson, leaders of the cyberpunk movement. This literary current was defined by its interest in information technologies but also its taste for a bohemian lifestyle and for new rock currents.[63] Whereas Toffler associated new technologies with new civilization, Gibson and Sterling (for whom Toffler was an intellectual guide[64]) articulated technique to literature. Unlike the counterculture of the 1970s that was resolutely ecological and antitechnological (although it did dabble in electronics at rock concerts and discovered computer technology in the following decade), the cyberpunk movement lived with technology. It was a stakeholder in its world: "This integration has become our decade's [1980s] crucial source of cultural energy. The work of the cyberpunks is paralleled throughout Eighties pop culture: in rock video; in the hacker underground; in the jarring street tech of hip-hop and scratch music; in the synthesizer rock of London and Tokyo. This phenomenon, this dynamic has a global range; cyberpunk is its literary incarnation."[65]

These novels were distinguished from traditional science fiction by the fact that the technique was no longer a sort of distant deus ex machina; on the contrary, it was surprisingly close: "It is pervasive, utterly intimate. Not outside us but next to us. Under our skin, often inside our minds."[66] Sterling considered that in Gibson's stories "we see a future that is recognizably and painstakingly drawn from the modern condition. . . . Rather than the usual passionless techies, . . . his characters are a pirate's crew of losers, hustlers, spin-offs, castoffs and lunatics. We see his future from the belly up, as it is lived not merely, as dry speculation."[67] This proximity between cyberpunk science fiction and the technical world was clearly apparent in computer technology. Alan Kay, researcher at Xerox Park and considered to be one of the founding fathers of the microcomputer, noted: "Computer science inverts the normal. In normal science you're given a world and your job is to find out rules. In computer science, you give the computer the rules and it creates the world. And so we have the reductionism dream. We can build the whole universe from just one principle."[68] It is also this exercise of production of a world from a few principles that science fiction performs.

Cyberpunk books were not only a product of closer ties between electronics and the counterculture; owing to their success, they were also agents of the computer scientists' openness toward pop culture. As Gibson so aptly put it: "I gave [computer nerds] the permission to wear black leather."[69] More generally, as critic Erik Davis wrote: "Gibson's work actually created a social space, organizing the desires and intuitions of people operating in the widely disparate fields of journalism, law, media, psychedelic culture and computer science."[70] Cyberpunk novelists were really mediators between computer science and art.

Gibson's Cyberspace

The world of Gibson's novels is highly coherent, which probably reinforced the influence of his work. From 1984 to 1988 this cyberpunk novelist published three novels and a series of short stories all set in cyberspace. He defined the term in two ways. First, cyberspace—which he also called the matrix—is an electronic "consensual hallucination"[71] experienced daily by a large number of individuals. But it is also a system for processing and "graphic representation of data abstracted from the banks of every computer in the human system."[72] These two meanings may seem antagonistic but are in fact profoundly complementary. Cyberspace is a complex collective fantasy that is also really operational. For the "Finn," one of the old wise men of this world, "it's just a tailored hallucination we all agreed to have, cyberspace, but anybody who jacks in knows, fucking *knows* it's a whole universe."[73] This electronic system "facilitates the handling and exchange of massive quantities of data"[74] belonging to giant multinational corporations and consisting of technical and industrial information but also personal data on partners. Armed with their consoles, Gibson's heroes—cyberspace cowboys—try to gain access to these data, to "crack" their protections. Cyberspace is thus profoundly ambivalent: on the one hand, it "was anything like the universe anyway, it was just a way of representing data";[75] and on the other, as Lucas in *Count Zero* explains to Bobby, who discovers this universe, it is the world[76], to which Slide remarks: "People here don't do *anything*, without jacking. This is where I *entertain*!"[77]

Cyberspace is also a communication network. "Is there no way to contact Sally through the matrix?" asks one of the heroines in *Mona Lisa Overdrive*, for example.[78] The normal mode of transmission is "the bodiless, instantaneous shifts,"[79] so that one doesn't have to move. "Travel was a meat thing,"[80] notes Case, the hero of *Neuromancer*. With his console he has direct access to both an American city and an artificial satellite. The identity of a person or a situation can thus be transmitted in space but also in time, through archiving in computer memories. Thus, the singer in *The Winter Market*, digitized in the central memory of a mainframe computer, carries on singing to cover the cost of her own archiving.[81] Likewise Marly, without leaving Brussels, talks to Virek who has been "confined for over a decade to a vat. In some hideous industrial suburb of Stockholm."[82] The meeting takes place in the Güell park in Barcelona. A little lower down one sees the spires of the Sagrada Familia. In fact, digital simulation replaces sensorial experience.

Instead of being transported by the network, computer intelligence can be loaded onto portable devices. It may consist in a microprogram that can be inserted into a connector placed under a flesh-colored patch pasted behind the ear. It is also possible to acquire relative fluency in a language that one has never learned.[83] For even more powerful programs, a "biochip" is used. Colin, a virtual character in *Mona Lisa Overdrive*, is in fact a "biochip personality-base . . . programmed to aid and advise the Japanese visitor to the United Kingdom."[84] In this science fiction world we thus find the description of telepresence or personal assistant services similar to those described by Negroponte or other futurologists.

References to computer technology are everywhere, but so are those to videogames, virtual reality, and total entertainment. "The matrix," we read in *Neuromancer*, "has its roots in the primitive arcade games, . . . in early graphics programs and military experimentation with cranial jacks."[85] When Gibson's characters want to relax they place "trodes" on their heads and link to a "simstim" console enabling them to experience all the sensations of the show they are watching. Fortunately "the commercial stuff was edited, of course" so that if the singer "got a headache, . . . you didn't feel it."[86] The spectator's body slides, in a sense, into the actors' sensorial world.

The cyberspace and matrix concepts were soon to become synonymous with the Internet. In 1990, John Quarterman entitled his book— the first to describe the various networks of the Internet—*The Matrix*.[87] Likewise, in 1993 the first section on the Internet in *Time* associated Gibson's cyberspace with Gore's information superhighways: "Both terms describe the globe-circling, interconnected telephone network that is the conduit for billions of voice, fax and computer-to-computer communications."[88]

Science Fiction, Shedding New Light on Reality

Cyberpunk novelists were also given a lot of space in *Wired*. But the magazine miscast them, in a sense, by sending them to do stories. In the first issue Sterling presented an extensive military simulation system:[89] by means of a computer reconstruction of the Gulf War environment, soldiers would be able to train and test their strategy or simply their coordination (see chapter 6). We are on the boundary here between science fiction and reality. In an article published a few years later on the beginnings of this military simulation system, *Wired* explained that it was not Gibson who had invented cyberspace but a military computer scientist, Jack Thorpe, who had launched the design of this interactive network of simulators in 1976.[90] In another paper Sterling presented a sort of hippie carnival of the 1990s in the Nevada countryside. In this "temporary autonomous zone," "it's just big happy crowds of harmless arty people expressing themselves," he wrote, adding "may be something like a physical version of the Internet."[91] Cyberspace was evidently never far from the hippie camp.

Other reporting by cyberpunk novelists took them abroad, where they were constantly on the lookout for cyberspace equivalents in the real world. In Prague Sterling found traces of another "temporary autonomous zone" that had united dissidents, rock musicians and authors of samizdats during the velvet revolution. He saw this dissident medium as "a spiritual ancestor of fanzines, bulletin board systems, Fidonet, the Internet."[92] One of Gibson's first nonfiction stories, published in *Wired*, was about Singapore, which he described as "a Disneyland with the death penalty."[93] Unlike the utopias that he usually imagined, this one was both clean and worrying.

Neal Stephenson, who also published a short story in *Wired*, defined an approach to reporting that could likewise apply to his novelist colleagues: "Our method was not exactly journalism nor tourism in the normal sense but what might be thought of as a new field of human endeavor called hacker tourism: travel to exotic locations in search of sights and sensations that only would be of interest to a geek."[94] Stephenson applied this type of trendy tourism to the construction of an underwater fiber-optic network. By exploring the different sites where the network emerges from the depths, he ended up visiting some of the founding sites of the history of communication: Alexandria and its famous library; Malaysia and its production of gutta-percha, a type of rubber that made it possible to isolate telegraph wires and consequently played a key part in the creation of undersea cables; Cornwall in Britain, from which undersea cables were laid; and so forth. This was a science fiction author who traveled not only in space but also in time. He moved around between a major futurologistic industrial project and key episodes in the history of communication.

Stephenson was not the only science fiction author interested in the past. Gibson and Sterling wrote an historical detective story, *The Difference Engine*,[95] inspired by Babbage's mechanical calculating machine, often considered to be the ancestor of computers. Moreover, Sterling (who in 1992 had published a book on the extensive FBI operation against hackers), launched a project with another author in 1995, to collect data on defunct media. He believed that to understand the future of new contemporary media it was essential to collect data on all old media. This information could be gathered cooperatively via the Internet.[96]

Thus, like futurologists, science fiction authors needed to situate their visions of the future in relation to a vision of the present and the past. Gibson saw his novels as an instrument of social critique: "What's most important to me is that it's about the present. It's not really about an imagined future. It's a way of trying to come to terms with the awe and terror inspired in me by the world in which we live."[97] As for Sterling, he wanted to produce a "sense of history," to reconstruct an ideological narrative based on observed phenomena. This goal appears clearly in his short and often cited article on the history of the Internet. In it we find two elements of the myth that had already appeared in the mainstream media. First, the military origins of the Internet, with the wish to have a communication device capable of withstanding a nuclear attack. Second, the libertarian and anarchistic organization of a network that had been able to move away from the military. Sterling wrote: "Why do people want to be 'on the Internet'? One of the main reasons is simply freedom. The Internet is a rare example of a true, modern, functional anarchy . . . It's rather like the 'anarchy' of the English language. Nobody rents English, and nobody owns English . . . The Internet belongs to everyone and no one."[98]

Builders of the Present

The essayists and writers to whom *Wired* turned for a definition of the future saw themselves above all as builders of the present. McLuhan urged intellectuals to adopt the new technological culture. Toffler compared his "practopia" to unrealistic utopias. Among the multiple technologies tried, Negroponte identified those which seemed most feasible and could be articulated to social demand. Gibson denounced the violence of our world. Sterling defended hackers and saw the appearance, in different sectors of society, of the same anarchic freedom that prevailed on the Internet.

Negroponte, who worked for the Media Lab on the realization of technical projects, was in a sense part of the same tradition as Licklider and Engelbart who wrote about a utopia that was to become an experimental project. By contrast, the other authors provided resources for readers who designed or used the technique. They proposed a set of justifications enabling computer scientists, artists, or users of the PC or Internet to explain their agendas in the digital world.

Some observers, such as anthropologist David Tomas, consider that Gibson influenced research on computer technology.[99] In the history of art, as in the history of techniques, the frequently evoked phenomena of influence remain very obscure. Even if we have difficulty seeing how Gibson could have been at the root of an IT discovery, he does provide some ideas for imagining a particular device or embarking on a project. I noted earlier that Juan Atkins called his music "techno," a term borrowed from Toffler, and that the founder of AOL learned of the existence of online services by reading the futurologist's writings. These are some of the modest resources that thinkers on the future provided for IT specialists. More important, they also provided a cultural space as a reference. Allucquère Rosanne Stone noted that *Neuromancer* "reached people who were technically cultured and socially discontent, seeking a social anchorage enabling them to combat the anomy characteristic of life in Silicon Valley. . . . Suddenly Gibson's powerful vision provided them with an imaginary public space and a community of debate that opened the way to new modes of interaction."[100]

This cyber-*imaginaire* also interested ordinary users. It provided them not with practical resources for entering into a new technical world, as in Rheingold's and the popularizers' myth, but with a general vision of cyberspace and the information society.

6

The Body and Virtual Reality

The prospective and futuristic discourses proposed by essayists and novelists seem to present a relatively uniform vision of the future. Yet closer examination of this new digital society reveals a wide diversity of viewpoints. Virtual reality (VR) is a particularly interesting case of the multiplicity of *imaginaires*.

The VR concept is probably one of the most polysemic in the literature on information technology and the Internet. Although agreement prevails that virtuality is opposed to reality, opinions on everything else differ. For computer scientists who developed VR, it is an IT device used to reconstruct the real by means of synthetic images and sounds. These are used to simulate situations for the purposes of learning or experimentation. On the other hand, artists see it as a means not for copying reality but for creating a new world. For certain hackers virtual reality is also a way of escaping the real world, either by living in an imaginary world or by trying to transfer their intelligence and, possibly, even their emotions onto their computers. Finally, the word "virtual" is also used in relation to communication via the Internet and primarily group communication where written messages are used to converse in a virtual space. These different meanings of virtual define it either as a tool for knowledge, action, and creation, or as a means for withdrawing into oneself and escaping into an imaginary world, or, last, as a means of communication.

Certain representations of VR relate to the individual's relationship with his or her computer. Is it possible to think, act, and communicate only via one's computer, and thus to disregard one's body? This theme is often present in VR discourse, which is why this chapter combines reflection on VR, human-machine interaction, and the role of the body in the use of information technology.

Discourses on VR are multiple. They are produced by hackers, computer scientists, and artists (visual artists, musicians, actors and, of course, science fiction authors). As usual, I chose those authors who had published or been interviewed in *Wired*. We will see that they represent a wide variety of viewpoints. Yet there is a common denominator: all of them were chosen by *Wired* as elements in the construction of the cyber-*imaginaire* discourse.

Before embarking on this reflection, we need to explore the technical apparatus of virtual reality. I do so briefly by examining the discourse of some of the founding fathers, and then look at how this project appeals to artists and those wanting to create a new medium. I then consider a fantasy shared by computer scientists and artists: the ability to abandon one's body. A similar project exists with the designers of robots, but there is probably no better example of disembodied communication, often called virtual communication, than that taking place on the Internet in various role games. This point is studied in the third part. Finally, I examine the utopias of virtual sex and travel.

Virtual Reality

Simulation
The idea of creating a copy of reality was widely diffused by science fiction. It was through simulation that this utopia first started to take shape, and flight simulators were some of the first techniques enabling users to test a real situation. During World War II the U.S. army mounted a cockpit on a dynamic platform which turned or tilted as the pilot moved the joystick. In the 1960s simulation was accompanied by a visual dimension with high-quality video images displayed on the cockpit windscreen. The camera's movements were synchronized with the pilot's actions.

These projects were boosted by the advent of computer technology that made it possible to unify the different components of simulators. The first step was the development of graphic computing through which visual models could be designed and displayed on the screen. Users could thus create images by means of an elementary interface, or pilot a computer via a graphic interface. In 1963 Ivan Sutherland developed one of the first graphic software packages, "Sketchpad." As Ted Nelson noted, it "lets you try things out before deciding. Instead of making you position a line in one specific way, it was set up to allow you to try a number of different positions and arrangements, with the ease of moving cut-outs around on a table."[1] Graphic computing thus made it possible to work by trial and error, to perform simulations. It also helped humans deal with complex problems. "In many cases," notes Sutherland, "we may be entirely unable to think through a problem, or even recognize one, without an appropriate picture. . . . An ability to construct, manipulate and observe complex pictures of computed phenomena may radically change our ability to grasp complex ideas."[2]

But even richer dialogue could be developed with computers. A few years after the creation of Sketchpad, Sutherland defined his vision of new computer interfaces in an article titled "The Ultimate Display": "The computer can easily sense the positions of almost any of our body muscles. So far, only the muscles of hands and arms have been used for computer control. There is no reason why these should be the only ones, although our dexterity with them is so high that they are a natural choice. Machines to sense and interpret eye motion data can and will be built. It remains to be seen if we can use a language of glances to control a computer. An interesting experiment will be to make the display presentation depend on where we look." He even considered that the computer should make use of as many senses as possible: "So far as I know, no one seriously proposes computer displays of smell or taste. . . . I want to describe for you a kinesthetic display. The force required to move a joystick could be computer controlled, just as the actuation force on the controls of a Link Trainer are changed to give the feel of a real airplane. . . . By use of such an input/output device, we can add a force display to our sight and sound capability."[3]

While Sutherland's goal was to multiply forms of human-machine dialogue in the flight simulator tradition, he initially focused on vision. He wanted to present users with an image that changed as they shifted their gaze. For that he had to create three-dimensional images and to develop a head-mounted display. Users thus had the impression of being immersed in a synthetic landscape in which they could navigate. This work, largely supported by ARPA, was to be continued in the 1980s as part of military and NASA research.

At the same time, in an air force laboratory, Thomas Furness developed a simulator based on the same techniques, that was to evolve into the "Super Cockpit" project. This program was based on the observation that fighter plane pilots had more and more information to process in a very short time. They also had less and less direct contact with the outside world, and they received increasingly abstract data which gave them no immediate references to pinpoint their position. To adjust to these changes, it was necessary to synthesize information transmitted to pilots and to give them the possibility of receiving it with all their senses. The "Super Cockpit" objective thus went further than simulation. According to Thomas Furness, it aimed to improve interactions with pilots in their machine, in both real and simulated situations: "Its thrust is to revolutionize the way that humans interact with machines by returning to the fundamental spatial and psychomotor capabilities of the operator." The project consisted of developing " 'a cockpit that the pilot wears,' such as a special flight helmet, gloves, and flight suit that contain control and display components which create an interactive virtual medium for the pilot. These components provide three dimensional stimulation of the visual, aural and tactile senses."[4]

Research on virtual reality thus took a big step forward, from simulation techniques to improved interfaces with reality. Situations were created in which real and simulated action not only corresponded more and more closely, but also used the same means to apprehend the outside world. These situations were nevertheless still structured by one question: the relationship between humans and machines. The next step in military simulation projects was to include aspects of coordination between individuals. It was the Simnet project that allowed tank simulators to wage virtual battles. The goal was no longer to learn to drive a tank, but to coordinate and react to enemy attacks. These techniques thus made it possible to simulate military maneuvers. The Pentagon, which owned a detailed data base on every square meter of Kuwait's and Iraq's territory, produced a "virtual reality version" of one of the Gulf War battlefields. Users of this type of simulation could move about on a

"Simnet flying carpet" and examine the battle from different angles. They could also change the parameters on the equipment or the Iraqi strategy and see the result. More generally, the data bases resulting from digitized satellite photos have enabled the U.S. army to train its different units on the digital version of any site in the world.

Bruce Sterling, who described this apparatus in the first issue of *Wired*, concluded as follows: " 'Simulate before you build.' They want to make that a basic military principle. Not just simulated weapons. Entire simulated defense plants."[5] But from the simulation of war to automated war is only one small step that General Westmoreland took when he said: "On the battlefield of the future, enemy forces will be located, tracked and targeted almost instantaneously through the use of data-links, computer-assisted intelligence evaluation and automated fire control. I see battlefields on which we can destroy anything we locate through instant communications and almost instantaneous application of . . . lethal firepower."[6]

How to Define Virtual Reality?

The previous examples of simulation give a clearer idea of what exactly VR is and how we represent it. For Negroponte, "Basically, VR makes the artificial as realistic as the real. In flight simulation, its most sophisticated and longest-standing application, VR is more realistic than the real. Pilots are able to take the controls of fully loaded passenger planes for their first flight because they have learned more in the simulator than they could in a real plane."[7] This play among artificial, real, and realistic is at the heart of VR. Let us take a closer look at how these notions fit together. VR makes it possible to simulate the real. In order to do so, one has to construct a copy of reality, an illusion. In the early 1980s Myron Krueger, one of the pioneers of this technology, used the concept of "artificial reality."[8] The technique is, indeed, based on synthetic sounds and images calculated and displayed by a computer.

During the same period Nelson used the term "virtual" in contrast to "real" and situated this production in the cinema tradition: "An interactive computer system is a series of presentations intended to affect the mind in a certain way, like a movie. . . . The *reality* of an interactive system includes its data structure and what language it's programmed in—

but again who cares? The important concern is, *what does it seem to be?*"[9]

Yet the idea was not only to show this artificial reality but also to interact with it. Research on VR therefore focused on human-machine interfaces—*interaction* being the second key element of VR. But users do more than just act on the program, they are completely immersed in virtual reality. As Brenda Laurel noted in the 1990s, "VR is utterly a first-person point-of-view medium."[10] This *immersion* is particularly intense in so far as all the user's senses are mobilized. For Laurel, "immersion is not just physical and perceptual; it is also cognitive and emotional."[11] Finally, the virtual environment with which interaction develops can be local or networked, in which case other humans can also be involved. We then talk of telepresence or, to emphasize the coordination of the different actors, copresence.

This relative complexity of VR explains why representations of this technique are so diverse, for VR associates different *imaginaries*. In the following section we examine the *imaginaire* of visual artists and musicians involved in the cyberpunk current.

Cyberpunk Art and Virtual Reality

Unlike the simulation model designed to produce artifices that are more real than reality, artists try to use VR to produce radically new works—not copies of the real but objects that are the product of their imagination.

The simulation of war that, as we have seen, is one of the main areas of research and use of VR techniques, also inspired the shows of Mark Pauline and his Survival Research Laboratories (SRL) workshop, although in a parodied form. These live shows presented giant robots made of objects salvaged from the California computer and aeronautical industries. In one of them, produced just after the Gulf War, an explosion of pressurized CO_2 shot a beer can with extreme violence from a missile launcher. The operator of the machine was wearing a head-mounted display. "SRL shows," Pauline explains, "are a satire of kill technology, an absurd parody of the military-industrial complex."[12] The show was organized so that the public could guess the operator's sensations: "The virtual reality display couples the operator more closely to the machine.

It feels like your head is mounted on the machine, like you're riding on the top of the missile."[13] Pauline's reflection on human-machine relations included the following: "The role model for the future of human interaction with machines, if we want to avoid our own destruction and regain control, is to start thinking of our interaction with technology in terms of the intuitive, the irrational."[14] It is by becoming the machine, by feeling it with one's body, and not by thinking one can manage it, that one is able to control it.

Although this comment conveys some optimism concerning human-machine relations, Sterling highlighted the pessimism underlying Pauline's vision in an article in *Wired*: "The invisible becomes visible, everything that is repressed in the sterile prison of so-called rational engineering returns in a hideous and terribly authentic guise of claws and spikes and fangs. Everything that industrial society would prefer to forget and ignore and neglect takes on a pitiless Frankenstein vitality. It isn't beautiful, it isn't nice, it isn't spiritually elevating. It casts the darkest kind of suspicion on the lives we lead and the twisted ingenuity that supports those lives. And it offers us no answers at all."[15]

Sterling's interest in Pauline's shows signals a relationship between this form of art and cyberpunk novels. Mark Dery considers that "Pauline pioneered *the* definitive cyberpunk art form."[16] In *Mona Lisa Overdrive* Gibson describes the character of Slick Henry who, in an old shed, builds strange robots resembling those of Pauline—for example, the Judge is a limping monster armed with electric saws.

New pop music also adopted cyberaesthetics by demonstrating its wish to combine computing and sensorial perceptions, in other words, to use virtual reality techniques. Like the authors of science fiction, these musicians drew their inspiration from cyberpunk. The new rockers had the same project as the computer pirates of *Neuromancer*: they wanted to connect their sensorial organs to computers—to the cyberspace matrix, as Gibson would say.

Paul Moore, a computer scientist and editor of a fanzine on the Internet, explained the link between science fiction and music: "I appropriated the term from science fiction and applied it to this music because, although nobody seemed to be talking about these bands in terms of a movement, there seemed to be a link between cyberpunk's hard-edged writing style and the edgy music made by bands like Clock DVA, etc."[17] But this resemblance was attested by more than the names of albums and groups—Nerve Net, Man Amplified and Tactical Neural Implant—it was also described by musicians. For instance, Bill Leeb from the group Front Line Assembly, said: "What journalists are calling 'cyberpunk' rock, stems from the idea of using machines to make music as well as the integration of technology into the human body, like in *The Terminator*." One of his colleagues added: "There are similarities between cyberpunk fiction and our music, especially the idea of breaking down the division between human and machine."[18]

David Myers, the inventor of the Feedback Machine (a black box with circuits designed to produce feedback loops), was explicitly inspired in his piece *Penetrating Black Ice* by a scene from *Neuromancer* where Case crosses the black ice, that is, the last level in the protection system of the matrix. "What really turns me on in cyberpunk literature," he explained, "is the idea of a data thief having a virtual reality experience. . . . For me, cyberpunk sensitivity isn't about leather and studs; it's about total immersion in an electronic reality. And in the same way that virtual reality is created by manipulating electrons, its musical analog has to be created electronically."[19] This electronic music can morph the sound characteristics of different instruments in real time. Virtual instruments are thus separated from their acoustic bodies.

Yet some musicians, such as Jaron Lanier, with his piece *The Sound of One Hand*,[20] or Tod Machover, researcher at the MIT Media Lab, also showed that they could use a data-glove to "play" electronic instruments. The movements of their fingers and hand in the glove enabled them to determine the tone of an instrument and the musical volume. In these different experiments a kind of music was created that could not be composed with traditional instruments, yet the composer's and musicians' role remained intact. Machover imagined an even more revolutionary system in which the musician no longer creates his or her own music but designs devices through which music can be made. "One of my dream for a long time," he said, "has been to have compositions which are like living organisms [made up of] musical agents, each of them a musical tendency, a melodic shape or harmonic progression or tone color. The trick would be to set up an environment with some kind of constraint language where you could put those things in motion. You might just push a button and watch it behave."[21]

Karl Sims realized a similar project on images, with a device called Genetic Images. The software proposed a number of image construction algorithms that could be combined like genes. As Kelly noted, "Sims sees a future for artists as agents who don't create specific images, but instead create novel processes for generating new images. The artist becomes a god, creating an Eden in which surprising things will grow."[22]

Virtual Reality, a New Medium?

The cyberpunk tradition inspired the aesthetic experiments previously presented. This was the tradition referred to by John Walker when he launched the Cyberpunk Initiative in 1988 in the company Autodesk. The idea was to develop a VR device for the public at large. In an article presenting the Cyberpunk Initiative project in 1988, the company Autodesk indicated that it wished to build "a doorway into cyberspace." In fact its slogan was "Reality isn't enough anymore."[23] One of the project managers, Randal Walser, defined virtual reality—what he called cyberspace—as follows: "Cyberspace is a medium that gives people the impression of being transported, with their bodies, from the ordinary physical world into worlds of pure imagination. . . . It enables the public not only to observe a different reality but also to enter into it or to experience it, as if it were real. Nobody can know what can happen from one minute to the next in cyberspace, not even the designer. At every instant, each participant has the possibility of creating the next event. Whereas the aim of the movies is to show a reality to a public, cyberspace is designed to give a virtual body and a role to each member of the audience. Printing and the radio tell you, theater and movies show you, cyberspace takes you there."[24]

Virtual reality thus seems no longer to be a copy of reality but a new medium characterized chiefly by the involvement of the viewer's body. This presence of the body not only distinguishes virtual reality from theater or cinema, it also constitutes the profound originality of this technique compared to computer technology. As Brenda Laurel so aptly put it in the early 1990s, computers "have evolved as a race of severed heads, without bodies, without a sense of pleasure, doomed by the arcana of their communication mechanisms . . . The idea of virtual reality is the antithesis of this state of affairs. It intends, regardless of how well it succeeds, to accommodate the body as well as the mind—in theory it refuses to distinguish between the two at all. VR is concerned with the *nature* of the body—how our senses work, how we move around, how we get the sense of being somewhere, and how the sense of physical presence affects us."[25]

Laurel is a profoundly original actor of VR who studied drama before going into computing (designing computer games and VR products). She published a book entitled *Computers as Theatre*, in which she developed the idea that theater can constitute an excellent analogy for understanding and conceiving relations between humans and computers. From her reflection on theater, she concludes that software designers must above all think about users' actions, rather than about objects or interfaces. In the field of art and games she suggests building "a system that would enable a person to participate in a dramatic action in a relatively unconstrained way, influencing the events and outcomes through his or her choices and actions as a character in the action."[26] This computer system must be capable of giving a sensorial representation of the environment and characters, of making inferences on these characters' strategies and possibly of creating random events. "Basically, the system functions like a playwright working with one bizarre constraint: one of the characters is walking around in the playwright's study, inserting actions and line of dialogue at will, which must be incorporated into a pleasing dramatic whole."[27]

To develop such a project one needs to apply the techniques of artificial intelligence, to design an expert system with knowledge on dramatic forms and structures and on the field in question. The designer must also define the appropriate interfaces which are not necessarily those used for simulation. In the final analysis, "the art of designing VR is really the art of creating spaces with qualities that call forth active imagination. The VR artist does not bathe the participant in content; she invites the participant to produce content by constructing meanings, to experience the pleasure of embodied imagination."[28]

The relationship that Laurel is trying to establish between theater and virtual reality can be understood only in a perspective in which theater is essentially a place of improvization, a situation in which the actor has a high level of autonomy. In this case, VR and theater can be considered as a "tool for thought" that can offer "the chance to discover parts of yourself that you wouldn't have found in the course of everyday life. It's like shining a flashlight around the dark part of your brain. It's a way of becoming larger than you might have been."[29] Finally, Laurel's creative thoughts and practices prompt one to consider VR as a means of artistic creation and a way of incorporating the body and, more broadly, the entire individual in the computing world.

Walser also read and commented on Laurel's book. He analyzes the body that VR mobilizes. Is it not a new body, a virtual one, very different from the real individual? "More than any mechanism yet invented, it will change what humans perceive themselves to be, at a very fundamental and personal level. In cyberspace, there is no need to move about in a body like the one you possess in physical reality. . . . In cyberspace your conditioned notion of a unique and immutable body will give away to a far more liberated notion of 'body' as something quite disposable and, generally, limiting. You will find that some bodies work best in some situations."[30] When we spend most of our time "embodied" in these different virtual bodies whose actions have specific effects, will we still be able to talk of the unity of our original personality? Will the body still be the medium for our identity?

Another computer specialist, Jaron Lanier, who is also a musician and designer of the first inexpensive VR system in the latter half of the 1980s, had another answer to these questions. He took the metaphor of music which was his second occupation. When one changes instruments, one gains new perspective enabling one to play differently. The same applies to VR as far as the relationship between one's body and its environment is concerned. He took the following example: "If you have a chance to experience your body and the control of it in the form of a grasshopper, and then you come back to being human, I think there is a broadening of experience and an opening of channels in increased sensitivity."[31]

Thus, whereas its designers saw virtual reality essentially as a tool for simulation and learning, various artists used it for a parodical simulation or a new creative tool. From their discourse, the characteristics of a new medium gradually emerged.

Let's Get Rid of Our Flesh and Blood Bodies

While virtual reality makes it possible to multiply one's body, some believe that cyberspace enables us to do without our bodies altogether or to connect them directly to machines. This idea is often expressed by nerds, young computer fanatics who spend their lives facing a screen. In an interview in the 1990s one of them said: "When I'm at a computer . . . I become detached from my physical self. This is not just mudding or playing games or being on the net; this is whenever I'm at a computer. I lose track of time, and don't feel hungry or tired. I often forget to eat and end up having meals at bizarre hours."[32]

Steven Levy noted that already in the late 1950s, those he called hackers "dazzled math teachers and flunked PE, . . . dreamed not of scoring on prom night but of getting to the finals of the General Electric Science Fair competition."[33] But hackers, like nerds, do not only forget their bodies and give themselves over to their passion; they actually consider that life is elsewhere; they see computing as something alive that must be worked at and improved, in short, a place of real life. As Levy remarked, "Systems are organic, living creations: if people stop working on them and improving them, they die."[34] To nurture this system one needs the best possible programming, that "could only be accomplished when every obstacle between you and the pure computer was eliminated—an ideal that probably won't be fulfilled until hackers are somehow biologically merged with computers."[35]

This idea of transplanting machines onto bodies is prevalent in cyberculture. In 1993 Gareth Branwyn quoted the following BBS message in *Wired*: "I am interested in becoming a guinea pig (if you will) for any cyberpunkish experiment from a true medicine/military/cyber/neuro place. New limbs, sight/hearing improvements, bio-monitors, etc. Or even things as simple as under the skin time pieces."[36]

The question of direct brain-computer connection appears not only in science fiction and among a few cranks; it is also on the frontiers of the scientific world, in brain simulation experiments. For *Wired*, " 'Neurohackers' are the new do-it-yourself brain tinkerers who have decided to take matters into their own heads." One of them explained to Branwyn:

"There is quite an underground of neurohackers beaming just about every type of field imaginable into their heads to stimulate certain neurological structures (usually the pleasure centers)."[37] It also seems that some beginnings of academic research can be found on the subject, which of course also fascinates the media. In *Time*'s special file on cyberpunk, published a few months before the *Wired* article and clearly inspired by *Mondo 2000*, a section was devoted to brain transplants defined as follows: "Slip a microchip into snug contact with your gray matter and suddenly gain instant fluency in a foreign language or arcane subject."[38] *Newsweek* published an article that quoted *Wired* at length, entitled "Computers as Mind Readers," with the subtitle "In the future (maybe), your PC will be connected directly to your brain."[39]

Thus, one can imagine not only directly connecting one's body to a computer but also freeing oneself from one's body. The idea of downloading one's mind was first put forward by a California New Age group, the "Extropians." The basic idea was that we have to struggle against entropy. Extropy, by contrast, would enable us to avoid the degeneration of individuals and society. To implement this program, the Extropian movement had five main principles: "Boundless Expansion, Self-Transformation, Dynamic Optimism, Intelligent Technology, and Spontaneous Order."[40] With this view of the world, they imagined that humans could be immortal. A computer specialist in the group considered that in the future one would be able to "download the entire contents of your mind into a computer—your memories, knowledge, your whole personality (which is, after all, just information)—you'd transfer all of it to a computer, make backup copies, and stockpile those copies all over creation. If at some point later you should happen to suffer a wee interruption of your current life cycle, then one of your many backups would be activated, and, in a miracle of electronic resurrection, you'd pop back into existence again, good as new."[41] The Extropians' dream was to become more than human, superhuman, transhuman, or posthuman: "Suddenly technology has given us powers with which we can manipulate not only external reality—the physical world—but also, and much more portentously, ourselves. We can become whatever we want to be."[42]

Entertainment and Science Fiction

The idea of connecting or disconnecting one's body is a subject of equal interest to artists. Among visual artists, the "body art" current wanted to display the body as a performance, in both senses of the word: a show and physical effort. One of the representatives of this current, Stelarc, became known for performances of suspension at great heights, over a huge drop. The pain was unbearable and it often took a week for his wounds to heal. He also did more hi-tech performances, swallowing sculptures and transmitting an image through two endoscopic video cameras.[43] He sums up his artistic project with the slogan "The human body is obsolete." These performances were soon limited, in the case of the former by the physical capacities for resistance of the body. In the latter case, he explained: "When the body is being hard-wired to the machinery then, at it's more successful moments, there is a kind of synergistic symbiosis where you really do lose a sense of self and become part of this operating system and the body." In fact, this unsuitable body needs to be cleared of its organs and replaced by machines. For Stelarc, "The body will become a host for micro-miniaturised machines, the body becomes a host, not only for virus and bacteria but also for a colony of nano-machines. We can re-colonise the human body."[44] In the final analysis, "the body's form is enhanced and its functions are extended."[45] More recently, Stelarc's performances made use of the Internet. In this way, "The body has been augmented, invaded and now becomes a host—not only for technology, but also for remote agents."[46]

Stelarc called his performances "sci-fi scenarios for human-machine symbiosis."[47] This idea of exchanging one's physical body for a virtual body is often found in cyberpunk science fiction. In Gibson's *Neuromancer* the hero Case, like the other cyberspace cowboys, professed "a certain relax contempt for flesh. The body was meat." Following a theft, his employers punished him by giving him a shot of a mycotoxin that damaged his nervous system. As a result, "Case fell into the prison of his own flesh."[48] Thus, the body has not disappeared; it has been devalued. When Gibson wants to glorify flesh he compares it to a machine, as when Case looks at his girlfriend Molly and notes that her hips have the "functional elegance of a war plane's fusilage."[49] Likewise, Julius Deane, a leading citizen in cyberspace, has a body that does not age. He is 135 years old and has a smooth complexion, for his metabolism is stimulated by weekly serums and hormones: "Sexless and inhumanly patient," he has lost all specific individuality.[50] In *Neuromancer,* real life is elsewhere, in journeys on the matrix, in the world of computerized data. When eventually, despite his nervous disorder, Case manages to connect himself, "This was it. This was what he was, who he was, his being. He forgot to eat." On awaking, "he'd go straight to the deck, not bothering to dress, and jack in. . . . He lost track of days."[51]

This is only one step away from leaving one's body. This theme was at the center of another cyberpunk novel, *Synners,* by Pat Cadigan. Like Case, Mark and Gabe, the two heroes, spend long hours on the Internet. Gradually they decide to stay connected all the time. Gabe "had been running around in simulation for so long, he'd forgotten how to run a real-life, real-time routine; he'd forgotten that if he made mistakes, there was no safety net program to jump in and correct for him."[52] He kept repeating: "I can't remember what it feels like to have a body."[53] As for Mark, despite the weak signs his body was sending him, asking him to come back, it became more and more difficult. One day, after an "interskull overheating," his mind is transferred onto the network. He is thus able permanently to leave that meat that he so detests. But he is the only human mind in a virtual data world. He could of course still have the feeling of skin-to-skin contact; he simply had to access it in his memory to experience pleasure but with it would be loneliness.[54] As Anne Balsamo comments judiciously in an analysis of the novel, Gabe and Mark are addicted to cyberspace for the release it offers from the loneliness of their material bodies.[55] By contrast, the two female characters, Sam and Gina, have a totally different view of relations between the body and technology "where technology isn't the means of escape from transcendence of the body but rather the means of communication and connection with other bodies."[56]

Robots and Thinking Neworks

For Balsamo, this is a feminist view of cyberspace that only a novelist could have. But the dominant vision of science fiction is rather one of a development of computer networks to the detriment of humans and their bodies. Mathematician and science fiction author Vernor Vinge considers that machines will end up dominating humans, like humans ended up dominating the animal world.[57] In another more recent article in *Wired*, he discusses his view of the future again. With continued growth of computer and network technology, he believes that even computer experts will no longer know what they are programming: "The largest control systems are being *grown* and *trained*, rather than written."[58] He conceived of a computer-garment that knew all the body positions of its owner and what he saw. Data display devices would be replaced by spectacles, so that users could superimpose artificial images over the natural images they received: "Cyberspace begins to leak into the real world. . . . Even when that is not explicit, there is growing use of synthetic intuition."[59]

This argument that computer networks constitute autonomous intelligence into which man can slip into like a garment is not far removed from that of philosopher Manuel De Landa. He based his vision on chaos theory to show that "singularities" (occurrences that trigger the emergence of a new order) appear in inanimate matter, and that strangely human cooperative behaviors emerge. The evolution of machines takes place in a nonlinear process in which they spontaneously move together. One can thus hope to facilitate "a symbiosis in which the evolutionary paths of humans and machines interact for their mutual benefit."[60] The Internet is a good example of this type of nonlinear development and could lead to the emergence of global artificial intelligence: "Past a certain threshold of connectivity, the membrane which computer networks are creating over the surface of the planet begins to 'come to life.' Independent software will soon begin to constitute even more complex computational societies in which programs trade with one another . . . , seed and spawn processes spontaneously."[61] This prospect brings to mind several California essayists' interpretation of Teilhard de Chardin.

Close to the theses of Manuel De Landa on the intelligence of computer networks, we find Moravec's speculation on intelligent robots. This robotics lecturer elaborated well-argued discourse on the future development of robots. After a first generation capable of performing mechanical tasks (reparation, maintenance, etc.), he foresees that robots capable of learning and adapting will appear in around 2020. He considers that their "success or failure will be defined by separate programs that will monitor the robot's actions and generate internal punishment and reward signals."[62] With the third generation, the robot will be capable of intelligent processes of planning and forecasting. "It will maintain an internal model not only of its own past actions, but of the outside world. This means it can run different simulations of how it plans to tackle a task, see how well each one works out, and compare them with what it's done before."[63] The robot could have reasoning that draws on psychological considerations: "A robot will express in its internal language a logical statement such as 'I must be careful with this item, because it is valuable to my owner, and if I break it, my owner will be angry.' This means that if the robot's internal processes are translated into human terms, you will hear a description of consciousness."[64]

Robots' form of intelligence will enable them to multiply simulations, so that these become far more numerous than original beings. "Therefore, statistically speaking, it's much more likely we're living in a vast simulation than in the original version."[65] Moravec has deduced that reality will no longer be distinguished from the real. Robots will then become equal to humans and would soon overtake them. To keep the human race on a par, Moravec has imagined humans downloading their minds onto computers: "You may choose to move your mind from one computer to another that is more technically advanced or better suited to a new environment."[66]

The fantasy of leaving one's body, finally to be reincarnated in a computer network or in a robot and to achieve immortality, is thus equally present in the ideas of engineers like Moravec or Vigne—for whom scientific activity is much the same thing as forecasting or writing science fiction—and in those of a strange sect like the Extropians. Likewise, the sensation of forgetting one's body appears both among cyberpunk artists and among computer fans or nerds.

Sometimes this refusal of the body is explained in psychological terms. Nerds are said to be asocial and maladjusted. For example, in an interview with *Wired*, Allucquère Rosanne Stone said: "For many people who tended to be socially inept and quite shy anyway, the quasi-intelligent character of the machine has replaced human social interaction. The interactive potential of the machine has created a novel social category of what I call quasi guys."[67] But she notes in her book on the birth of the virtual age that *Neuromancer* life in cyberspace is, in a sense, guaranteed by real life. One cannot exist in it if one does not live in the other world, and when one dies in the real world one also dies in the virtual one. Thus, despite the loathing for "meat," one can never totally reject one's body.[68] In the final analysis, there is always a gap between cyberspace and the real world, and while the former can be an escape, it can also provide assets for returning into real life, which she suggests when she questions whether cyberspace is not "a base camp for some kinds of cyborgs, from which they might stage a coup on the rest of reality."[69]

Social Virtual Reality

The play between the virtual and real worlds takes place not only through man-machine dialogue but also through communication between individuals. The confusion that sometimes exists between virtual reality and cyberspace is a reminder that, as we all know, computer technology, when linked to a network, allows individuals to communicate. This communication, at the center of the Internet, is generally delayed but can also take place in real time. In chats or Internet Relay Chats (IRCs), the interlocutors join chat groups and converse in writing. By contrast, in Multiuser Dungeons (MUDs), they build an imaginary world together. We could say that they are together in a virtual place and that, in this case, communication among individuals is simply a new opportunity for virtual reality. We could also say that the interlocutors are in a situation of copresence. They interact but, unlike in real life, they can use only some of their senses. They communicate by means of texts or drawings, sounds or images. This virtual place in which individuals are in copresence constitutes what Turkle calls "a social virtual reality."[70] *Time* magazine, in a report on this phenomenon in 1993, considered that it is "a sort of poor virtual reality."[71] For another observer, "The experience of networked, text-based virtual reality can be at least as intense as that of multi-sensory VR."[72]

It is not surprising that this social virtual reality appeared through a collective fiction, that of role play. In 1980 a British student, mad about the game "dungeons and dragons," made a computer version. This collective game was diffused on the Internet as MUD, and it became the matrix of collective communication in real time. MUDs, wrote Kelly and Rheingold in one of the first issues of *Wired*, "have become a medium for consensual virtual reality."[73] Interactions among players take place exclusively through texts that each one enters in their computer. A spatial metaphor, the room, is used to denote each of the subsets of the MUD. These different zones relate to a situation and give the players in them the possibility of interacting at will and inventing their own story. Each zone is described in a few sentences. Players move from one space to the next by keying in instructions such as: go north, enter the castle, and so forth. Players can interrupt and restart the game at will. The action has no end.

More recent games allow players to add elements of programs, with an object-oriented computer language. They can create a new room and new objects, or introduce links among these different elements. These new MUDs are called MOOs (MUD object oriented). For the past few years, some MUDs also offer a graphic environment that allows users to create a setting.

MUDs are a good illustration of Laurel's theories on computer technology as a theater. Users are both authors and audiences of their own plays. As a young hacker notes: "What we are doing here is creating our own environment. Virtual reality is the wave of the future, but we are experiencing it now, in an object-oriented text format, where our imagination takes control."[74]

There is, however, a considerable difference compared to a theatrical tradition such as the comedia del arte, in that the participants themselves define who they are. It is through the dynamics of interactions that they construct their identity. As one of them told Turkle: "You can be whoever you want to be. You can completely redefine yourself if you want. . . . It's easier to change the way people perceive you, because all they've got is what you show them. They don't look at your body and make assumptions. They don't hear your accent and make assumptions. All they see is your words."[75]

While the MUD is a sort of collective online improvisation, it also has another characteristic distinguishing it from an ordinary remote communication device, and that is the possibility that participants have to make several avatars act (write). Participants thus assume several identities.

One of them commented: "I'm not one thing, I'm many things. Each part gets to be more fully expressed in MUDs than in the real world. So even though I play more than one self on MUDs, I feel more like 'myself' when I'm MUDding."[76] These different lives can take place simultaneously in different windows of the same computer screen. "I split my mind," said one of the players. "I can see myself as being two or three or more. And I just turn on one part of my mind and then another when I go from window to window."[77] The virtual thus seems to be not only like a simulation of reality but also like a set of images that appear in distorting mirrors. It is a series of representations of I that can be multiplied to infinity. Are we heading for an identity crisis, as Walser predicted, or can we consider, like Turkle, that this coexistence of different identities is one of the characteristics of our postmodern age? The virtual world or, rather, virtual worlds thus seem to be far more complex and diversified than the real world that, in the eyes of Turkle's interviewee, is no longer very much: "just one more window, and it's not usually my best one."

Robots that Join in Conversations

Thus, MUDs are not simply a collective game based on writing and played over a distance. The fact that a participant can have several avatars clearly indicates that we have left a situation of distance communication to enter into a new world—a virtual one. But this virtual world has another feature distinguishing it from the real one: some of the talk that appears in MUDs is generated not by human participants but by a computer program. These programs, called bots, are the software equivalent of robots. In the late 1980s Michael Maudin, a computer scientist at Carnegie Mellon University, created a set of bots called Maas-Neotek, the name of the multinational corporation in Gibson's novels. Julia, the best known of these bots, can hold a conversation. "Although Julia is programmed to interact like a human, she has special abilities that most humans lack,"[78] notes Turkle. According to *Wired*, Maas-Neotek "could explore their ever-expanding environment and register which characters (human or otherwise) were present or what was going on in each room of the MUD. They could be used as secretaries to log all conversations held in the MUD, or as police officers with the power to automatically 'kill' the account of MUDders who violated a rule. They could even be spies—a so-called gossipbot could listen in and record the conversation between two other MUD visitors, and then later, in response to a question like 'What did so-and-so say?,' regurgitate the conversation to someone else."[79]

Bots are not only used as troublemakers or policemen; they sometimes play a key role in MUDs. For example, an educational MUD is structured around teaching robots. In an experimental project launched at the University of Texas, Pt.MOOt, at one stage over 50 percent of the participants were bots.[80] With bots, the imaginary world of MUDs becomes a space in which humans and nonhumans mingle. The utopias of virtual reality are thus realized.

Cybersex and Virtual Journeys

Of the many activities taking place on MUDs, flirting and seduction are unquestionably a key element. Kelly and Rheingold note in *Wired* that "Flirtation, infatuation, romance, and even 'TinySex' are now as ubiquitous in MUD worlds as on real college campuses."[81] One of the findings of Turkle's study is that virtual sexuality on MUDs "consists of two or more players typing descriptions of physical actions, verbal statements, and emotional reactions for their characters. In cyberspace this activity is not only common; for many people it is the centerpiece of their online experience."[82] That is also what one of Quittner's interviewees remarks: "Sex is the real virtual lure."[83] These sexual games are no novelty in telecommunications and *Wired* has devoted several articles to sex chatlines,[84] seduction via email,[85] sadomasochist newsgroups,[86] online striptease,[87] and the sex industry in general.[88] But in our inquiry on the computing *imaginaire*, the fantasy of a sexual cyberact needs to be examined more closely. In *Mondo 2000* Barlow notes: "I have been through eight or ten Q&A sessions on virtual reality, and I don't remember one where sex didn't come up. . . . And I did overhear the word 'DataCondom' at one point. . . . Maybe the nerds who always ask this question will get a chance to make it with their computers at long last!"[89] This fantasy also appears strange to R. U. Sirius, who considers that sexuality is what prevents man from getting rid of his body to download it into cyberspace. In his view, "Sex is the only good excuse for embodiment."[90]

At the end of his book on virtual reality, Rheingold gives an exact description of what cybersex could be. He imagines that individuals wear skin-tight bodysuits equipped with thousands of sensors capable of transmitting and receiving tactile sensations. When the entire system is linked to the Internet, each of the partners has access to a multisensorial representation of the other's body: "Your representations are able to touch each other, even though your physical bodies might be continents apart. You will whisper in your partner's ear, feel your partner's breath on your neck. You run your hand over your partner's clavicle and 6,000 miles away, an array of effectors are triggered, in just the right sequence, at the right frequency, to convey the touch exactly the way you wish it to be conveyed."[91]

We have thus attained the ultimate goal of virtual reality in which it is possible to simulate the action of all the senses, to create not a relationship between man and the computer, but the most intimate relations that exist between humans. Yet this simulation has a limit that appears at the end of Rheingold's description: "If you don't like the way the encounter is going, or someone requires your presence in physical reality, you can turn it all off by flicking a switch and taking off your virtual birthday suit."[92]

Thus, this virtual sex that Rheingold believes is not technically perfect is distinguished above all from real sex by the fact that it requires no commitment by the partner in the relationship. This is the peep show tradition, except it is no longer a case of "look but don't touch" but of "touch but don't get involved." Virtual lovers do not build a relationship that would commit them even for a short space of time. In these new games of love and chance, one can skip from one window to another at any time.

The heralds of virtual sex emphasize the fact that it is risk free, and therefore suited to the generation confronted with AIDS. This goal of developing risk-free human relations also appears in the writings of the futurologist Gilder who considers that tomorrow's computer networks will enable us to "visit third-world countries without drinking their water."[93] Gilder has the same fantasy as nerds or Gibson's heros: living in one's computer screen, acting through the keyboard and mouse, without taking the risks of real life. But this cyberlife seems singularly atrophied, poor, and stunted, compared not only to real life but also to that of the characters in science fiction. As we have seen, Gibson's characters suffer in their bodies for choices they have made in cyberspace.

Let us pause for a moment on this example of cybertourism that, unlike cybersex, generates fewer fantasies and is starting to be achieved. Laurel has suggested launching "surrogate travel," using virtual reality. In this case, "VRs are a compromise—a concession to time and convenience."[94] Cybertourists who, from their living room armchair or from a special hall in their town, visit the big American nature parks will be able to do so without being surrounded by hordes of tourists, and will be able to go where they like, to climb the highest cliffs, see sunsets over and again, and so on. "But surrogate travel is different from actual travel. . . . Surrogate travel is for people who can't, or who don't want to, actually *be there*."[95] "Physical" travel, by contrast, involves the traveler's body with all its senses, its pleasure, and its fatigue. It requires time and may involve unexpected events.

Cyborgs

As the boundaries between real and virtual, body and mind, nature and science fade, debate on these issues can also open new avenues. Thus, the reflections of Donna Haraway on cyborgs further our understanding of the role of the body in the virtual reality perspective. She uses the word cyborg created in 1960 by two scientists who combined cybernetics and organism to denote an individual capable of self-regulation in an artificial environment such as the conquest of space,[96] but gives it a different meaning to that of science fiction or space research engineers. The idea is not to create a semi- or completely artificial being, but to become aware that relations between humans and technology are so close that it is not possible to say where one stops and the other starts. This perspective introduces a whole new vision of technology that is no longer completely outside the individual with whom a relationship has to be constructed. "The machine is not an it to be animated, worshiped, and dominated. The machine is us, our processes, an aspect of our embodiment."[97]

From this viewpoint, the cyborg is a hybrid not only of machine and organism but also of material reality and imagination. Haraway refuses the traditional opposition between humans controlling machines and machines dominating humans. "It is not clear," she explains, "who makes and who is made in the relation between human and machine."[98] In the final analysis, our immersion in technoculture makes us cyborgs. Haraway draws an essential conclusion for action: "taking responsibility for the social relations of science and technology means refusing an anti-science metaphysics, a demonogy of technology, and so means embracing the skilful task of reconstructing the boundaries of daily life, in partial connection with others, in communication with all of our parts."[99] The task of coconstructing technology will be facilitated if its evolution is not determined by its history. Thus, the military origins of virtual reality do not mean that it will always be an instrument of oppression. The machine is not something that is given in advance; it is not imposed on us. Humans and machines are coconstructed simultaneously through the constant evolution of their interactions, the merging of a technical project and individuals' experience. For Haraway, "The cyborg is a matter of fiction and lived experience."[100]

This view of the cyborg that had an audience in the culture of the Internet generation, since *Wired* devoted an article to it,[101] is particularly interesting in so far as it allows us to explain the position of computer technology and, more particularly, virtual reality, in relation to the body and human-computer articulation.

First, machines are not the antithesis of the imaginary: "The boundary is permeable between tool and myth. . . . Indeed, myth and tool mutually constitute each other."[102] Virtual reality and the Internet are hybrids involving interaction between technical opportunities and imaginations. These are expressed primarily in science fiction which, for Haraway, has become a major literary genre of our time, comparable to the naturalist novel in the industrial era.

Liberating Utopia and Ideology of Illusion

Of all the *imaginaires* blossoming around virtual reality or body-machine relations, some are utopias which foresee an opening toward new technical or artistic devices, while others are profoundly mystifying illusions. We see two main facets of these discourses emerging: on the one hand, a mobilizing utopia that proposes the construction of computer systems capable of simulating reality, of creating experiences with enactment; on the other, an isolationist and security-oriented ideology that gives the impression of being able to manipulate the world through one's computer.

As regards utopias, we find all the rhetoric of simulation, the idea that objects, human activities, and human-machine relations can be shaped and reproduced artificially. Virtual reality can serve as a knowledge and learning tool, but it can also be a means for artistic production, a new medium. The idea is then to go beyond simulation and to create another reality: other sounds, images, and involvement of bodies in computer technology. Distant individuals are also able to act together in games. Participants of these interactions can thus bring into play different facets of their personality.

As regards ideology, we find the idea that individuals can get rid of their bodies and become a pure computer mind, that there is no longer any difference between enactment and reality, and that one can surf on human relations without getting involved. Cybersex is the prime example of this ideology. The illusion does not stem from the fact that people use techniques in the context of their most intimate relations. Contraceptive techniques are at the heart of contemporary sexual practices. Haraway is right to remind us that we are all cyborgs, beings made up of both flesh and techniques. But the virtual *imaginaire* becomes ideology when it imagines that one can put one's body on hold, that computer technology can create bodiless human relations, disconnected from any engagement of the body in space and time, and that one can develop human relations that involve only enrichment and pleasure, without any solitude or pain.

Cyberwar is the second example of this ideology. We find the idea of a war with zero deaths (at least for the United States) one of the principles of the Kosovo war. Automated war is supposed to make it possible to conduct war from a command post consisting largely of computer and telecommunications technology. Here again, this is a way of waging war without risks or human involvement.

We find the same debate between liberating utopia and ideology of illusion in the issue of the disappearance of the body and its possible replacement by an artificial being. Gibson uses his novels to denounce the erring ways of a world in which digital technologies dominate man. Moravec, on the other hand, builds his discourse around the domination of man by machines, based on a very elementary scenario of the miniaturization of components and the growth of computer power. It is the same type of technical ideology that conceals the fact that technology is also a human construction.

Yet the virtual *imaginaire* and the body cannot be split into two areas with motivating utopia on the one hand and mystifying ideologies on the other. These two facets of the *imaginaire* merge at all times. Cyberpunk novelists, to better denounce the ravages of our computer society, invented the theme of rejection of the flesh. This appealed to nerds who, failing to see Gibson's demystifying project, found in this theme one of the basic references of their new culture. Likewise, cyberpunk musicians who became the eulogists of neuron interfaces and human-machine fusion clearly saw the potential of using sound synthesis to create a new distinct type of music. By contrast, ideologies like Moravec's, with the disappearance of the flesh and the victory of robots, successfully developed from modeling techniques and simulation of particular body functions. In the final analysis, just as we should not fight against cyborgs but all recognize ourselves as cyborgs, virtual reality shows that computer technology should not play down the body. The idea is not only to create human-machine interfaces but to promote a body-to-body or a body-to-computer affordance. If the virtual can do away with bodies, it can also involve them deeply.

7

The End of Politics

The designers of computer-mediated communication, Usenet and the first BBS saw these online debates as a process of elaboration of knowledge and, more broadly, of shared opinions. But they also suggested that this process of construction of opinions could be applied to the political sphere. In so far as BBS were used as a tool for cooperation in certain rural areas and for local democracy in average-sized towns, why not conceive of the Internet facilitating or even overhauling the democratic process on a larger scale?

Cyberdemocracy and the New Public Sphere

Howard Rheingold's book, *The Virtual Community*—which constructed the first Internet myth, based on experiments—defined the perspective: "the political significance of computer mediated communication lies in its capacity to challenge the existing political hierarchy's monopoly on powerful communications media, and perhaps revitalize citizen-based democracy."[1] Futurologists, like Gilder or Toffler, believed that it was necessary to conceive of a policy suited to the third wave. Toffler wrote: "We should attempt to devise new forms of democratic practice that can handle the levels of complexity and speed our society requires."[2] He believed that a possible third way existed, between representative and direct democracy.

The idea of creating new communication channels between the people and their leaders soon diffused within political leadership. Ross Perot, an independent candidate in the 1992 presidential elections, proposed electronic municipalities and local direct democracy. Clinton and Gore who, as we have seen, made information superhighways one of their main campaign slogans, suggested in June 1993 that citizens correspond with them by email. System manager Jock Gill explained: "This administration was committed to changing things to involve citizens more in governance. This would involve communication between the citizens and the White House free from filters and third-party interpretations. With the White House email system, more citizen access would lead to less top-down message dependence."[3]

Republican leader Newt Gingrich wanted to use these technologies to promote a "grassroots democracy." *Business Week* rightly commented that "Gingrich has a populist notion that with information technology, angry, disenfranchised people will be empowered to take more control over their government."[4] This theme was also taken up by other media. In a spring 1995 special issue of *Time*, entitled "Welcome to Cyberspace," Kevin Phillips imagined a virtual Washington, "a wired, cyber-spatial capital in which U.S. Representatives and Senators could participate from their states or districts, while citizens, too, would have any information, debate at their fingertips."[5] But this vision was Contested by another *Time* journalist who maintained that government's and Congress' problem was not their disconnection from the people but, on the contrary, the constant pressure of lobbies that were bound to become even stronger with digital technologies. Cyberdemocracy would result in hyperdemocracy.[6]

While Phillips presented his vision as a "high-tech version of Athenian democracy," most reflection on cyberdemocracy referred rather to the founding fathers of U.S. democracy and especially Thomas Jefferson, author of the Declaration of Independence, whose philosophy was close to that of the Enlightenment thinkers. Jefferson had imagined an agrarian and decentralized republic. He was often cited by the digerati because he seemed to be the representative of a society based essentially on the life of small local communities. In *Wired*, Mitchel Kapor, one of the leaders of the Electronic Frontier Foundation, mused about what a Jeffersonian information policy might be like: "In fact, life in cyberspace seems to be shaping up exactly like Thomas Jefferson would have wanted: founded on the primacy of individual liberty and a commitment to pluralism, diversity, and community."[7]

Wired journalist Jon Katz believed that Thomas Paine, considered to be the founder of American political journalism, "should be resurrected as the moral father of the Internet."[8] For him, as for Jefferson, "the media existed to spread ideas, to allow fearless argument, to challenge and question authority, to set a common social agenda."[9] In the same spirit, he considered that "the Internet has, in fact, redefined citizenship as well as communications. It is the first worldwide medium in which people can communicate so directly, so quickly, so personally, and so reliably. In which they can form distant but diverse and cohesive communities."[10] By contrast, today's mainstream media and especially television, with its law of maximum audiences, have made all in-depth public debate impossible.[11] Televiewer does not have the means to check statements made or to compare them with other opinions. On the other hand, commented computer scientist and musician Jaron Lanier observed that with the Internet "people can have personal contact with the truth, perhaps through a series of other people."[12]

Virtual Communities and Democratic Debate
Can we consider that the Internet enables us to recreate the public sphere of the Enlightenment and the fledgling U.S. democracy, and that the centralized mass media are simply a passing phase? To answer this question we need to revert to online community practices. For Rheingold, who first conceived of virtual communities, "there is an intimate connection between informal conversations, . . . in the coffee shops and computer conferences, and the ability of large social groups to govern themselves without monarch or dictators. This social-political connection shares a metaphor with the idea of cyberspace, for it takes place in a kind of virtual space that has come to be known by specialists as the public sphere."[13] By contrast Elizabeth Reid, who observed online communities from the early 1990s, found that "virtual communities are not the agora, that they are not a place of open and free public discourse. It is a mistake to think that the Internet is an inherently democratic institution or that it will necessarily lead to increased personal freedoms and increased understanding between people."[14] She noted that online communities had difficulty reaching the compromises needed for self-management of the group. This she linked to the flame wars in which individuals very

quickly formed opinions that they were subsequently unwilling to change. If the conflict became too violent they dropped their initial identity and returned to the debate with a new one.

This coexistence of identities, studied by Turkle (see chapter 6), seems to have been one of the major causes of the difficulty that online communities had in developing a common viewpoint. In real life the different facets of an individual are unified by their inscription in the same body, in face-to-face interactions, with each interlocutor sensing the other's complexity and being able to rely on that complexity to reach an agreement. By contrast, virtual communities encourage rigid, rather than flexible, points of view.

By way of a different approach, historian Mark Poster[15] reached similar conclusions in an article published in *Wired*. If we consider that the public sphere has three characteristics—debate between equals in which rational arguments prevail and where consensus is sought—the Internet fits with only the first of these. Internauts can indeed debate on an equal footing, but this type of interaction is far from being the rule. We know, for instance, that many insults circulate on the Internet. The debate tends not toward reaching consensus but rather toward a multiplication of contradictory points of view. This fragmentation of opinions is further reinforced by the fact that Internauts' identities are fuzzy and unstable. Not only do interlocutors use nicknames and create a virtual identity for themselves, they can also change identities or even have several at the same time. Hence, a key element distinguishing the Internet from the public sphere of the Enlightenment is the question of the body. The source of an individual's identity is their body, which stabilizes their standpoints. "Pure computer minds" cannot create deliberative democracy. In this respect the Internet is neither a new public sphere nor a place that can revive the democratic debate.

In all this reflection the key issue is relations between the Internet and real life.[16] The Internet is unquestionably a world apart that developed in a self-managed context and must continue to do so. But is it completely independent from real life? In the following section I examine this thesis. If the Internet is in fact linked to real life, we can conceive of two positions. Either ordinary life is a stakeholder in the Internet since it is a locus of political life, citizenship, and business, and in that case the laws of society must apply to it as well, or cyberspace is the model of a new society and gradually its laws will have to apply to the real world. I study these two points of view and then examine, in more concrete terms, how Internauts mobilized to prevent the state of intervening on the Internet.

A Particular Social Sphere

In order to affirm the fact that the Internet is different from the rest of society and that the same laws could not be applied to it, John Perry Barlow, cofounder of the Electronic Frontier Foundation (see chapter 4), wrote a "declaration of independence," just as Jefferson did. He published it in February 1996 during the Davos forum that brought together the world's ruling elite. Barlow's declaration was addressed to the governments of the industrial world and warned of "the global social space we are building to be naturally independent of the tyrannies you seek to impose on us."[17] Governments have neither legitimacy nor competence to intervene in this domain, he claimed. They "derive their just powers from the consent of the governed. You have neither solicited nor received ours. We did not invite you. You do not know us, nor do you know our world. Cyberspace does not lie within your borders. . . . Your legal concepts of property, expression, identity, movement, and context do not apply to us. They are based on matter, There is no matter here."[18] The fact that the Internet was part of an immaterial world, of minds and not matter or bodies, enabled Barlow to argue more soundly in another document where he affirmed that no democratic government could claim to control its citizens' thoughts.[19]

Barlow pointed out that cyberspace is a world apart with different rules: "We are forming our own Social Contract. This governance will arise according to the conditions of our world, not yours. . . . Ours is a world that is both everywhere and nowhere, but it is not where bodies live. We are creating a world that all may enter without privilege or prejudice accorded by race, economic power, military force, or station of birth. We are creating a world where anyone, anywhere may express his or her beliefs, no matter how singular, without fear of being coerced into silence or conformity.[20] In this new world the pioneers believed that "from ethics, enlightened self-interest, and the commonwealth, our governance will emerge."[21]

From Public Sphere to Market

Although Barlow claimed to jettison the laws of states, his cyberrepublic nonetheless lacked some form of governance. In fact, this digerati had little to say about rules for a society that combined individual freedoms with community life. The only law that he cited, and that he turned into a golden rule, was netiquette. But can a society really be based on a code of savoir-vivre? Certain jurists developed a set of ideas that were used to support Barlow's intuitions. For instance, David Post proposed "reinvent[ing] primitive forms of a-geographical lawmaking."[22] He considered that it was necessary to construct a "a distinct doctrine, applicable to a clearly demarcated sphere, created primarily by legitimate, self-regulatory processes."[23] The main difference between cyberspace and the real world derived from the fact that individuals are not physical or legal entities, as in our legal system, but beings of another nature. The user IDs or domain names that correspond to individuals in this new space are in fact Internet addresses. By regulating these addresses, one regulates basic Internet units without initially taking into account the links that may exist between these cyberindividuals and physical or legal entities in the real world.

In this new space the notion of community also takes on another meaning. Not only do established territorial partitions no longer apply to virtual communities, but the classical functioning of democracy is also inappropriate. The fundamental difference between cyberspace and an ordinary space is the fact that Internauts are completely mobile. They can instantaneously change sites and engage in several activities at the same time under different identities. New sites or communities can likewise appear at any moment. It is through this mobility and not through votes that everyone can express their collective preferences. "In the online context, the check against sysop tyranny is not 'one person, one vote' but, rather, ease of exit. And there is reason to believe that the combination of decentralized rule-making by means of (1) the unilateral actions of sysops to define online spaces and (2) the unilateral decisions by users to join or leave such spaces, will arrive at a good solution to the collective-action problem."[24] We thus have a model where citizens' opinions are expressed in the same way as those of consumers: by rejecting the unwanted product or site. Public opinion is not built up by a series of debates and interactions; at any point in time citizen-consumers vote with their feet or, more exactly, their mouse.

In this decentralized mode of governance individuals have no need for representatives, they can act by themselves. For David Post, not only is the Internet an autonomous space, independent of the authority of nation-states, it also has to be regulated according to specific forms intended for individuals who are not real people. This legal utopia paves a new way for regulation of the Internet; it takes into account the fact that actors in the network are not people but avatars, and that the law must incorporate that fact. Conversely, another facet of this discourse constitutes a mask ideology. By proposing to reduce the economic to the political, it creates the illusion that there is no difference between economic liberalism and political liberalism. The initial legal utopia erases all specificity of the political sphere.

Regulating the Internet

If we consider, on the other hand, that the Internet is not a world apart and that it is constantly interacting with the rest of society, we address the issue of regulation differently. The specific nature of the Internet obviously needs to be recognized. Jurist Lawrence Lessig considers that "software code—more than law—defines the true parameters of freedom in cyberspace. And like law, software is not value-neutral."[25] He notes that the Internet can be characterized by its "architecture of liberty."[26] In fact, he adds, "Who someone is, where he is, and whether law can be exercised over him there [are all] questions that government must answer if it is to impose its will. But these questions are made impossibly difficult by the architecture of the space."[27]

As previously shown, this situation can be explained by the history of the Internet. On this point Lessig hardly differed from Post. Yet he believed that the situation could evolve rapidly since the software on which the Internet was based could be amended, turning a structure of freedom into one of control. Certain laws aimed at preventing the circulation of pornographic documents or illicit activities on the Internet (drug trade, terrorism, etc.) could lead there, but governments had not yet managed to establish such forms of control. On the other hand, commerce was very likely to impose identification structures with the same effect. Commercial activity required all actors to identify themselves, thus putting an end to anonymity, a basic ingredient of freedom of the Internet.

The academic Internet of the 1970s and 1980s was profoundly democratic since the broad lines of the architecture and software were discussed collectively and produced by a large number of participants. By contrast, the new software produced for commercial purposes was created by programmers working for a small number of companies in whose interests it was to promote an architecture allowing control over activities on the Internet. In these conditions, "the values of free speech, privacy, due process, and equality define who we are. If there is no government to insist upon these values, who will do it?"[28] Thus, times have changed, Lessig tells us. Today, those who can violate the freedom of the Internet are no longer governments but businesses, and the law becomes a guarantor of freedom. This jurist, who at the end of 1997 was appointed as an expert in the antitrust lawsuit against Microsoft, believes that in the current situation public intervention is essential to defend the initial values of the Internet.

It is precisely this capacity of political action to formulate a common will that other jurists, like Post, challenge. In a critique of Lessig's book he notes that the original values of the Internet, which he also defends, "can best be protected by allowing the widest possible scope for uncoordinated and uncoerced individual choice among different values and different embodiments of those values; we need not 'a plan' but an infinity of plans from among which individuals can choose. It is indeed 'the market,' and not action by the global collective, that is most likely to bring that plenitude to us."[29]

Post's critique is interesting, for it shows that the thesis of independence in cyberspace is unable to withstand analysis. In fact this jurist, who, like Barlow, defended the idea that the Internet must govern itself autonomously, also recognized that it had to defend its operating principles and that, in order to do so, it required modes of regulation that were not peculiar to cyberspace. On this point he agreed with Lessig. Yet they differed as to the choice of regulatory action, since Post preferred the action of the invisible hand of the market to state intervention.

Post forgot one of the essential dimensions of economic liberalism. In fact, if the state does not intervene in private affairs (the laissez-faire doctrine), it does nevertheless set rules governing economic activity to prevent large companies from acquiring dominant positions that they could abuse. Economic liberalism is in no way synonymous with the big capitalist enterprise. Lessig, as a player in the antitrust lawsuit against Microsoft, knew full well that only the state could prevent large corporations from misusing their leading positions. Behind the Lessig/Post dichotomy, we find the opposition between Democrats and Republicans. Although they defend the right to free enterprise, the former have always granted special importance to antitrust legislation. The latter, by contrast, defend complete freedom of big business.

Finally, the Lessig/Post debate enables us to identify the two rival political views on cyberspace. The dominant view, that of the libertarians, adopted by a large fraction of the Republican Party, associates the utopia of an independent cyberspace governed by its members, with market regulation. Since this link is never clearly indicated, the independence utopia becomes a neoliberal ideology. The visceral antistatism of libertarians prevents them from seeing that the cyberspace citizen's freedom is threatened far more by big business than by the state. Another view corresponds to a liberal perspective (in the American sense), one that is, on the whole, supported by the Democratic Party, in favor of state intervention to avoid abuses by large corporations.

The Internet, a Model for a New Stateless Society

Cyberlibertarians willingly associated their vision of complete independence of the Internet with that of a cyberspace model of the future society. Barlow, in an article in *Time* in which he denounced the ban on retransmission of pornographic newsgroups by CompuServe, in the name of independence of cyberspace, wrote: "What the Net offers is the promise of a new social space, global and anti-sovereign, within which anybody, anywhere can express to the rest of humanity whatever he or she believes

without fear."[30] But, according to a group of futurologists, including Toffler and Gilder, cyberspace is more than a place for free expression, "it
can be one of the main forms of glue holding together an increasingly
free and diverse society."[31]

The idea of this new society is present in the work of many authors.
Katz believed that he was witnessing the slow agony of the existing political system and the birth of a new digital nation. This new form of citizenship was direct democracy. The members of this nation no longer
needed intermediaries. He noted: "On the Net . . . I saw positions soften
and change when people were suddenly able to talk directly to one
another, rather than through journalists, politicians, or ideological mer-
cenaries."[32] Digital citizens could also become autonomous compared to
the paradigms of the media and old political ideologies; they no longer
needed to conceive of social issues in terms of Left/Right or Democrat/
Republican opposition. As at the time of the Enlightenment, they could
exercise a new rationality. Yet Katz also noted that this was often by no
means the case, and that misinformation and insults were commonplace
in many open newsgroups. It was only in restricted spaces such as the
academic world that this new rationalism was evident and particularly
productive: "If this notion works for science, could it work for politics? . . . But I've seen the process work; it can be done."[33] This type of
statement nevertheless remained a petition of principle. Katz gave very
few examples of the transfer of the academic model into the political
domain.

This vision of what he called "post-politics" was explained in another
part of his article where he defined the digital nation as a new social
class. It was for this new elite that *Wired* claimed to be the mouthpiece.
These new citizens "are young, educated, affluent . . . Still, some of their
common values are clear: they tend to be libertarian, materialistic, toler-
ant, rational, technologically adept, disconnected from conventional
political organizations . . . They are not politically correct, rejecting
dogma in favor of sorting through issues individually, preferring discussions to platforms . . . the digital young are revolutionaries. Unlike the
clucking boomers, they are not talking revolution; they're making one.
This is a culture best judged by what it does, not what it says."[34] This
new ruling class had a new view of politics and wanted to implement it.

Its members were not interested in swearing allegiance to a party that would more or less force its program onto them. On the contrary, they wanted to deal with political affairs rationally, like one sorts out a technical problem. In a second article, Katz refined his description of the digital citizen. An opinion poll commissioned by *Wired* showed that the most frequent users of the Internet were also the most politically active ones. These data helped to challenge many received ideas on the Internet. Katz remarks: "Digital Citizens are not alienated, either from other people or from civic institutions. [They] appear startlingly close to the Jeffersonian ideal—they are informed, outspoken, participatory, passionate about freedom, proud of their culture, and committed to the free nation in which it has evolved."[35]

It was precisely this digital elite that Canadian Marxist, Arthur Kroker, denounced as the "virtual class." He considers that "the virtual class is the class that comes to power on the back of cyberspace or the internet. . . . This class is working two agendas all at the same time. Their most immediate agenda is what I would call an ideology of facilitation. They say 'Come on aboard the information superhighway,' and who would be an idiot to refuse what they're offering. . . . But as soon as they've got us interested in the information superhighway and the possibilities, for example, of the internet . . . they begin to deliver the grim message, like *Wired* magazine came out recently and said, you know, 'The age of the net utopia is over. . . . It's now time to get back to the good old American business of making money on the internet.'"[36]

For Kroker, the new digital society for all was simply an ideology masking market domination. The dichotomy that he established between Internet utopia and ideology may seem appealing, for it highlights the role of the imaginary at the beginning of the Internet design process and in the extension phase. However, by suggesting that all initial utopias have been "harnessed" by capitalism it oversimplifies the issue. According to Kroker, the inventiveness of hackers simply served to create big companies like Microsoft. Yet we know that the initial profusion spawned widely diverse computing practices. For instance, data collated by universities or even private individuals on their personal sites is available to all at no cost, and certain newsgroups constitute forums for very rich debate. Computer-mediated communication has made it possible to set up new cooperative and creative devices. Owing to this diversity of practices and discourses attending them, the virtual class is less an illusion than a way of legitimizing the new technology and mobilizing new actors. Moreover, we see that the commercialization of the Internet is a complex process, in no way identical to the commercialization of the preceding media.

Disappearance of the State?

The new society created by the cyberlibertarians constructed not only a new vision of politics but also a new vision of the state. In a synthesis of their view of cyberspace, futurologists Toffler and Gilder, in association with Dyson and Keyworth, noted that with the emergence of the "Third Wave" it was necessary to rethink the state's role entirely: "The reality is that a Third Wave government will be vastly smaller (perhaps by 50 percent or more) than the current one—this is an inevitable implication of the transition from the centralized power structures of the industrial age to the dispersed, decentralized institutions of the Third."[37] But for these futurologists this huge reduction of the state's role did not mean its disappearance.

Louis Rossetto, managing editor of *Wired*, believed that we are facing an unavoidable Copernican revolution. In these times of change, he said, "we need to question everything including that most sacred of sacred cows, the state. What is obsolete, what is necessary?"[38] He started that questioning by examining the education system: "Schools are obsolete. We should be doing all we can to liberate children from the slavery of the classroom." Rossetto's solution consisted in allowing families to buy educational services suited to their children. This argument had already been developed in the first issue of *Wired*, where Lewis Perelman wrote: "Education is the last great bastion of socialist economics. . . . Schools and colleges are as productive and innovative as Soviet collective farms."[39] The solution would be "to form a coalition that demands the commercial privatization of the entire education sector."[40] But it was also the entire social welfare system that Rossetto said should be scrapped: "The idea that we need to worry about anyone being 'left out' is entirely atavistic to me, a product of that old economics of scarcity and the 19th century social thinking that grew out of it."[41] This particularly virulent position was not as new as it may have seemed, for it reflected libertarian political theses, theorized mainly by Robert Nozick in the 1970s.[42]

This antistatism was obviously fiercely contested. In *Wired* Kline and Burnstein, for instance, accused the cyberlibertarians of throwing out the baby with the bathwater. In an article entitled "Cyberselfish," a former journalist with the California magazine, pointed out the state's role in the creation of the Internet and denounced the "techno-libertarians creaming the profits from public resources."[43] She accused them of being like nineteenth century California capitalists who misappropriated federal grants for building a railroad.

Two British post-Marxist sociologists, Richard Barbrook and Andy Cameron, published a short essay along the same lines, entitled "The Californian Ideology." They argued that this ideology was the outcome of "a bizarre fusion of the cultural bohemianism of San Francisco with the hi-tech industries of Silicon Valley. . . . It combines the free-wheeling spirit of the hippies and the entrepreneurial zeal of the yuppies."[44] These two authors also showed that "despite the central role played by public intervention in developing hypermedia, the California ideologues preach an antistatist gospel of hi-tech libertarianism: a bizarre mish-mash of hippie anarchism and economic liberalism beefed up with lots of technological determinism."[45]

All these people who crossed swords with Rossetto and *Wired* identified a key contradiction in the cyberlibertarians' position. The Internet had developed outside the market for over a quarter century, owing to public funding (ARPA, NSF, state governments, universities). These public or semipublic funds made it possible to invent and build the network, but also facilitated experimental and then large-scale use within the academic sphere. Although the success of the Internet owes much to the intellectual investment of its designers from university, it was decentralized state investments that allowed this new intellectual tool to be made available throughout the academic community.

Apart from the Internet itself, this debate took a more operational turn with regard to the new telecommunications law. On this point the digerati formed two opposing currents of thinking that simultaneously tried to lobby the Democratic and Republican parties. The Electronic Frontier Foundation (EFF) helped to draft the first reports on information highways (see chapter 1). EFF President Mitch Kapor focused not so much on defending the idea of strong state intervention in infrastructures as proposing new regulatory principles around the idea of an "open platform." This would consist in organizing a general interconnection of all telecommunications transporters (telephone, cable, satellite) and of making it mandatory for each of them to distribute all existing services (the common carrier principle). "An open platform for information services will enable individuals and small organizations, as well as established information distributors, to be electronic publishers on a local, national and international level."[46] He also proposed that the universal service, that is, the subsidized service for low-income groups, limited to the telephone, be extended to all digital services and thus to the Internet. This topic of universal service and support for the have-nots of the information society, often taken up by other authors,[47] coincided with the Democrat's position of state intervention to promote equality for all.

The Progress and Freedom Foundation (PFF), intellectually close to Toffler and run by George Keyworth, former scientific advisor to Reagan, proposed a very different policy that strongly inspired Gingrich,[48] Republican Speaker of the House of Representatives from 1995 to 1999. Like Al Gore, Gingrich was taken with new technologies. The foundation wanted to put an end to market regulation of telecommunications: "Like a Soviet-era good under Gosplan, no one really pays the true cost of the phone services they use. The replacement model puts a halt to this muddle."[49] The idea was to scrap the various regulations weighing on each of the communication systems and to mark the policy change by entirely doing away with the FCC, the regulatory authority. This is a precise illustration of the reduced state in the Third Wave of which Toffler dreamed.

While the two foundations had antagonistic positions that inspired the two main currents in U.S. political life, the digerati slid back and forth between the two. Dyson, Barlow, and Brand alternated their support for one or the other. When at one stage the EFF envisaged establishing "a Net political party," Dyson, a member of its governing board, considered that "organized political parties won't be needed if open networks enable people to organize ad hoc, rather than get stuck in some rigid group."[50] She personally put this flexibility into practice by cooperating with the PFF. Barlow and Brand likewise moved closer to Gingrich.[51]

This switching of political partners reflected both an opportunistic attitude (as a pressure group the digerati wanted to influence the political parties) and a much deeper trend. At the very beginnings of the Internet, government funding seemed to be one of the conditions for the development of the computer republic, and dreams of a state that built the basic elements of information highways open to all were possible. However, with the massification of the Internet and the arrival of commercial enterprises on the network, state intervention became less necessary and even futile, and the libertarian position triumphed. The California ideology consequently forgot its debt to the state.

Hackers Launch an Attack on the State

Private Secret, Public Secret

The digerati's collaboration with the political class was always partial and often swung around. After flirting with the Clinton administration they launched a right-wing campaign in *Wired* in April 1994 for the protection of privacy. The following extract sums up the magazine's argument: "This is a pivotal moment in history. The national security state, with the backing of the Clinton-Gore administration, is attempting a stealth strike on our rights. . . . Then lend your support to help stop the government from extinguishing the Bill of Rights in cyberspace."[52]

At the origin of this mobilization lies the issue of cryptography. Federal security agencies, fearing new encrypting techniques that might prevent them from spying on communication among terrorists and other criminals, proposed to the government a system allowing all users of digital phones or computers the use of encrypted transmissions that would nevertheless allow the police to continue their surveillance work. This system would be based on the "clipper chip." The encryption key would be held by a public institution and could be used by the police when necessary, with authorization by the courts.

The debate was twofold. First, did the state have the right to keep a watch on private communications? Second, should it regulate cryptography? Let us examine these two questions. Behind the government's project was the fear that the police might no longer be able to listen to conversations or decode computer data, and would thus no longer be able to carry out its surveillance duties. To be able to access encrypted conversations, it was necessary for the state to have the keys, that is, the codes enabling it to decrypt messages. But the digerati saw the shadow of Big Brother looming. Faced with the raison d'état, they perceived a worrying violation of individual freedom. To stop criminals, there was a risk of eventually sinking into totalitarianism. Barlow clearly summed up the debate by saying that the government was prepared to defend Americans' security at the expense of their liberty.[53] Sterling commented that "even the Four Horsemen of Kidporn, Dope Dealers, Mafia, and Terrorists don't worry me as much as totalitarian governments. It's been a long century, and we've had enough of them."[54] This anticlipper chip campaign was relayed by direct actions by Internauts. An electronic petition against the project obtained close to 50,000 signatures.[55]

The clipper chip project also restored the state's central role in the area of cryptographic regulation, since it banned certain types of encryption and the export of such technologies. For the cryptorebels or cryptopunks, hackers specialized in cryptography, any state intervention in this domain was perfectly illegitimate. Steven Levy summed up their point of view: "In the Cypherpunk mind, cryptography is too important to leave to governments or even well-meaning companies."[56] They considered that the possibility of encrypting their messages was part of individuals' basic rights. According to the "Crypto Anarchist Manifesto," "two persons may exchange messages, conduct business, and negotiate electronic contracts without ever knowing the true name, or legal identity of the other." Of course, "these developments will alter completely the nature of government regulation, the ability to tax and control economic interactions, the ability to keep information secret, and will even alter the nature of trust and reputation."[57] In a sense, cryptoanarchists were as aware as government officials that the regulation of cryptography was at the heart of society's organization. They nevertheless had difficulty explaining what society would be like if trust had to be continuously renegotiated, since one would never know with whom he or she was dealing.

But the cryptorebels did more than produce manifestos; like many hackers they also implemented their project. Former antinuclear activist Phil Zimmerman, for example, developed a sound encryption algorithm called "Pretty Good Privacy" (PGP) and circulated it on the Internet in the early 1990s. His intention was to hinder planned legislation to ban mass use of cryptography. Zimmermann presented his work as follows: "If privacy is outlawed, only outlaws will have privacy. Intelligence agencies have access to good cryptographic technology . . . But ordinary people and grassroots political organizations mostly have not had access to affordable 'military grade' public-key cryptographic technology. Until now. PGP empowers people to take their privacy into their own hands. There's a growing social need for it. That's why I wrote it."[58]

Other cryptorebels developed rerouting systems that erased the sender's name.[59] Welcome to a completely anonymous opaque society where the state can no longer watch over its citizens. But how can relationships of trust and cooperation be established in such a society? How can social links be constructed?

Information Free for All

Along with secret access to private communications, the digerati wanted free access to public information. This new issue was another source of conflict with the Clinton administration. In the framework of reflection on information superhighways (see chapter 1), the government prepared a White Paper on intellectual property rights that largely corresponded to the demands of audiovisual and literary publishers for control over the use of their products. The White Paper called into question the principle of "fair use" that allowed users to make private copies for their own personal use and to lend them to friends. It furthermore stipulated that the temporary copy of a file (text, sound, or image) from the Web, on the live memory of a computer[60]—necessary to be able to open it— was illegal.[61] The project ran counter to the Internet culture and was strongly opposed by academic circles, some digerati and certain companies.[62] This coalition succeeded in blocking it in Congress and at the Geneva conference in 1997.[63]

The debate was revived with new vigor two years later, with the success of Napster and the exchange of musical files on the Internet. Barlow returned to his keyboard to criticize a judgment that threatened to close down Napster: "Her decree transformed an evolving economy into a cause, and turned millions of politically apathetic youngsters into electronic Hezbollah. . . . No law can be successfully imposed on a huge population that does not morally support it and possesses easy means for its invisible evasion. . . . The war is on, all right, but to my mind it's over. The future will win; there will be no property in cyberspace."[64]

Protest against intellectual property rights concerned not only the possibility of making private copies and exchanging them, but also the extension of IP rights to the computing domain. Use of patents on software is a major constraint for computer scientists. Theirs is a world of perpetual change, where patents are multiple and badly listed, and sometimes refer to principles that are common throughout the profession. Simon Garfinkel, Richard Stallman, and Mitchel Kapor concluded their article "Why Patents Are Bad for Software" with the following recommendation: "Nearly all programmers view patents as an unwelcome intrusion, limiting both their ability to do their work and their freedom of expression. . . . Congress should feel justified in eliminating this barrier to innovation."[65]

From Control of Pornography to Control of Content

In regard to content, it was not only intellectual property rights that the digerati were challenging but also censorship. In 1995 the American press presented a new image of the Internet. It focused on exchange, dialogue, and worldwide communication less than in the previous year, more frequently presenting the network as a tool for the free distribution of pornographic documents that were starting to be accessible to children, and even as a tool for the organization of pedophile networks.[66] Certain universities, for instance Carnegie Mellon, started to ban the use of pornographic newsgroups on their campus computer networks.[67]

The campaign against cyberporn also caused concern among politicians. Two senators proposed an amendment to the telecommunications law under discussion: the Communications Decency Act (CDA). In terms of this amendment it would be illegal not only to put pornographic documents on the Web but also to use lewd or filthy vocabulary in emails and newsgroups whenever a minor might be concerned, in other words, all the time. The amendment was passed with a large majority by the Senate and the law in its entirety was promulgated by President Clinton in February 1996. The two legal models that served as a reference were radio-television and telephone harassment. The former case concerned two of the mass media directly accessible to all, and the content of which the legislator wished to regulate, while the latter concerned an intrusion into the intimacy of telephone users.

The CDA triggered the opposition of the digerati community which immediately claimed that the political authorities had failed to understand the specific nature of the Internet. It was neither like television nor like the telephone. Moreover, it was an international communication device that the U.S. government would not be able to regulate alone. For Barlow, who protested immediately, "They are a government of the completely clueless, trying to impose their will on a place they do not understand, using a means they do not possess."[68] More profoundly, this struggle against cyberpornography was perceived by the digerati as an attack on freedom of expression. EFF jurist Mike Godwin wrote during the first censorship operations of Carnegie Mellon university: "It is precisely because the Net holds the promise of being the most democratizing communications medium in the history of the planet that it is vital we prevent the fearful and the ignorant from attempting to control your access to it."[69]

During the debate in Congress on the CDA the digerati circulated electronic petitions. Web sites that supported the campaign displayed a blue ribbon, an analogy with the red ribbon symbolizing the fight against AIDS. When the law was promulgated the digerati observed a day's mourning by putting a plain black background on their computer screens. Apart from such symbolic actions, legal action was taken by ACLU, the largest civil rights organization, the EFF, librarians' associations, *Wired*, and such firms as Internet service providers Microsoft and Apple.

At the end of the trial the Philadelphia appeal court judge explained his ruling: "Cutting through the acronyms and argot that littered the hearing testimony, the Internet may fairly be regarded as a never-ending worldwide conversation. The Government may not, through the CDA, interrupt that conversation. As the most participatory form of mass speech yet developed, the Internet deserves the highest protection from governmental intrusion . . . The absence of governmental regulation of Internet content has unquestionably produced a kind of chaos, but as one of plaintiffs' experts put it with such resonance at the hearing: 'What achieved success was the very chaos that the Internet is. The strength of the Internet is that chaos.' Just as the strength of the Internet is chaos, so the strength of our liberty depends upon the chaos and cacophony of the unfettered speech the First Amendment protects. For these reasons, I without hesitation hold that the CDA is unconstitutional on its face.'[70] A year later the Supreme Court upheld that decision.

Not only had cyberlibertarians won their battle against the state, the judge had actually used their arguments. For Katz, the CDA "galvanized a diverse coalition of idiosyncratic individuals into a cohesive political force." Like the Stamp Act that mobilized the independence movement in the late eighteenth century, "the CDA did the same for the digital world, giving credence to the notion of the birth of a Digital Nation."[71] For Katz, the CDA was the Internet's war of independence!

The cyberlibertarian utopia switched over into ideology here, for it was less the citizens' struggle that got rid of the CDA and the "clipper chip" than corporate hostility. Internet access providers both supported and financed the legal action against the CDA, a real threat to their business. Likewise, the manufacturers of microcomputers and telephone sets opposed the "clipper chip" which would have increased the prices of their terminals. During this period when the Internet was starting to become an economic issue, firms vigorously opposed any attempts by government or Congress to restrict it.

Can we conclude that cyberlibertarians were orchestrated by big business? Clearly not. The wish to express oneself freely is not only one of the essential components of the Internet *imaginaire* but also a basic feature of the U.S. political culture. More important, although the CDA was a case where cyberlibertarians and firms had the same interests, on the issue of intellectual property rights, their positions were diametrically opposed: while the ones defended property rights, the others struggled for free use of software and cultural products.

Withdrawal of the Digerati

Katz's discourse on the digital nation masks another illusion, that of the founding nature of cyberlibertarians' political actions. Is it enough to strive for freedom on the Internet and to combat liberticidal laws or projects in order to found a new vision of politics? *Wired* carried out a brief survey on its readers' political identity. The results gave an extremely varied picture in which two-thirds of readers identified with the following: "liberal, progressive, libertarian, anarchist, and conservative." Even stranger were the ambiguous terms that appeared, the new oxymorons of politics: "progressive conservative," "virtual populist," "market-oriented progressive." Although a strong libertarian sentiment was clearly apparent, it seems doubtful that politics was indeed an important issue for the digerati. As Jay Kinney notes in her comments on the survey: "Where do politics fit into this new world, when leaving the Internet becomes as unthinkable as no longer breathing?"[72] Even though at one stage they considered founding a "Net political party," the digerati lost interest in politics and participated only when their interests were at stake. Cyberlibertarianism was simply an Internaut lobby.

A similar analysis that reduces discourse on the digital nation to pure illusion fails to do justice to militant actions such as those of the EFF, set in the tradition of the civil rights movement founded in the 1960s and 1970s. In this perspective, cyberlibertarianism is a movement to defend freedoms, not the bedrock of new global politics.

We can therefore conclude that, on the whole, citizens of the Internet have little interest in politics. On the other hand, they have some strong convictions regarding the role of the state which, in their view, should under no circumstances regulate content transmitted on the Internet. Most consider that the state should intervene as little as possible and that any necessary regulation should be provided by the market. In their opinion we are witnessing the end of the nation state. For Lawrence Wilkinson, cofounder of Global Business Network, a think tank close to *Wired* (see chapter 4), "It was during the Enlightenment that the nation state ousted the church and became the dominant seat of power. The nation state is now making way for the market. Note that its power is everywhere, at local and global level, . . . independent of national borders."

This is a difficult change. National rivalries "will end up being replaced by kinds of tribal and commercial conflicts. What will remain of nationalism?"[73] For Wilkinson, the answer is clear: residual nationalism will resemble loyalty to a brand or a sports club. We are in the world of global economics where the only remaining conflicts will be between megafirms. Constant reference to the market appears fuzzy since it is no longer clear who sets the rules of the game, and huge corporations, especially U.S.-based, readily turn to the state to obtain competitive advantages. Market regulation is thus very weak compared to power struggles between big companies.

Alongside this largely dominant position, a smaller group believes, on the contrary, that the state must intervene in cyberspace, either to promote the launching of new technologies, as was formerly the case with Arpanet, or to avoid excesses by dominant economic players in the process of conquering the Internet.

From Science to the Market

In the final analysis, the digerati's conception of relations between society and cyberspace are complex. They consider both that the Internet is a world apart in which the state must not intervene, and that it should constitute the model for tomorrow's society. Yet, on closer inspection, we see that these two positions are less antagonistic than they seem. The freedom that the digerati demand for the Internet is not that of a separate space in which a different society could be tried and tested just for fun; it is a virtual world in which tomorrow's reality can be simulated (in the sense of a mock-up of the real world). The consistency of these two positions is found in the concept of virtual reality which is both an unrestricted space and a place in which a future society can be prepared. Cyberspace makes it possible to test and shape these utopias so that they can be materialized in tomorrow's world.

In the 1970s and 1980s these claims for freedom of action to prepare the future were difficult to obtain from the economic world and the state seemed to be the guarantor of independent research. It was the state that enabled the academic world to create the Internet; the first Internauts were in favor of its intervention. Today, as the Internet has lost its experimental status and the state can legitimately intervene in this new field, it appears more like an enemy. The digerati tend to be even more opposed to state control. They would readily see former self-regulation by competency replaced by regulation by commercial success. The principle of regulation has shifted from science to the market. In this new context, citizens of the Internet have a lot in common with libertarians. They imagine a system without state intervention, as in the case of protection of individual data, in which firms define the commitments that they undertake to observe. But by staking everything on market regulation, citizens of the Internet could be confronted by the power of big business. Should they trust in the state again, to avoid abuses by certain large groups in a dominant position?

8

The New Economy

For nearly twenty years the Internet developed outside the market economy. Free-of-charge products and cooperation were at the heart of the Internaut culture and market exchange was even proscribed. But a new commercial and economic discourse gradually shifted onto the network of networks. In this chapter I present its origins and examine a new component of the cyber-*imaginaire*.[1]

For a long time free sharing was not an issue; it was taken for granted. The Internet was a project of university researchers and hackers, and as such was expected to yield freely available products. By contrast, in other areas of information technology firms were increasingly protecting their software with patents and various legal devices. In the 1980s some computer scientists, steeped in the academic tradition of openness and freedom, and opposed to the principle of intellectual property rights on software, were the first to theorize the principles of cooperation and free exchange underlying the Internet. Their reflection was to lay the foundations of the freeware utopia and an alternative economic theory.

In parallel with this utopia other Internauts had the idea, in the mid-1990s, of doing business on the Internet. They saw it as a medium like any other that should be available for advertising and trade. A head-on collision between the two views resulted: free access and even free sharing versus payment and business. It was this debate that spawned the idea of the Internet as the bedrock of new commercial relations and thus of a new economy. The two conflicting perspectives were poles apart: Internet pioneers and hackers defended a model close to that of open source, free software, while the newcomers wanted a business model based on that of the mass media, with financing via advertising and e-commerce. Discourse on the new economy was inspired by these contradictory views. The outcome is, in a sense, a hybrid of the two.

This discourse opened new perspectives for the development of the Internet and was profoundly innovative from an economic point of view. Even if economists often evoked the impact of technological innovation on equilibriums between capital and labor, and on growth, none of them had hitherto imagined that a new technology could revolutionize the very principles of economic activity. The digerati were the first to reason this way and to find economic grounds for their arguments. This was clearly a break from traditional thinking on new technologies. It was also an opportunity for debate between the digerati and professional economists.

Freeware, a New Public Good

In the first chapters of this book I showed that the designers of the Internet and, especially, hackers on the fringes of the university world believed that information had to be free and shared by all. In 1983 Richard Stallman, an academic computer specialist and hacker, sent a message to one of the Usenet newsgroups, entitled "Free Unix": "I am going to write a complete Unix-compatible software system, called GNU (for Gnu's Not Unix), and give it away free to everyone who can use it . . . I consider that the golden rule requires that if I like a program I must share it with other people who like it . . . If I get donations of money, I may be able to hire a few people full or part time. The salary won't be high, but I'm looking for people, for whom knowing they are helping humanity is as important as money."[2] This founding statement contains some of the essential features of the freeware movement:

First, the ambition to build a complete computing system with an operating system similar to Unix and a full range of application software such as a text editor and graphic interface. Although Unix, the most widely used operating system in the research community, was easily accessible in the academic world, its user license prohibited changes to the software. Moreover, AT&T, which following its breakup had obtained the right to develop computer-related activities, had started to extract value from its rights on Unix.

Second, the notion of freedom, which is often confusing. It relates to the absence not of payment but rather of secrecy, and thus to the possibility of sharing. The word "free" in this sense comes from the tradition of civil rights movements in the 1960s and 1970s.[3] In the world of computing, it means the opposite of ownership. Thus, freeware is a computer program whose sources (i.e., complete set of instructions) are accessible. The freeware movement is therefore clearly opposed to computer companies that it sees in the following light: "The rule made by the owners of proprietary software was, 'If you share with your neighbor, you are a pirate. If you want any changes, beg us to make them.' "[4] By contrast, it proposes the following: "You have the freedom to run the program, for any purpose . . . to modify the program to suit your needs . . . to redistribute copies, either gratis or for a fee . . . to distribute modified versions of the program, so that the community can benefit from your improvements."[5] These principles of freedom are codified in a system called "copyleft" in which copyright legislation is used for a diametrically opposed purpose. "Copyleft," defined in a license (General Public License) attached to every piece of free software,[6] specifies the rights of program users who may use, copy, and disseminate the software. They may also change it but may under no circumstances protect the changes they make. These must circulate freely, like the original software: "If you distribute copies of such a program, whether gratis or for a fee, you must give the recipients all the rights that you have."[7]

Finally, the third feature of the freeware movement was the wish to mobilize hackers wanting to participate in the project. Stallman defined this type of hacker not as a pirate but as "someone who loves to program and enjoys being clever about it."[8] Thus, it is above all for the pleasure of programming freely and being judged primarily by peers that computer specialists write freeware. We have here a model very similar to that of the Internet. In order to pay computer specialists not financed by a university, Stallman created a fundraising foundation in 1985, the "Free Software Foundation," although financial gain derived from business creation was not the prime motive of these hackers. Stallman's project was above all societal; he wanted to build a public good. In an interview in *Byte*, he noted: "The principle of capitalism is the idea that people manage to make money by producing things. . . . But that doesn't work when it comes to owning knowledge. They are encouraged to do not really what's useful, and what really is useful is not encouraged. I think it is important to say that information is different from material objects like cars and loaves of bread because people can copy it and share it on their own and, if nobody attempts to stop them, they can change it and make it better for themselves." He therefore considered that "the law should recognize a class of works that are owned by the public."[9] This Stallman model, well known to freeware specialists, is the same as the model of scientific production, university work, and the Internet.

To define these public goods, Stallman took the example of a space station[10] where the cost of producing air is so high that it may seem fair to charge for its consumption. This would make it necessary to supply each consumer with a gas mask and to check that nobody cheated. To avoid such a breach of individual freedom, Stallman considered it preferable to finance the production of air by means of a tax. In a more recent interview, he repeated his idea of a public good, comparing the freeware movement to protection of the environment: "the goal is to end a certain kind of pollution. But in this case, it's not pollution of the air or the water, it's pollution of our social relationships . . . the willingness to cooperate with other people."[11]

In the early 1990s GNU consisted of many programs but still lacked a core operating system. *Wired*, which devoted an article to Stallman in its first issue,[12] suggested that the project was stalling and would fail to meet its goal. However, during the same period Linus Torvalds, a student at Helsinki University, wrote the core of an operating system similar to that of Unix. Unlike the Unix tradition, he used not a mainframe computer but a PC. Owing to the collaboration of hundreds, then thousands, and finally tens of thousands of voluntary computer specialists[13] who readily became involved because they needed only a PC to do so, Linux was soon fleshed out. The original ten-thousand-line code would swell to one million lines six years later. Linux, articulated with GNU, offered a real alternative to commercial software, and by 1997 it had about five million users.[14] In the words of the *Wired* journalist who studied the project: "The Linux approach is deceptively simple. All hackers are free to work on any additional features or improvements. Even in the earliest stages, new code is freely downloadable for users to try and critique: beta-testing is not a last-minute attempt to catch the worst flaws, but an integral part of the process. When several people work on the same area, they may compete or combine; if they compete, the best code wins through raw Darwinian selection."[15] With the participation of tens of thousands of hackers, Linux constituted a large-scale cooperative project that combined coordination and anarchy. It was necessary to allow the expression of each hacker's creativity while maintaining sound coordination. What bound the partners together was shared understanding of the software. Meetings among a large number of designers and the participation of users throughout the process also helped to detect errors more easily. According to *Wired*,[16] that is what Eric Raymond, the movement's philosopher, calls the Linux Law: "Given enough eyeballs, all bugs are shallow."[17]

Like the designers of GNU or the Internet, those of Linux tried above all to obtain peer recognition: "For most hackers, the goal is to create neat routines, tight chunks of code, or cool apps that earn the respect of their peers."[18] In more economic terms, we could consider, like Raymond,[19] that Linux constituted a market in which hackers tried to maximize a function of particular utility: their own intellectual satisfaction and their reputation within the community. Open coordination, far more effective than a centralized plan, was thus established.

This community nevertheless needed a coordination tool. The Internet was the obvious answer. Debates took place on Usenet and bits of software circulated on the Web: "Anybody anywhere on the Net could obtain the basic Linux files. Email enabled them to comment and offer improvements, while Usenet provided a forum for discussion. Beginning as the product of one mind, Linux was turning into a tapestry, a movement of like-minded hackers."[20] But the link between Linux and the Internet was even stronger since much Internet support software was freeware.

In the late 1990s the freeware principle was no longer just a utopia, it was embodied in concrete achievements. But is it, for all that, a feasible economic solution? The allegory of the commons is often used, especially by economists,[21] to show that collective exploitation is an impossible resource. Rational behavior of farmers who share such ground is to let their cattle graze intensely, so as to extract the maximum value from the resource before everyone else. The pasture inevitably turns into a dam of mud. To avoid such an outcome, there are only two alternatives: either the collectivist model where an authority imposes shared exploitation, or the field is divided into private allotments. But for freeware advocates like Raymond, computing is a case where the allegory does not apply.[22] The value of software does not decline with its exploitation; on the contrary, it increases. The more people use freeware, the more advantageous its use becomes. At the same time, producers derive prestige and reputation for their skills which can enable them to obtain higher salaries in the job market. GNU and Linux thus show, in the Internet tradition, that cooperation can be rational and effective. New economic behaviors are unquestionably at play. This observation has been made not only by hackers but also by Thomas Malone, professor at the Sloan School of Management, who wrote in the *Harvard Business Review*: "The Linux community, a temporary self-managed gathering of diverse individuals engaged in a common task, is a model for a new kind of business organization that could form the basis for a new kind of economy."[23]

Finding a Business Model for the Internet

Hackers and Internauts, in general, who subscribed to the cooperative principles of freeware in the early 1990s were also reluctant to see the Internet used for commercial purposes. At the time, the network of networks was used essentially by the academic world, and Nsfnet (see chapter 2), which constituted the heart of the system, precluded any commercial use. Yet the idea of commercialization was starting to take shape. Initially, reflection focused on payment of access to the network—the theme of a seminar at Harvard in 1990.[24] Two years later three private regional networks created the Commercial Internet Exchange enabling them to bypass Nsfnet. Gradually Internet infrastructures were privatized and the commercial sector showed an interest in the network. In 1994 and 1997 successive proposals for business models were witnessed: mass advertising, the Internet as a marketplace, the push media, one-to-one marketing, and virtual communities. We will now examine these different models.

Advertisers Invade the Internet

Although the aim was thus to open up to the business world, the idea of using the Internet for purely commercial purposes was so foreign to Internet culture that few actors even considered it. A trial run in April 1994, the cause of a lot of fuss in the Internaut community, clearly illustrates attitudes at the time. Two Phoenix lawyers and Internet users, L. Canter and M. Siegel, offered their services to people wishing to obtain residence in the United States. When they posted their messages on Usenet to several thousand newsgroups, Internauts were outraged. The two lawyers' email boxes were immediately saturated with complaints. One computer specialist wrote a short program that automatically erased copies of the advertisement in machines on the network. In the final analysis, it was less the fact that Usenet was used for advertising that caused the outcry than this general diffusion. As one commentator remarked: "Usenet is not a common carrier such as television or the radio. . . . What Canter and Siegel did was only a violation of community values, abusing the cooperation of others. But cooperation, helping others to speak and exercising some restraint in ones own speech, is the only thing holding the Usenet community together, and the only law it really has. If mass advertising is allowed to continue, and others join in (as they already have) this fragile structure may well dissolve, and Usenet as we know it will cease to exist."[25]

On the strength of this highly controversial experiment, Canter and Siegel founded a company called Cybersell, which specialized in advertising consultancy on the Internet. A few months later they published a book, *How to Make a Fortune on the Information Superhighway,*[26] which gave a number of practical tips on how to advertise on the network of networks. It was a weapon in their struggle to get commercial activities onto the Internet and to impose their model of functioning, irrespective of Internauts' traditions. They often used the frontier metaphor. Cybersellers were said to be new pioneers who had to set up businesses in "underdeveloped" countries of cyberspace. They were opposed to "natives," those academics who had raised voluntarism and the gift economy to the status of behavioral norms.[27] Canter and Siegel considered it necessary to discipline that group, so quick to enrage people, if the interests of business were to be safeguarded.

Naturally, the pioneers held the natives' culture in contempt and saw no reason to adopt it. The two blatantly provocative authors wrote: "Some starry-eyed individuals who access the Net think of Cyberspace as a community, with rules, regulations and codes of behavior. Don't you believe it! There is no community. . . . Along your way, someone may try to tell you that in order to be a good Net 'citizen,' you must follow the rules of the cyberspace community. Don't listen."[28] Behind the colonial metaphor lay the idea that the Internet was a medium like any other and as such could be used for advertising.

A New Marketplace

Several e-commerce guides were published in the same year. The idea that one just had to open a cybershop to make money was widespread. As the title of one chapter so neatly put it:[29] "If you build it they will come." The same position can be found in the few rare newsmagazine articles published at the time on business on the Internet[30]. *Time*, which cited the Canter and Siegel affair at length, also published the views of an advertiser: "I think the market is huge. . . . There's a place for advertising on the network."[31] In *Business Week* John Verity wrote: "Today, after two decades of use by engineers, scientists and, lately, by adventurous PC owners, the Internet is at a turning point. Although some old-timers object, the network is going commercial—if only because it's there, it works, and it's essentially free for businesses to use."[32] A few months later he interviewed one of the actors of these new projects: "With the Internet, the whole globe is one marketplace. . . . It also will create all kinds of opportunities to save money. By linking buyers and sellers and eliminating paperwork, the cost per transaction will go through the floor."[33] We thus see a theme emerging that had already been present in the literature on information highways, namely, the electronic marketplace in which buyers and sellers could get together at very little cost.

The question was how to organize this marketplace so that buyers could find their bearings. The answer was to group businesses together. Canter and Siegel, for example, noted that "the most popular marketing idea in Cyberspace today is the virtual mall."[34] In early 1995 a journalist for *Time* wrote that "online shopping centers are springing up everywhere, inviting customers to use their credit cards to buy on impulse, without even leaving their chairs."[35]

Push Media

Another commercial Internet model, the push media system, appeared two years later. Instead of fetching data off a website, users received information corresponding to their profile of interests directly on their computers. For *The Wall Street Journal*, the Internet "has been a medium in search of a viable business model. Now it has found one: television."[36] As one observer remarked, "It makes the Web relevant to the masses."[37] For *Business Week*, "that ability to 'narrowcast' is transforming the Net into a personal broadcast system."[38] Thus, even if push invented a small channel, it pointed the way back to a regular media paradigm.

The authors of the first books on e-commerce, like the first press articles on the subject, believed that the Internet was a new medium that had particular characteristics but which could, like preceding media, be used for advertising and commerce. They thought that, as with radio in the 1920s, professionals in these two business lines would gradually oust the first Internauts along with their anarchic and noncommercial practices. But failure of early attempts to commercialize the Internet, through advertising, online selling, and later push media, prompted observers to doubt seriously the future of e-commerce. Steven Levy, in the 1995 end-of-year issue of *Newsweek*, summed up the situation as follows: "Businesses salivate at the prospect of reaching customers worldwide from a virtual storefront. But the Net economy will force every company to change its ways."[39] Rheingold commented that "publishers never understood that people didn't want their content, they wanted a global jam session"[40]—an opinion shared by other digerati.

One-to-One Advertising

Debate on e-commerce was not limited to early Internauts versus cyberspace colonists. Marketing specialists were wondering about the low returns from mass advertising. They were particularly interested in interactive media that were more topical than the Internet in the early 1980s. In 1993 Don Peppers and Martha Rogers published the book *The One to One Future: Building Relationships One Customer at a Time.*[41] In an article in *Wired* a few months later[42] they explained that tomorrow's marketing would be individualized. Advertising would become a dialogue between potential buyers and sellers. It could also come in the form of useful information, similar to the yellow pages. Businesses could thus develop long-term relations with consumers.

In the same issue Michael Schrage reflected on the connection between the Internet and advertising. He asked: "Is advertising finally dead?" For him, unlike Canter and Siegel, there was no doubt that "tomorrow's soft-ads are going to reflect the values of the Net more than tomorrow's Net will evolve into a digital regurgitation of today's advertising."[43] Was this encounter of two cultures likely to trigger conflict? Schrage took up the cyberpunk novelist David Brin's idea of advertising viruses: "No doubt, some netcrawlers will be virulently anti-advirus. They'll want Lysol-like software to scour and disinfect adviruses from any program before it can be displayed. We'll see an epidemiological battle between the forces of digital commercialism and purists who think commerce has no place on The Net. Of course, we all know who'll win that battle, don't we?" In the final analysis, it seems that "the Net becomes the key medium for both community and commerce."[44]

In early 1996 Evan Schwartz drew conclusions in *Wired* from the first Internet advertising experiments. He described the characteristics of a very specific Web economy, webonomics—"You just have to forget everything you ever learned about business"[45]—and highlighted three key principles:

• "The quantity of people visiting your site is less important than the quality of their experience." Loyal and regular Internauts must therefore be given priority;

• "Marketers are not on the Web for exposure, but results." The idea is not only to show a product but to describe its characteristics and uses. In this perspective, the advertiser is paid not according to the number of visitors to the site (the equivalent of diffusion) but according to sales;

• "Customers must be rewarded when they disclose information about themselves." Since the Internet allows specific dialogue with consumers, businesses can take advantage of that to collect precise information about them. But they can gather such information only if they reward customers with discounts, complementary services, or gifts.

Here we find Peppers's and Rogers's idea of targeted and individualized marketing. Schwartz associated these ideas with the emergent characteristics of the Internet.[46]

Virtual Communities

By contrast, in *Net Gain*, McKinsey consultants John Hagel and Arthur Armstrong considered webonomics from the point of view of a particular characteristic of Internet culture: virtual communities. As attentive observers of The Well, they knew that "most of these initiatives were motivated by passion not profit"[47] and that "there was a strong anticommerce culture in the online world." Yet they believed that virtual communities were not necessarily averse to commerce. In their view, these communities were like individuals who shared the same interests and wanted to build real personal relationships or explore virtual worlds together. Balanced exchange resembling information bartering was one of the elements of the original Internet culture, codified in netiquette. Small ads had existed on the network from the outset. It was therefore natural for virtual communities to make space for commercial transactions. In fact, "commerce can actually reinforce community."[48]

The virtual community thus became a new economic agent enhancing consumers' power. This created a "reverse market" situation "where customers seek out vendors and deal with them on a much more level playing field in terms of information access."[49] In this way, the virtual community is a device for aggregating buying power. Information on the product or service offering is collected by users and not by experts (specialized journalists, publishers of guides, etc.), who make their own quality assessments. But the community also provides information on the demand, which it can structure itself. It thus produces value (its members' commercial profile) that is normally produced by firms' marketing services. Hagel and Armstrong's intuition was that this economic activity of virtual communities could not be achieved in the context of information cooperation initially present on the Internet. It was necessary to create commercial communities that were real business enterprises, with investors, managers, and employees. These communities "will be the most competitive commercial online format,"[50] they said. "Virtual communities are not an opportunity that executives can choose to address or to ignore. They represent a profound change that will unalterably transform the business landscape and benefit only those who confront it head on."[51]

This somewhat peremptory judgment on the future of commercial virtual communities was based essentially on an economic argument. It concerned an activity which, unlike most industries, had increasing returns and even combined several forms of increasing returns: low marginal costs (the initial investment is high but additional costs are limited), considerable learning effects (as the activity develops, organization improves and costs are reduced), and network effects (the greater the number of participants, the more attractive the community). To better understand the relevance of this reasoning, consider the way in which income was to be generated: subscriptions for use, advertising, and commission on commercial transactions. It was primarily from the latter source of revenue that large-scale development of virtual communities could be expected.

This project was therefore based on an economic and sociological gamble. Although the dynamics of increasing returns can be highly profitable, they require continual investments, whereas income is low for a long time. Moreover, unlike other economic activities with the same characteristics, such as software and telecommunication networks, a first level of economic equilibrium could not be reached with high prices and a small customer base. In fact, like other economic projects on the Internet, the gamble was potentially very profitable but also very risky.

To reduce this risk, Hagel and Armstrong suggested using the multiple noncommercial possibilities of the Internet. Initially, to create traffic, the initiator of a community could propose a repertory of available resources on related topics, with the relevant hypertext links. Next, "bulletin boards and chat areas are the elements of the community most effective in engaging members. A virtuous circle is often unleashed once members start contributing to these areas of the community. The act of contributing creates a feeling of involvement and ownership that draws members in one more tightly to the community and motivates them to contribute even more actively over time."[52] Since newsgroup moderators are usually volunteers, commercial communities fitted into the Internet culture and benefited from noncommercial services from the outset, enabling them to reduce their initial losses. Creators of commercial communities thus had to maintain a delicate balance between seemingly antagonistic concerns: those of business and those of free exchange. Hagel and Armstrong concluded one of their chapters with the following advice: "The team should always remember the principle of 'community before commerce,' to keep the organization's eye on what matters most—the members' interests and their relationships with one another."[53]

This confusion between community life and commerce was also reported in a special issue of *Business Week* entitled "Internet Communities: How They Have Shaped E-Commerce."[54] Robert Hof developed the idea that, faced with the confusion that was starting to reign on the Web, communities constituted landmarks and stabilized use of the medium. Several specialists of online communities, like Rheingold or Morningstar,[55] explained that a community was a complex collective construct built up over time. An AOL executive who launched many newsgroup and chat services noted that "the community is the Velcro strip keeping people there."[56] But with these stabilized Internauts it was also possible to do business, provided one could play by the rules of collective life on line. Rheingold, Figallo,[57] and other pioneers of The Well contributed their expertise to the new entrepreneurs of commercial communities.

Apart from online communities, the media started to forecast a great future for e-commerce—the "click here economy," as *Business Week* put it in a special issue entitled "Doing Business in the Internet Age." "Indeed, the Net is deconstructing the fundamental nature of business transactions. As every link in the supply chain is wired, the traditional roles of manufacturers, distributors and suppliers are blurring, and buyers will be the ultimate winners."[58] These profits reaped by both consumers and businesses stem from increasing competition (buyers can compare prices more easily) and reduced transaction costs (negotiation between buyers and sellers is more direct).

To conclude this reflection on advertising and e-commerce, we note that these two activities have not developed naturally, with the Internet being substituted for other media, as Canter and Siegel forecast. Other forms of advertising and commerce have been invented that are more in keeping with the history and culture of the network of networks, incorporate the new prospects of a more individualized form of marketing, and fit into more general economic upheavals. In the final analysis, it seems that the Internet is less a novel means for expanding traditional business than a new way of actually doing business.

Toward a New Economy

Although the free software perspective was initially radically opposed to that of the Internet commercial model, the two were to merge with the idea of a new economy. In 1994–1995 the economy of the immaterial was an attempt to turn free sharing into a business strategy.

To explain this process, we need to revert to the early years of the network. Even though the pioneers of the Internet developed a world of free sharing and cooperation, they were less removed from the economic sphere than they seemed. This was particularly true of the hippie and community currents on the Internet. As Brand notes, "Since we started dropping out of college, one of the things we missed was academia's disdain for business and money: 'do your own thing' translated into 'start your own business.' Carried by a vaster social movement, the hippies were readily accepted by the small business world."[59]

We will proceed chronologically in our analysis of this nascent new economy ideology. Reflection on the economy of the immaterial, published in 1994–1995, constitutes the base of the ideology that tried to merge free software with the commercial Internet model. In the years from 1996 to 1998, the new economy as a topic appeared more and more explicitly, and some authors tried to develop a theory. From 1999 onward, the new economy theme was associated with the Internet boom, followed by the bursting of the bubble.

Conceiving an Economy of the Immaterial

One month before Canter and Siegel's ad operation, Barlow published an article in *Wired* on the ideas economy in the digital era. This article, subsequently published in numerous collective volumes, was probably the first reflection by the digerati[60] on intellectual property on the Internet and, more broadly, on the information economy. Barlow based his reflection on the fact that with digital techniques information is detached from a physical medium, so that the copy can no longer be distinguished from the original: "Notions of property, value, ownership, and the nature of wealth itself are changing more fundamentally than at any time since the Sumerians first poked cuneiform into wet clay and called it stored grain."[61] Current intellectual property laws were totally unsuited to the situation and trying to apply them, regardless of that inappropriateness, would amount to limiting freedom of expression.

In order to lay the new foundations of intellectual property, Barlow defined his idea of information. He saw it as fundamentally different from a good that could be stored. It is action, movement. Similar to life itself, it is part of a dynamic, yet perishable. It is also fundamentally collective. The model of the author of a book can be considered an exception. In today's digital culture, which in this respect resembles yesterday's oral culture, "most information will be generated collaboratively by the cyber-tribal hunter-gatherers of cyberspace."[62]

Unlike material goods, there is no link between value and rarity. The value of a software package, for example, increases with its diffusion. There are nevertheless cases where time creates phenomena of rarity—that is, the first to receive information can take advantage of it, compared to those who do not yet have it.

Based on these different characteristics of information, Barlow devised an economic model that articulates payment and gratuity, exclusivity and free dissemination, and emphasizes additional services. Exclusivity is possible only if it corresponds to a particular service: priority in reception or a special quality. Cryptography is more appropriate for implementing it than legal weapons.[63] In respect of music, Barlow recalls the experience of his rock group, the Grateful Dead, which charged for tickets to their concerts but let pirated recordings circulate: "Instead of reducing the demand for our product, we are now the largest concert draw in America, a fact that is at least in part attributable to the popularity generated by those tapes."[64] For software, it is advisable to offer the latest version and various forms of assistance and training free of charge: "Once a program becomes central to your work, you want the latest version of it, the best support, the actual manuals, all privileges attached to ownership. Such practical considerations will, in the absence of working law, become more and more important in getting paid for what might easily be obtained for nothing."[65]

That is exactly the strategy that Netscape (at the time called Mosaic) was developing at that stage. In an interview in October 1994 with *Wired*, Jim Clark, one of the two founders, explained that he had provided the first version of his navigator freely and was preparing a more complete update that would then be sold.[66] The effectiveness of that strategy was clear, since in the spring of 1995 six million copies of the navigator had been downloaded. The new managing director later commented to *Wired*, "I don't know of a company that's created a brand quicker than we have. And by the way, over a period of a year and a half we have never run an ad."[67]

Barlow's intuition, tested in a sense by Netscape, was presented in more complete form in an article by Dyson. From the outset she asserted that content should be provided freely so that complementary services could be sold by building up a network of relations. This did not reflect a wish to apply the ethical rules of the Internet; rather, it was the result of a reasoned commercial strategy: "This 'generosity' isn't a moral decision: it's a business strategy."[68] "The trick is to control not the copies of your work but instead a relationship with the customers—subscriptions or membership. And that's often what the customers want, because they see it as an assurance of a continuing supply of reliable, timely content."[69]

What we have here is a "new economy" (the term appears in the text), in which "intellectual property" can be considered like ownership of land that produces no rents if it is not exploited in any way. It is the "intellectual value" that has to be sold. Dyson cites the case of a company that sells freeware of the "Free Software Foundation." Its service consists in installing software and training and advising users: "In the end, the only unfungible, unreplicable value in the new economy will be people's presence, time, and attention."[70] To attract the attention of Internet users and make them spend their time, service providers will need mediators. One of "the most promising businesses in the Net world will be services and processes. They will include selecting, classifying, rating, interpreting, and customizing content for specific customer needs. . . . Much chargeable value will be in certification of authenticity and reliability, not in the content. Brand name, identity, and other marks of value will be important; so will security of supply. Customers will pay for a stream of information and content from a trusted source."[71]

In short, creators will be able to earn a living by proposing either choice content at a high price or additional services associated with free content: "Of course, this new world will distribute its benefits differently than how they are distributed today. But as long as the rules are the same for everyone—and predictable—the game is fair."[72] Thus, in the information field, the new economy functions on really different bases.[73]

The idea that in the Internet world free services must be articulated to paid services also appeared at the first international conference on e-commerce (May 1994), which, incidentally, had a very explicit subtitle: "Making Money on the Internet." In particular, Laura Fillmore developed the argument that with the advent of the Web, we have moved from an "economy of rarity" to an "economy of abundance" in which very different intellectual services can be offered, from direct, "live" intellectual work, at very high prices, to standard knowledge that is already widely disseminated and proposed freely.

This idea of articulating free information to payable information is at the heart of the Web economic model. At the end of 1994, 42 percent of the 2.5 million host computers connected to the Internet in the United States were business machines, while 39 percent were for educational purposes and 13 percent belonged to government organizations.[74] Five years later the proportion of commercial hosts had increased substantially, but 86 percent of Web pages were still noncommercial. These pages accounted for 51 percent of the audiences (i.e., pages read).[75] If we take into account the fact that the motive for visiting a large number of commercial sites (portals, search engines) was consultation of noncommercial sites created either by universities or on a voluntary basis, we see that the noncommercial sector was still central when it came to content on the Internet. Moreover, the flourishing new Internet businesses were not, strictly speaking, media that transmitted information, but rather intermediaries providing access to information collected and formatted in a nonmarket context. The peer-to-peer promoted by Barlow (see chapter 7) clearly fits this model.

Principles of the New Economy

Until this point the main economic reflections on the Internet and computer technology concerned intellectual property rights. It was only in 1996–1997 that the subject of the new economy started to appear, in another context. The term was first coined by *Business Week*[76] in 1996 in connection with skyrocketing high-tech stock prices and the sustained growth of the U.S. economy under the impetus of information technologies. In 1997 Kevin Kelly, editor in chief of *Wired*, published an article entitled "New Rules for the New Economy."[77] The central idea was that with the new digital world, new economic principles were emerging.

In the following year, he expanded the article to a book.[78] The "twelve dependable principles for thriving in a turbulent world" were less economic laws than precepts drawn from experience. Kelly's thinking was organized around two main themes: the first, technical and economic, consisted in analyzing all the impacts of the network's functioning; the second, a sort of radicalization of the Schumpeterian theme of creative destruction.

According to Kelly, the network's strength appears primarily in its technical components, chips, which are connected to one another and proliferate in computers and in many other machines. This law of increasing connection applies not only to chips but also, more generally, to humans. As the network expands and "as the number of nodes increases arithmetically, the value of the network increases exponentially."[79] With the law of abundance, "more gives more." This exponential growth of the network, which has never really been proved, has become one of the characteristics of the new economy. Thus, the law of increasing returns, which corresponds to self-reinforcing network effects, bears no relation to traditional economies of scale in the industrial era. The latter were linear, whereas the former correspond to exponential growth. There is, moreover, a law of exponential value in terms of which the success of Internet businesses is not linear. These different network effects result in a drop in prices of information and communication services as their quality increases. This law of inverse pricing leads to the law of generosity in terms of which all information and communication services end up being free.

Innovation is clearly fundamental in this type of model, for it allows firms to make huge profits before the ineluctable drop in prices. Although Kelly had interviewed two neo-Schumpeterian economists in previous issues of *Wired*,[80] his view of innovation was inspired above all by biology. In a book published a few years earlier[81] he had explained that the principles governing biological systems could also apply to technical systems and especially to networks, and he pursued that analysis in his new work. In terms of the law of devolution, goods and services inevitably deteriorate. At global level (law of displacement) "all transactions and all products tend to obey the network logic."[82] Firms therefore need to be innovative all the time. This is the law of churn which is "like the Hindu god Shiva, a creative force of destruction and genesis."[83] Firms have to look for situations of "sustainable disequilibrium" and constantly create new spaces. The priority is no longer, as in the industrial era, to improve productivity and solve production problems (law of inefficiencies), but to find new opportunities afforded by networks.

Kelly was clearly not claiming to produce economic theories. His discourse was rather prospective. He cited very few economists (Paul Romer and Brian Arthur[84]) and based his reflection on futurologists such as Toffler, Gilder, and Drucker, who were often given space in the magazine, or on consultants like Hagel and Armstrong. Kelly's new economy was a technological utopia like virtual society or online democracy.

Reflection in *Wired* was continued in 1998 in the March, April, and May issues. These contained an "encyclopedia of the new economy"[85] comprising a hundred or so articles classified in alphabetical order. The tone was more or less the same. In the introduction the two authors, John Browning and Spencer Reiss, stress the key role of innovation and the fact that intelligence is becoming the main factor of production. This radically new world is presented as being fundamentally unsure: "We don't know how to measure this new economy. . . . We don't know how to manage its companies. . . . We don't know how to compete in it. . . . A final thing we don't know is where—or how—the revolution will end."[86] This is more than a treatise; it is advice for the pioneers of this new frontier.

Eleven of the terms used are general economic concepts: capitalism, deflation, free market, monopoly, and so forth; twelve others apply more specifically to the new economy: technological lock-in, network externalities, winner takes all; and eighteen define the characteristics of the new networked world: e-cash, e-commerce, electronic markets, information theory, narrowcasting, and so forth. Last, the encyclopedia also contains twelve technical terms: PC, microprocessors, bandwidth, convergence, and so forth. Whereas this part of the encyclopedia is fairly close to Kelly's discourse, the remaining terms differ insofar as they apply the previously mentioned concepts to four particular domains: finance (9 terms), commerce (8), corporate organization (7), and knowledge management (5).

First, in regard to finance, the authors point out the appearance of a world market (big bang), that is permanently open (trading limits) and functions in real time (Bloomberg box). But they also cover development of microfinance in third-world countries, insofar as these experiments are opposed to the banking establishment. Second, when it comes to commerce, the encyclopedia puts the accent on marketing: brands, online communities, data mining, disintermediation. Third, the principles of corporate organization proposed by Browning and Reiss correspond essentially to contemporary managerial rules: restructuring, outsourcing, decentralization and "enabling people to continuously share information and coordinate themselves informally."[87]

Last, in order to be able to run a business along these lines, knowledge management is necessary: "If knowledge is the only real asset, why not manage it like any other?"[88] Education is therefore a requirement. "Training—acquiring the skills necessary to do a specific job—is the most important form of investment in an information economy."[89] But this has to be done efficiently, through just-in-time learning that "delivers the right tools and parts when people need them. Instead of spending months in boring classrooms, people can use networks and clever databases to answer questions and solve problems as they crop up."[90] Along with these four areas of application of the new economy, the encyclopedia notes several principles for state action, namely, deregulation and privatization. The basic tenets of liberal economic policy are thus reaffirmed.

Of the hundred or so words in this encyclopedia, only six proper nouns—three firms and three economists—add a concrete dimension to the content. First, the breakup of AT&T marks the beginning of competition in the telecommunications sector and an international grasp of a nationally segmented market. Second, Microsoft is cited as an emblematic case of network externalities and technological lock-in, while Netscape is seen as the "the new economy's corporate poster child."[91] Adam Smith is described as "the grandfather of the new economy"[92] since networks correspond to a situation in which the invisible hand of the market is unquestionably at its optimum. Hayek is presented as the "free-market seer,"[93] and Schumpeter's "creative destruction" is defined as "the battle cry of today's entrepreneurial Davids as they topple corporate Goliaths."[94]

At first sight, Browning's and Reiss's new economy hardly seems all that new. It is a collage of diverse considerations: neoliberalism, new marketing, and management principles, and a vision of technological development. The link among these different elements is never demonstrated. But the strength of this discourse is precisely its assertion that the Internet can function efficiently only in a neoliberal economy and that network information technologies entail a new mode of functioning of financial markets, a new organization of firms, direct relations between sellers and buyers, and new modes of access to knowledge. This discourse is intended not to enhance economic theory but to mobilize actors around these techniques and to give the new Davids the stones they need to attack the incumbent Goliaths.

A New Age of Growth

In this respect *Wired*'s vision is not that different to the one found in *Business Week* during the same period. "By the New Economy," wrote Stephen Shepard, "we mean two broad trends that have been under way for several years. The first is globalization of business," which translates into "freer trade and widespread deregulation. . . . The second trend is the revolution in information technology," which results in the appearance of new economic activities but "affects every other industry. It boosts productivity, reduces costs, cuts inventories, facilitates electronic commerce. It is, in short, a transcendent technology, like railroads in the 19th century and automobiles in the 20th."[95]

It was the same long-term perspective that Chip Bayers proposed in a paper entitled "Capitalist Econstruction." He likened the changes under way to those observed by Braudel with the beginnings of the capitalist market: "As we re-create capitalism—this time, as one global market rather than the many regional exchanges Braudel chronicled—we are erasing the inefficiencies that have developed in the last 500 years."[96] The idea was not to generalize the success stories of eBay or Amazon to the entire economy but to exploit the potentialities of the network economy in day-to-day business. Consumers and traders could use bots to compare prices. Even the status of money could change. You could replace real money with virtual currency. And in the future, money itself may disappear. Some sectors of the economy might become a new barter system.

Since the market and bartering mobilize far more information in the electronic world than in the brick and mortar world, will consumers be prepared to spend their time and energy on processing it, or will they prefer to trust the most well-known brands and companies? This e-construction of capitalism is still largely unfinished.

The Internet Boom

The September 1999 issue of *Wired* devoted a large portion of its special report to the economic boom of the end of the century. A contributing writer, Peter Schwartz, presented his most recent book *The Long Boom: A Vision for the Coming Age of Prosperity*, while an article entitled "Prophets of the Boom" contained an interview with Harry Dent who had just published *The Roaring 2000s*.[97] The lead article in the section, written by Kevin Kelly, was entitled "The Roaring Zeros."[98] The often cited subtitle—"The good news is, you'll be a millionaire soon. The bad news is, so will everybody else"—became the symbol of the aberrations of the new economy rhetoric. In subsequent issues, letters to the editor expressed some readers' indignation: "I'm flabbergasted that a seemingly educated, intelligent person could be so naïve."[99]

Were the authors of this report really so naive? They did mention the possibility of a stock market crash and were aware of the cyclic nature of the stock market, but they saw slumps as periods of adjustment. It was therefore not on this point that they concentrated. Most important, for Kelly and his colleagues, was the fact that the Western economy was on the brink of a major change that would lead to a long period of growth. This growth would be based on four main conditions. The first was demographic. The United States had well-educated and prosperous classes, capable of mastering productivity gains and attracted by new types of consumption. The second factor was new information and communication technologies. Not only was innovation developing very fast, the effects of the huge corporate investments in ICTs were expected to be considerable. Third, the revolution in financial markets was far from over. Last, global openness was amplified very quickly. In the final analysis, this discourse was a continuation of that of previous years on the new economy. The fact of being at the peak of the Internet bubble enhanced its euphoric character. Yet, at the same time, the September 1999 issue was, in a sense, the last shift in discourse on the new economy. It no longer concerned only the Internet or the digital economy but a new macroeconomic perspective, and that was possible because digital technologies were generic technologies.

Not all the gurus of the Internet shared Kelly's unshakeable optimism. In an article in *Red Herring*, Peter Schwartz studied several development scenarios of the new economy, from a rosy picture of "a world of mostly winners . . . where rewards are more often measured in equity than cash," to one "where the new economy is principally an illusion" or even a crash situation "where almost everyone is a loser."[100]

In 2001 *Wired* published an article entitled "Death of the New Economy," in which the author seemed to believe that the crash scenario was happening. He noted: "The trouble with the term new economy is its McLuhanesque slipperiness. It means whatever you want it to mean. Too often, that has translated to wishful thinking: new rules, new paradigms, new riches."[101] He further stated that the economy had fundamentally changed in the previous few years and that the financial crisis of the early 2000s was simply a phase. Structurally, the U.S. economy had experienced constant, substantial productivity gains from the mid-1990s, and in 2000–2001 that was still the case. This trend, at the heart of the new economy, did not preclude sharply accentuated business cycles: "Job cuts are likely to be deeper and more frequent. An economy driven by equity investment is more vulnerable to excesses of speculation." Finally, for this author, as for the gurus of the new economy, the bursting of the Internet bubble was simply an episode that in no way undermined the development of the new economy.

A few months later *Wired* raised the question of whether "The New Economy Was a Myth, Right?"[102] The author noted that even if, in the public imagination, the new economy was associated with the stock market and in particular the Nasdaq, the real winners were, in fact, consumers and workers. Unemployment had decreased and in the private sector salaries had increased far quicker in the 1990s than in the previous decade. The gains of the late 1990s were sustainable; in the first quarter of 2002 productivity gains increased steeply. Thus, it seemed that the success of the new economy was not limited to a few cases directly related to the Internet, such as Amazon, Dell, or Cisco, but affected all business. From this point of view, the idea of a new economy makes sense.

The author of an article published in August 2003, "Don't Worry about Deflation," noted that U.S. firms had bought more computer hard- and software than ever before: "The boom of the 1990s continues."[103]

In less than ten years, discourse on the new economy changed profoundly. Whereas at the outset the idea was to find a business model suited to the new technology that had developed outside the market economy, the discourse gradually got carried away. The new economy became the flag of all those who had developed a passion for the Internet, and, finally, it became a subject of more general reflection on the information society.

Economists Show an Interest in the Internet

As the idea of a new economy rapidly spread from *Wired* to the national press, professional economists joined the debate. In 1998 two academics at Berkeley, Carl Shapiro and Hal Varian, published a "strategic guide to the network economy"[104] in which they consider that "you don't need a brand new economics."[105] Work on price discrimination, related sales, filters, licenses, lock-in, and network economies provides a whole range of theoretical elements that are perfectly applicable to computer technology and to the Internet. The same was true a century ago when certain contemporary actors were under the impression that electricity and the telephone completely undermined existing economic models. One point of agreement with the *Wired* journalists is the fact that the world is facing major technological change. On the other hand, while Shapiro and

Varian consider that economic laws apply perfectly to this new situation, Kelly, like Browning and Reiss, believes that they are dealing with new economic principles. In fact, their disagreement relates less to theory than to the presentation of the phenomena. The *Wired* team was familiar with some of the economic laws described by Shapiro and Varian, and they had interviewed several prominent economists in the field,[106] but these laws seem more meaningful when presented as the base of a new economy, as in *Wired*.

Shapiro and Varian's book, like the writings discussed earlier, is presented essentially as a guide offering advice to Internet entrepreneurs. The various economic principles described are illustrated by numerous practical examples. In certain respects, this book on economics resembles Hagel and Armstrong's volume on marketing, but, in addition, a strong scientific ambition is affirmed. For example, in the introduction the authors state their wish to "seek models, not trends; concepts not vocabulary; and analysis not analogies."[107]

Shapiro and Varian, above all specialists in industrial economics, study the ways in which firms can differentiate prices of goods or services in relation to their customers/clients, and in which standards are the instruments of cooperation or competition. They focus on the way in which a product or standard is imposed in a market through a feedback or snowball effect, and consider that self-realizing prophecies are one of the main components of this effect: "Companies participating in markets with strong network effects seek to convince customers that their products will ultimately become the standard, while rival, incompatible products will soon be orphaned."[108]

I believe that this theory of self-realizing prophecy can be extended beyond new products to the entire information technology and Internet sector. Discourse on the new economy also serves to promote these new IT activities and to discredit others, the "old economy." They are therefore at once a watershed utopia and a project utopia. Skillful use of anticipation furthermore serves to influence entrepreneurs and the general public as potential customers and potential stock market investors. It is an ideology that legitimizes new business practices but that also masks the huge inequalities and major uncertainties characterizing this new economic activity.

Ambivalence of the Internet

In the early 1990s the Internet was used only in the academic world and in certain communities of the California counterculture. Diffusion in the general public and incorporation into the market economy appeared in 1993–1994 and was not in any way a natural development. On the contrary, it was a total break that challenged existing Internauts and ushered in new actors and practices. To mobilize those already immersed in the Internet, it was necessary to show that the network of networks could be developed on the basis of economic rules that took into account the specific characteristics of this new universe (cooperation, free circulation, community, etc.). Doing business on the Internet did not mean getting rid of former ideals and practices but incorporating them into a new framework. It also meant winning over new actors and showing them that the Internet was far more than simply a new industrial sector; it was the base of a new mode of functioning of the economy.

In fact, the idea was neither to remain outside the market economy nor to transform the Internet into a medium like any other. Industrialists were trying rather to take advantage of the assets and competencies of a nonmarket cyberspace. Cooperation seemed to triumph over conflict. We could consider that cohabitation was established between the nonmarket and the market sectors, although this has not precluded violent competition between certain actors. In the market sector modes of financing are at this stage more diverse than for the traditional media: subscription, which is exceptional except for pornographic sites; advertising, which has assumed two main forms (banners and corporate sites); and, last, e-commerce. In the latter case the activity can be direct or indirect (a site can sell itself or be an intermediary for a market site). In the nonmarket sector the Internet is still a place where many actors offer and exchange information free of charge.

The novelty of the Internet derives from the fact that this communication system allows both private and public interaction, concerning both cooperation at work and sociability with family and friends; it is simultaneously a recreational device and a system of trade. This is its real originality, its richness and the source of all dangers. The main risk in this world of abundance is not the triumph of a single model, as in the case of radio-television, but the eventuality of one actor managing to align all the different uses for its own benefit, capturing all the surplus from the combination of different social activities of the Internet, to the detriment of other actors; of newsgroups all depending on commercial media sites; of a particular sought-after content being accessible only via a single site which monitors and commercializes information on users' visits; and so on. Unlike radio-television which, in the United States, soon standardized around an economic model and a media format, the Internet is fundamentally heterogeneous. This diversity is a key asset.

Conclusion

When, after this long journey through the cyber-*imaginaire*, we return to the Internet in daily life as proposed by firms and experienced by ordinary Internauts, we may have the impression of leaving a world of fantasy and illusion, and landing back on the more temperate shores of reality. The utopias of the digital society then seem so distant that we wonder if it was not simply a past *imaginaire* that played a part in the design of computer networks but no longer has a role today. From this point of view, the cyber-*imaginaire* has above all provided subject matter for science fiction movies, novels, and shows. After a period of agitation and confusion, we are finally reverting to an efficient social division of work in which engineers and managers design and diffuse the technique while visionaries and artists transform their dreams into works of art or political and social projects. Other observers might consider, on the contrary, that the Internet utopias have been betrayed, like those of radio in the 1920s.[1] They may say that another, more cooperative, society was about to be born, thanks to computer networks, but that the project was hijacked by large corporations which harnessed the innovation and restructured it to suit their own mode of organization.

Last, technical utopias may be considered by some to be either useless or even harmful, or simply raw material for artists or new social and political movements hoping to change society. For them, the dream is now over and we have to get back to reality. Everything will end up back to normal; new techniques will replace old ones and adapt to society's demands.

Well, no, the age of imagination is not over. Utopias are not opposed to reality; on the contrary, they are one of the elements on which it is built. They are involved not only in the period in which techniques are developed, but also in their diffusion when users and even an entire society have to construct their relationship with the new tool. If, as Paul Ricœur believes, the identity of a human community has a prospective dimension, utopia is one of its essential components.[2] The social *imaginaire* enables a society to construct its identity by expressing its expectations for the future. A society without a vision would therefore be dead. The study of the technical *imaginaire* shows that it always has two functions: building the identity of a social group or a society, and providing resources that can be reinvested directly in the preparation and implementation of projects.

The *Imaginaire* Is at the Heart of Technical Debate

In the traditional history of techniques, inventions are always associated with an inventor's intuition. By contrast, contemporary sociology and history of techniques are built on a radically different hypothesis, namely, the idea that technology is the result of an articulation of countless human and nonhuman elements and that the innovator's strength derives from his or her capacity to articulate all these elements effectively. In this schema opportunities count far more than projects. Through its reflection on the Internet *imaginaire*, this book rehabilitates the notion of a project, not in the sense of the inventor's brilliant *eureka*, but of a collective project of a group of engineers such as users of Unix or Arpanet, hackers, and so forth.

In the case of the Internet, such projects can materialize very quickly since new software can circulate on computer networks and be used immediately. Not only can a utopia rapidly turn into a project; it can also be embodied in achievements. In this new situation, the issue of users' mobilization is so crucial that a new ideology is produced. It is this ideology that is used to legitimize the new technique, to attract and integrate new users, to provide a framework for use of the innovation. It also affords a set of justifications that enable designers and users alike to explain their engagement in the digital world. The *imaginaire* is at the center of design and use of the Internet. As Michel de Certeau noted, "Narratives precede social practices and pave the way for them."[3]

But the fact that this *imaginaire* plays a key part in the technical actions of designers and users does not necessarily imply its unity. On the contrary, it is characterized by diversity and riddled with contradictions. Traces of these differences can be found in both technical achievements and social debate. For example, academics and hackers did not have exactly the same representation of communication networks, and the specific systems they built were completely different from the system of centralized and hierarchical communication imagined by IBM at the time.

Utopias are thus embodied in technical choices. But the multiplicity of the cyber-*imaginaire* also appears in debate on the role of the body, the regulation of cyberspace, and its commodification. Certain positions open new avenues by breaking away from existing systems. Others ensure that conflict is avoided around concrete problems. In some cases, mobilizing discourse can be a rhetoric of illusion. On all these points, public debate is essential; it helps counter the many illusions and fantasies circulating on the Internet.

If the definition of a future is a key element in the definition of our collective identity, it seems to follow that, in a democratic society, this debate should be organized in the political sphere. After all, is it not politicians' role to define society's future prospects? The example of information highways reminds us that this type of debate can be rich, but parliaments and task forces cannot channel all debates on the utopias of a digital society. These debates take place in a wide variety of places, and it is preferable to let them proliferate rather than trying to direct them. The creators of utopias are diverse; they produce not only discourses but also cultural products (novels, shows, etc.) and software packages in which their vision is inscribed in algorithms. The technical *imaginaire* cannot be reduced to a public debate; it is also expressed in experiments.

An American *Imaginaire*

While utopias are a way of forecasting the future, they are also part of representations which sometimes stem from the past and appear to be characteristic of a particular culture. Many features of the Internet *imaginaire* unquestionably refer to the United States. Consider the following three themes—the frontier, the community, and individual initiative—and their specific place in the U.S. cultural sphere.

The idea of a frontier is associated with the discovery and development of new virgin territory where pioneers can grasp original opportunities and mobilize their competencies, enthusiasm, and ability to innovate while setting their own social rules. Considering the frontier as a value means opting for mobility and change as opposed to stability. Cyberspace is obviously seen as this new virtual frontier where Internauts will be able to settle. In the meantime, hackers and Gibson's cowboys are already living there totally freely, and have set the first rules of collective life.

The community is a constant in U.S. life; it is an element of the citizen's roots at a local level. That is where shared values take shape. For some of the founding fathers of U.S. democracy, like Jefferson, the rural community was the basic unit of democracy. Later, with the proliferation of ethnic and religious groups in twentieth-century urban America, geographic mobility became commonplace and the word "community" took on new meaning, that of a community of interests. In this context the new media often appeared as a way of binding these communities and even of forming them. Radio, cable television, and video were perceived as community media. Finally, there is widespread reflection in the United States today on the "revitalization" of communities. The promoters of "community development" naturally see the Internet as a new way of strengthening existing community ties or even of creating new ones.

In *De la démocratie en Amérique,* Tocqueville defines individualism as a "well thought-out and calm feeling that disposes each citizen to isolate himself from the mass of his kind and to withdraw with his family and friends so that, after thus creating a small society for himself, he willingly leaves society at large to itself."[4] This definition, which he applied to Americans of the 1830s, reflects continuity between attachment to the community and individual initiative, and can be applied to entrepreneurship. The model of a dynamic U.S. economy driven by entrepreneurs creating their own firms made a recent comeback with the development of startups and other dot.coms. In reality the business creation model, dating back to the nineteenth century, was strongly revived well before the advent of the Internet, with the electronic and computer industry. Many startups had already set up around certain universities, such as MIT and Stanford. This attachment, shared by most entrepreneurs who managed to set up their own businesses, probably explains why a part of U.S. public opinion sympathizes with firms, such as Microsoft, that have a quasi-monopoly, and opposes antitrust lawsuits against them.

New frontier, community, entrepreneurship: these three themes are at once totally American and completely universal. The theme of the pioneer who builds not only technical devices but also a new society is obviously not peculiar to the United States. Nor are the ideas of strengthening community life or setting up one's own business in a field where one can start out with small investments yet be at the cutting edge of modernity. This is probably where a major ambiguity in the development of the Internet lies. The Internet *imaginaire*, like the technology accompanying it, was born in the particular context of the United States but subsequently became universal. Wherever one is in the world, logging on to the Internet is, in a sense, plugging into modernity and the country that best symbolizes it. The success of cybercafés in many towns and cities throughout the world is a clear illustration of this. In Lima, for example, 40 percent of households state that at least one of their members uses the Internet and, for the vast majority, this takes place in local versions of cybercafés that abound in the favellas.[5]

Notes

Introduction

1. Bruno Latour, *Science in Action: How to Follow Scientists and Engineers through Society* (Cambridge, Mass.: Harvard University Press, 1987).

2. See Kim Clark and Steven Wheelwright, "Organizing and Leading 'Heavyweight' Development Teams," *California Management Review*, Spring 1992, 9–28.

3. Susan Star and James Griesemer, "Institutional Ecology, Translations and Boundary-Objects: Amateurs and Professionals in Berkeley's Museum of Vertebrate Zoology (1907–1939)," *Social Studies of Science* 19 (1989): 393.

4. Thomas Hughes, *Rescuing Prometheus* (New York: Pantheon Books, 1998), 305.

5. John Staudenmaier, *Technology's Storytellers: Reweaving the Human Fabric* (Cambridge, Mass.: MIT Press, 1985), xx.

6. Leo Marx, *The Machine in the Garden: Technology and the Pastoral Ideal in America* (New York: Oxford University Press, 1964).

7. Rosalind Williams, *Notes on the Underground: An Essay on Technology, Society, and the Imagination* (Cambridge, Mass.: MIT Press, 1990).

8. Carolyn Marvin, *When Old Technologies Were New: Thinking about Electric Communication in the Late Nineteenth Century* (New York: Oxford University Press, 1988); Susan Douglas, *Inventing American Broadcasting (1899–1922)* (Baltimore, Md.: Johns Hopkins University Press, 1987); Joseph Corn, *The Winged Gospel: American Gospel with Aviation 1900–1950* (New York: Oxford University Press, 1983).

9. Douglas, *Inventing American Broadcasting*, xvii.

10. Joseph Corn, ed., *Imagining Tomorrow: History, Technology, and the American Future* (Cambridge, Mass.: MIT Press, 1986), 228.

11. Charles Bazerman, *The Languages of Edison's Light* (Cambridge, Mass.: MIT Press, 1999), 333.

12. Joanne Yates, *Control through Communication: The Rise of System in American Management* (Baltimore, Md.: Johns Hopkins University Press, 1989).

13. Rob Kling, ed., *Computerization and Controversy: Value Conflicts and Social Choices*, 2nd ed. (San Diego: Academic Press, 1996).

14. Roland Barthes, *Mythologies* (Paris: Le Seuil, 1970), 195–202. [Mythologies. Selected and translated from the French by Annette Lavers (New York: Hill and Wang, 1972).]

15. Ibid., 204 (our translation).

16. Ibid., 207 (our translation).

17. Paul Ricœur, *Lectures on Ideology and Utopia* (New York: Columbia University Press, 1986), 12.

18. Ibid., 310–314.

19. Ibid., 311.

20. Ibid., 312.

21. Patrice Flichy, *L'Innovation technique* (Paris: La Découverte, 1995), 226–228.

22. Flichy, *L'Innovation technique*, 228–230.

Chapter 1   Information Highways, or the Difficulty of Transforming a Utopia into a Technological Program

1. Clifford Stoll, *Silicon Snake Oil: Second Thoughts on the Information Highway* (New York: Anchor Books, 1996), 9.

2. *The Nation*, 18 May 1970, 602.

3. In 1972 Smith developed his theses in a book: *The Wired Nation: Cable TV: The Electronic Communication Highway* (New York: Harper & Row).

4. This was how William Bresman, director of a cable company, entitled his speech in 1973 to the San Francisco Society of Security Analysts (quoted in Mark Surman, "Wired Words: Utopia, Revolution and the History of Electronic Highways," Internet Society Conference, Montreal, 1996).

5. See, in particular, the electronic counterculture magazine *Radical Software*.

6. Starr Roxanne Hiltz and Murray Turoff, *The Network Nation: Human Communication via Computer* (Reading, Mass.: Addison-Wesley, 1978), xx.

7. Jacques Vallée, *The Network Revolution: Confessions of a Computer Scientist* (Berkeley, Calif.: And/Or Press, 1982), 198.

8. Anne W. Branscomb, "Beyond Deregulation: Designing the Information Infrastructure," *Information Society Journal* 1, no. 3 (1982): 170.

9. Lawrence E. Murr, James B. Williams, and Ruth-Ellen Miller, *Information Highways: Mapping Information Delivery Networks in the Pacific Northwest* (Portland: Hypermap, 1985).

10. Educom Networking and Telecommunications Task Force, "A National Higher Education Network: Issues and Opportunities," White Paper, no. 1, May 1987, quoted in Richard Mandelbaum and Paulette Mandelbaum, "The Strategic Future of the Mid-Level Networks," in *Building Information Infrastructure*, ed. Brian Kahin (New York: McGraw-Hill, 1993), 70.

11. National Research Council, *Toward a National Research Network* (Washington, D.C.: National Academy Press, 1987).

12. *High-Performance Computing Act*, 1991, Section 2 § 6.

13. Albert Gore, *Remarks on the NREN*, National Net '90, Washington, D.C., 14–16 March 1990 (published in *Educom Review*, Summer 1990, 12–16).

14. Rick Boucher, *The Challenge of Transition*, National Net '92 (published in *Educom Review*, September/October 1992, 30–35).

15. See, in particular, "An Information Superhighway?" *Business Week*, 11 February 1991; "How Do You Build an Information Highway?" *Business Week*, 16 September 1991.

16. Ohio Department of Administrative Services, *Communication of Information: The Key to Future Development*, August 1990; Iowa Communications Network, "Information Highway of the Future," in *Information Infrastructure Sourcebook*, ed. Brian Kahin (Cambridge, Mass.: John F. Kennedy School of Government, Harvard University, 1994), 297–304.

17. James Keller, "Public Access Issues: An Introduction," in *Public Access to the Internet*, ed. Brian Kahin and James Keller (Cambridge, Mass.: MIT Press, 1995), 35.

18. Robert B. Cohen, *The Impact of Broadband Communications on the U.S. Economy and on Competitiveness* (Washington, D.C.: Economic Strategy Institute, 1992).

19. *Business Week*, 6 April 1992, 70.

20. In its 12 April 1993 special issue on information highways, *Time* noted: "During the 1992 presidential campaign, Clinton and Gore made building a data superhighway a centerpiece of their program to revitalize the U.S. economy."

21. Albert Gore, *Remarks at National Press Club*, 21 December 1993.

22. William Clinton and Albert Gore, *Technology for America's Economic Growth: A New Direction to Build Economic Strength* (Washington, D.C.: U.S. Government Printing Office, 1993), 28. Available at http://www.iitf.nist.gov/documents/speeches/gore_speech122193.html.

23. Ibid.

24. Gore, *Remarks at National Press Club*.

25. John Schwartz, "The Highway to the Future," *Newsweek*, 13 January 1992, 57.

26. Robert Samuelson, "Lost on the Information Highway," *Newsweek*, 20 December 1993.

27. Robert Allen, "Technology for a New Renaissance," *Educom Review*, Winter 1990, 22–25.

28. Smart Valley, "An Electronic Community: A Vision of Our Future," 14 May 1993, in Kahin, *Information Infrastructure Sourcebook*, 259–364.

29. *Vision 2000: Public Policy Requirements to Achieve Technology Vision* (Washington, D.C.: United States Telephone Association, 1993).

30. *Perspectives on the National Information Infrastructure: CSPP's Vision and Recommendations for Action* (Washington, D.C.: Computer Systems Policy Project, 1993) (the CSPP, founded in 1989, has a more important strategic and political role than an ordinary employer's union; thirteen of the chairmen of the main computer companies are members); *National Information Infrastructure: Industry and Government Roles* (Arlington, Va.: Information Technology Association of America, 1993).

31. *Vision for a 21st Century Information Infrastructure* (Washington, D.C.: Council on Competitiveness, 1993); Frank Splitt, *The U.S. Information Industry: Creating the 21st Century* (Chicago, Ill.: National Engineering Consortium, 1993).

32. *Perspectives on the National Information Infrastructure*, 4.

33. *Vision for a 21st Century Information Infrastructure*, 1.

34. *Perspectives on the National Information Infrastructure*, 14.

35. On this point, see *The National Telecomunications and Information Administration Infrastructure Report, Telecommunications in the Age of Information* (Washington, D.C.: U.S. Department of Commerce, 1991).

36. Queens and Orlando for Time Warner, CastroValley for Viacom, Denver for TCI, Cerritos for GTE, Virginia for Bell Atlantic (*Time*, 12 April 1993).

37. See the section in the 12 April 1993 issue of *Time*: "The Info Highway. Bringing a Revolution in Entertainment, News, and Communication."

38. The 7 March 1994 issue of *Time* subtitled the announcement of this failure as follows: "The collapse of the Bell Atlantic-TCI deal may slow but not stop construction of the information highway."

39. James Duderstadt, "An Information Highway," *Educom Review*, September–October 1992, 36–41.

40. John Markoff, "Building the Electronic Superhighway," *New York Times*, 24 January 1993.

41. In 1990, during the drafting of the law on NREN, Al Gore wrote in the *Washington Post*: "The private sector can't build [the network] any more than a turnpike company could have financed the interstate highway system" and further on, "At first, the network would be supported by the federal government" (Al Gore, "We Need a National Superhighway for Computer Information," *Washington Post*, 15 July 1990).

42. Henry Perritt, Jr., quoted in Markoff, "Building the Electronic Superhighway."

43. Ibid.

44. Clinton and Gore, *Technology for America's Economic Growth*, 29.

45. Marc Levinson, "Cutting Edge?" *Newsweek*, 8 March 1993.

46. *The National Information Infrastructure: Agenda for Action* (Washington, D.C.: Information Infrastructure Task Force, 1993), 8.

47. The Telecommunications and Information Infrastructure Assistance Program had $26 million in 1994 and $36 million in 1995. Brian Kahin, "The U.S. National Information Infrastructure Initiative: The Market, the Net and the Virtual Project," in *National Information Infrastructure Initiatives, Vision and Policy Design*, ed. Brian Kahin and Ernest Wilson III (Cambridge, Mass.: MIT Press, 1997), 175.

48. I have borrowed this title from Robert Samuelson, who wrote in an editorial in the 20 December 1993 issue of *Newsweek* called "Lost on the Information Highway": "What now passes for the information superhighway is a slogan in search of a mission."

49. Ibid.

50. United States Advisory Council on the National Information Infrastructure, *Kickstart Initiative: Connecting America's Communities to the Information Superhighway* (Washington, D.C.: U.S. Department of Commerce, 1996).

51. Gore, *Remarks at National Press Club*, 3.

52. Albert Gore, *Remarks at the Superhighway Summit*, Los Angeles, 11 January 1994, 5–6. Available at http:www1.whitehouse.gov/WH/EOP/OVP/other/super hig.txt.

53. *Business Week*, 24 January 1994, 89.

54. Albert Gore, *Remarks at International Telecommunications Union*, Buenos Aires, 21 March 1994, 2–3. Available at http://www1.whitehouse.gov/WH/EOP/OVP/html/telunion.html.

55. Richard Shaffer, *Technologic Partner*, quoted in Michael Meyer, "The Hyperactive Highway," *Newsweek*, 29 November 1993, 56.

56. Ibid.

57. Philip Elmer-Dewitt, "Play . . . Fast Forward . . . Rewind . . . Pause," *Time*, 23 May 1994, 46.

58. "Interactive TV: Not Ready for Prime Time. Time Warner's Technology Still Needs Tinkering," *Business Week*, 14 March 1994.

59. Philip Elmer-Dewitt, "First Nation in Cyberspace," *Time*, 6 December 1993, 62.

60. Evan I. Schwartz, "Is the Info Superhighway Headed the Wrong Way?" *Business Week*, 20 December 1993, 15.

61. "Live Wires," *Newsweek*, 6 September 1993; "The Strange New World of the Internet: Battles on the Frontiers of Cyberspace" (cover story), *Time*, 25 July 1994; "How the Internet Will Change the Way You Do Business" (cover story), *Business Week*, 14 November 1994.

62. "Coming Soon to Your TV Screen: The Info Highway. Bringing a Revolution in Entertainment, News, and Communication" (cover story), *Time*, 12 April 1993; "Interactive: A New Technology That Will Change the Way You Shop, Play and Learn. A Billion Dollar Industry (Maybe)," *Newsweek*, 31 May 1993.

63. Steven Levy, "How the Propeller Heads Stole the Electronic Future," *New York Times Magazine*, 24 September 1995, 59.

64. *Time*, 25 July 1994, 50; *Business Week*, 24 October 1994, 18.

65. Even Schwartz, "Power to the People: The Clinton Administration Is Using the Net in a Pitched Effort to Perform an End Run around the Media," *Wired*, December 1994, 88–92.

66. On this point, see Patrice Flichy, Dynamics of Modern Communication. The Shaping and Impact of New Communication Technologies (London: Sage, 1995).

Chapter 2   The Internet, the Scientific Community's Ideal

1. Richard Civille, "The Internet and the Poor," in Kahin and Keller, *Public Access to the Internet*, 184–185.

2. An earlier version of which was published in the journal *Réseaux* 17, no. 97 (1999).

3. Thomas Hughes, *Networks of Power: Electrification in Western Society* (Baltimore, Md.: Johns Hopkins University Press, 1983).

4. Maurice Wilkes, "Introductory Speech," in *Proceedings of the International Conference on Information Processing* (Paris: Unesco, [1959] 1960), quoted in Arthur Norberg and Judy O'Neill, *Transforming Computer Technology: Information Processing for the Pentagon (1962–1986)* (Baltimore, Md.: Johns Hopkins University Press, 1996), 81.

5. From the MIT Computation Center, "Progress Report Number 4 of the Research and Educational Activities in Machine Computation by the Cooperating Colleges of New England," 1958, quoted in Norberg and O'Neill, *Transforming Computer Technology*, 82.

6. Howard Rheingold, *Tools for Thought: The People and Ideas behind the Next Computer Revolution* (New York: Simon & Schuster, 1985), 138

7. Joseph Licklider, "Man-Computer Symbiosis," in *IRE Transactions on Human Factors in Electronics*, March 1960. Reedited in *In Memoriam: J.C.R. Licklider 1915–1990* (Palo Alto, Calif.: Digital Systems Research Center, 1990).

8. On relations between computer technology and the military, see Paul Edwards, *The Closed World: Computers and the Politics of Discourse in Cold War America* (Cambridge, Mass.: MIT Press, 1996), especially chapters 3 and 8.

9. Martin Greenberger, ed., *Management and the Computer of the Future* (Cambridge, Mass.: MIT Press, 1962), 205.

10. Joseph Licklider and Robert Taylor, "The Computer as a Communication Device," *Science and Technology*, April 1968. Reprinted in *In Memoriam*, 1990, 4.

11. Ibid., 2–3.

12. Greenberger, *Management and the Computer of the Future*, 324.

13. The rest was from the universities' own income or generated by contracts with the private sector. In 1968 the ARPA budget alone, namely, the defense ministry's fundamental research budget, was equivalent to half of that of the National Research Foundation.

14. Quoted in Katie Hafner and Mathew Lyon, *Where Wizards Stay Up Late: The Origins of the Internet* (New York: Simon & Schuster, 1996), 68.

15. Licklider interview at Charles Babbage Institute.

16. Fernando Corbato and Robert Fano, "Time-Sharing on Computers," in *Information, a Scientific American Book* (1966), quoted in Michael Hauben and Rhonda Hauben, *Netizens: An Anthology*, chapter 5. Available at http://www.columbia.edu/~rh120.

17. Joseph Licklider, "Memorandum for Members and Affiliates of the Intergalactic Computer Networr," ARPA, 23 April 1963. Available at http://www.fixe.com/wizards/memo.html.

18. Joseph Licklider, "Position Paper on the Future of Project MAC," October 6, 1970.

19. Stanislas Ulam, *A Collection of Mathematical Problems* (New York: Interscience Publishers, 1960).

20. Simon Ramo, "The Scientific Extension of the Human Intellect," *Computers and Automation*, February 1961.

21. Rheingold, *Tools for Thought*, 180.

22. Douglas Engelbart, *Augmenting Human Intellect: A Conceptual Framework* (Menlo Park, Calif.: Stanford Research Institute, 1962), 1. Available at http://www.histech.rwth-aachen.de/www/quellen/engelbart/ahi62.html.

23. Ibid., 23.

24. For a study of the interfaces conceived by Engelbart, see Thierry Bardini, *Bootstrapping: Douglas Engelbart, Coevolution and the Origins of Personal Computing* (Stanford, Calif.: Stanford University Press, 2000).

25. Douglas Engelbart and William English, "A Research Center for Augmenting Human Intellect," in *Proceedings of the AFIPS Fall Joint Computer Conference*,

San Francisco, Calif., 1968, 2. Available at http://www.histech.rwth-aachen.de/www/quellen/engelbart/ResearchCenter1968.html.

26. Douglas Engelbart, *Study for the Development of Human Intellect Augmentation Techniques* (Palo Alto, Calif.: Stanford Research Institute, 1968), 40. Available at http://www.histech.rwth-aachen.de/www/quellen/engelbart/study68.html.

27. Licklider and Taylor, "The Computer as a Communication Device," 21.

28. Ibid., 38–40.

29. Letter from Tom Marill to Lawrence Roberts, quoted in Hafner and Lyon, *Where Wizards Stay Up Late*, 68.

30. Thomas Marill, "A Cooperative Network of Time-Sharing Computers: Preliminary Study," June 1966, quoted in Arthur Norberg and Judy O'Neill, *Transforming Computer Technology: Information Processing for the Pentagon (1962–1986)* (Baltimore, Md.: Johns Hopkins University Press, 1996), 158.

31. Thomas Marill and Lawrence Roberts, "Toward a Cooperative Network of Time-Shared Computers," in *Proceedings of the AFIPS Fall Joint Computer Conference* (Montvale, N.J.: AFIPS Press, 1966), 428, quoted in Janet Abbate, *Inventing the Internet* (Cambridge, Mass.: MIT Press, 1999), 66.

32. Norberg and O'Neill, *Transforming Computer Technology*, 162.

33. Hafner and Lyon, *Where Wizards Stay Up Late*, 41–42.

34. IEEE, *Annals of the History of Computing* 14, no. 2 (1992): 35, quoted in Hauben and Hauben, *Netizens*, chapter 5.

35. Licklider and Taylor, "The Computer as a Communication Device," 31–32.

36. Roberts had participated with Tom Marill in the first experiment of distant liaison between computers.

37. Leonard Kleinrock, *Communication Nets: Stochastic Message Flow and Delay* (New York: McGraw-Hill, 1964).

38. Some authors have concluded, somewhat hastily, that the ARPA network was built to enable the U.S. army to maintain communication links in the event of Soviet attacks. In fact, as indicated earlier, this network was primarily intended to link the different university computing centers working for ARPA—which is very different. We note, however, that once it had been built the network was also used by the military. On the connection between ARPA and the Rand project, see Norbert and O'Neill, *Transforming Computer Technology*, 161, and Hafner and Lyon, *Where Wizards Stay Up Late*, 76–77. On the link between academic and military research, see Paul Jon Edwards, *The Closed World: Computers and the Politics of Discourse in Cold War America* (Cambridge, Mass.: MIT Press, 1996).

39. Thomas Hughes, *Rescuing Prometheus* (New York: Pantheon Books, 1998), 278.

40. University of California, Los Angeles (UCLA); Stanford; University of California, Santa Barbara; and University of Utah.

41. Requests for Comments, 3 April 1969. Available at http://www.isoc.org/ftp/rfc/0000/rfc3.txt.

42. Ibid.

43. Ibid.

44. Stephen Carr, Stephen Croker, and Vinton Cerf, "Host-Host Communication Protocol in the ARPA Network," in *Proceedings of the AFIPS Spring Joint Computer Conference* (Montvale, N.J.: AFIPS Press, 1970), 589–590, quoted in Abbate, *Inventing the Internet*, 74.

45. Robert Braden, *Who's Who in the Internet*. Requests for Comments 1251, 1991, 3–4. Available at http://www.njc-archive.org/get-jc.php?njc=1251.

46. Carr et al., "Host-Host Communication Protocol in the ARPA Network," 79, quoted in Abbate, *Inventing the Internet*, 68.

47. Abbate, *Inventing the Internet*, 70–71.

48. Lawrence Roberts, "Network Rationale: A Five Year Reevaluation," *IEEE Computer Society*, 1973, quoted in Norberg and O'Neill, *Transforming Computer Technology*, 176.

49. Lawrence Roberts and Barry Wessler, "Computer Network Development to Achieve Resource Sharing," in *Proceedings of the AFIPS Spring Joint Computer Conference* (Montvale, N.J.: AFIPS Press, 1970), 543, quoted in Abbate, *Inventing the Internet*, 96.

50. Fifteen to twenty percent of use of Multics computers (one of the main time-sharing computer languages). It seems that other machines were used even less in this way (*Arpanet Completion Report*, 1978, quoted in Abbate, *Inventing the Internet*, 97).

51. RCA Service Company, *Arpanet Study Final Report*, 1972, 9, quoted in Abbate, *Inventing the Internet*, 86.

52. Lawrence Roberts, "Multiple Computer Networks and Intercomputer Communication," in *Proceedings of the ACM Symposium on Operating System Principles*, 1967, 1, quoted in Abbate, *Inventing the Internet*, 108.

53. Hafner and Lyon, *Where Wizards Stay Up Late*, 194.

54. T. H. Myer and D. W. Dodds, "Notes on the Development of Message Technology," Berkeley Workshop on Distributed Data Management and Computer Networks, LBL-5315, Lawrence Berkeley Laboratories, 1976, 145, quoted in Ian Hardy, "The Evolution of ARPANET Email" (Ph.D. diss., Berkeley, 1996), 18. Available at http://www.ifla.org/documents/internet/hari1.txt.

55. Raymond Panko, "An Introduction to Computers for Human Communication" (paper presented at the NTC '77 Conference Record, IEEE, New York, 1977), 21, quoted in Hardy, "The Evolution of ARPANET Email," 18.

56. Joseph Licklider and Albert Vezza, "Applications of Information Networks," *Proceedings of the IEEE* 66, no. 11 (November 1978): 1331.

57. On this point, see Janet Abbate, "An Archeology of the Arpanet" (paper presented at the MIT Conference, 14 April 1993), 7. Available at http://www.rci .rutgers.edu/jea/papers/Artch.html.

58. Norberg and O'Neill, *Transforming Computer Technology*, 178.

59. Panko, "An Introduction to Computers for Human Communication," 21.

60. T. H. Myer and John Vittal, "Message Technology in the Arpanet" (paper presented at the NTC '77 Conference Record, IEEE, New York, 1977), 21.

61. Myer and Dodds, "Notes on the Development of Message Technology," 145.

62. Hafner and Lyon, *Where Wizards Stay Up Late*, 205–208.

63. I am referring here only to academic use of Arpanet, which was its main use and the one with the most media coverage. Arpanet was, however, also used by the military. From 1975 the network was run by the Defense Communications Agency. In 1982 40 percent of all sites were military. In 1984 the military part was separated to form Milnet. Alexander McKenzie and David Walden, "Arpanet, the Defense Data Network, and Internet," in *Encyclopedia of Telecommunications*, ed. F. Froehlich and A. Kent (New York: Marcel Dekker, 1991), 365–367.

64. Roy Amara, John Smith, Murray Turoff, and Jacques Vallée, "Computerized Conferencing: A New Medium," *Mosaic*, January–February 1976, quoted in Rheingold, *Tools for Thought*, 308.

65. Andrew Feenberg, "L'organisation de réseaux et l'animation de conférence," in *Gestion et communication*, Paris, January 1986, 7.

66. Hiltz and Turoff, *The Network Nation*.

67. Ibid., xxvii–xxiv.

68. Diane Crane, *Invisible Colleges: Diffusion of Knowledge in Scientific Communities* (Chicago: University of Chicago Press, 1972).

69. Hiltz and Turoff, *The Network Nation*, 49.

70. Brock Meeks, "An Overview of Conferencing Systems," *Byte*, December, 1985, 170.

71. Joshua Lederberg, "Digital Communications and the Conduct of Science," *Proceedings of the IEEE* 66, no. 11 (November 1978). Reprinted in Mark Stefik, *Internet Dreams* (Cambridge, Mass.: MIT Press, 1997), 168.

72. Lynn Conway, "The Multi-Project Chip Adventures: Experiences with the Generation of VLSI Design and Implementation Methodologies" (paper presented at the second Caltech Conference on Very Large Scale Integration, January 1981). Reprinted in Stefik, *Internet Dreams*, 155.

73. Ibid., 156.

74. Unix is a distant descendent of the MIT time-sharing project, MAC (see earlier). In 1964 MIT formed a partnership with General Electric and Bell laboratories to write an operational computer language, Multics. In 1969 Bell labs withdrew from the project and developed Unix.

75. On the history of Unix, see David Mowery, *The International Computer Software Industry. A Comparative Study of Industry Evolution and Structure* (New York: Oxford University Press, 1996).

76. Dennis Ritchie, "The Evolution of the Unix Time-Sharing System," *ATT, Bell Labs Technical Journal* 63, no. 8 (October 1984), quoted in Hauben and Hauben, *Netizens,* chapter 5.

77. John Quarterman, *The Matrix: Computer Networks and Conferencing Systems Worldwide* (Bedford, Mass.: Digital Press, 1990), 253.

78. Ibid., 244.

79. Stephen Daniel, James Ellis, and Tom Truscott, *USENET, a General Access Unix Network*, Duke University, 1980, quoted in Quarterman, *The Matrix*, 243.

80. G. Spafford, "Usenet History," *IETF Meeting*, October 1, 1988.

81. Ibid.

82. Bruce Jones, Henry Spencer, and David Wiseman, *The Usenet Oldnews Archives*. Available at http://www.google.com/googlegroups/archive_announce_20 .html.

83. Arpanet had launched "Messages services groups" (MsgGroups) in 1975.

84. Interview with Ray Tomlinson, 10 April 1996, quoted in Hardy, "The Evolution of ARPANET Email," 29.

85. Donald Austin, "Introduction," Berkeley Workshop on Distributed Data Management and Computer Networks, LBL-5315, Lawrence Berkeley Laboratories, 1976, quoted in Hardy, "The Evolution of ARPANET Email," 29.

86. Richard Roistacher, "The Virtual Journal," *Computer Networks* 2 (1978).

87. Article from 8 April 1982, Usenet Oldnews Archives.

88. Brian W. Kernighan and John Mashey, "The Unix Programming Environment," *Computer*, April 1981, 20, quoted in Hauben and Hauben, *Netizens,* chapter 9.

89. Ibid.

90. Steve Sends, "English Murdering and Flame about Human Telecommuting," in *Human-nets*, Usenet Oldnews Archive, 15 May 1981.

91. An organizational backbone since in Usenet, unlike Arpanet, the standard telephone network is used, rather than special links.

92. DEC was created by two MIT computer scientists. It had a policy of selling its minicomputers to universities at very low prices. These consequently constituted the majority of machines running on Unix.

93. Available at http://www.vrx.net/usenet/history/bjones.net-explodes.txt 6 (message from Gene Spafford).

94. Hauben and Hauben, *Netizens*, chapters 10, 16.

95. Ibid.

96. Brian Reid, "Corregida to the History of the Net," 23 September 1993, quoted in Hardy, "The History of the Net." Available at http://www.ijla.org/documents/internet/met_hist.txt.

97. Post from tower@bu-it.bu.edu, 26 October 1990, 17. Available at http://www.vrx.net/usenet/history/bjones.net-explodes.txt.

98. Robert Zakon, *Hobbes' Internet Timeline*. Available at http://www.info.isoc.org/guest/zakon/Internet/History/HIT.html.

99. But 30 percent of the files transmitted. This difference is probably because there were many files with pictures.

100. Brian Reid, Usenet Readership Reports for June 92, articles 3653 and 3724 of news.lists.

101. Lee Sproull and Samer Faraj, "Atheism, Sex and Databases: The Net as a Social Technology," in Kahin and Keller, *Public Access to the Internet*, 71.

102. Quoted in Hafner and Lyon, *Where Wizards Stay Up Late*, 240.

103. Quarterman, *The Matrix*, 364.

104. Quoted in Barry Leiner, Vinton Cerf, David Clark, Robert Kahn, Leonard Kleinrock, Daniel Lynch, Jon Postel, Lawrence Roberts, and Stephen Wolff, *A Brief History of the Internet*, 8. Available at http://www.isoc.org/internet-history/brief.html.

105. Vinton Cerf and Robert Kahn. "A Protocol for Packet Network Interconnection," *IEEE Trans. Comm. Tech.* 22, no. 5 (1974): 627–641.

106. Leiner et al., *A Brief History of the Internet*.

107. Quarterman gives the following definition: "The Internet is an internetwork of many networks all running the TCP/IP protocol." Quarterman, *The Matrix*, 278.

108. Norberg and O'Neill, *Transforming Computer Technology*, 185.

109. National Science Foundation Network Technical Advisory Group, *Requirements for Internet Gateway*, 1986, RFC 1985.

110. Grace Tolido and Dale Dougherty, *Using UUCP and Usenet News* (Sebastopol, Calif.: O'Reilly and Associates, 1986), 11.

111. Quarterman, *The Matrix*, xxiii.

112. Vannevar Bush, "As We May Think," *Atlantic Monthly*, July 1945, section 1. Available at http://www.w3.org/History/1945/vbush.

113. Ibid., section 6.

114. Joseph Licklider, *Libraries of the Future* (Cambridge, Mass.: MIT Press, 1965). Report produced in 1963. Reprinted in Stefik, *Internet Dreams*, 27.

115. Ted Nelson, *Dream Machines*, 1974. Reprinted by Microsoft Press, 1988, 46–47.

116. The first public presentation of this concept was at the Association for Computing Machinery congress in 1965.

117. Nelson, *Dream Machines*, 45.

118. Ibid., 56.

119. Gary Wolf, "The Curse of Xanadu," *Wired*, June 1995, 202.

120. Robert Kahn and Vinton Cerf, *The Digital Library Project*, vol. 1, *The World of Knowbots* (Reston, Va.: Corporation for National Research Initiatives, 1988); extract published in Stefik, *Internet Dreams*, 33–38.

121. Tim Berners-Lee, *Information Management: A Proposal* (Geneva: CERN, 1989).

122. Tim Berners-Lee and Robert Cailliau, *World Wide Web: Proposal for a HyperText Project* (Geneva: CERN, 1990).

123. See Licklider and Taylor, "The Computer as a Communication Device."

124. See Hiltz and Turoff, *The Network Nation*.

125. Corbato and Fano, "Time-Sharing on Computers."

126. Ritchie, "The Evolution of the Unix Time-Sharing System."

127. Amara et al., *Computerized Conferencing*.

128. Lederberg, "Digital Communications and the Conduct of Science."

129. Conway, "The Multi-Project Chip Adventures."

130. *Wall Street Journal*, 30 November 1984, 18, quoted in Theodore Roszak, *The Cult of Information* (New York: Pantheon Books, 1986), 60.

131. Roszak, *The Cult of Information*, 58.

132. Myer and Vittal, "Message Technology in the Arpanet."

133. John King, Rebecca Grinter, and Jeanne Pickering, "The Rise and Fall of Netville: Institution and Infrastructure in the Great Divide," in *Culture of the Internet*, ed. S. Kiesler (Mahwah, N.J.: Lawrence Erlbaum Associates, 1997), 1–33.

134. This policy of closure on the academic world also stemmed from the fact that Congress reportedly refused to allow government grants to be used for commercial purposes.

134. Hauben and Hauben, *Netizens*, chapter 12.

Chapter 3   Communities, a Different Internet *Imaginaire*

1. For Levy, "hacker" meant a computer enthusiast. Today the word tends to be used to refer to software pirates.

2. Steven Levy, *Hackers: Heroes of the Computer Revolution* (New York: Dell, 1985), 40–45.

3. See, in particular, Paul Freiberger and Michael Swaine, *Fire in the Valley: The Making of the Personal Computer* (Berkeley: McGraw-Hill, 1984).

4. Michael Rossman, "What Is Community Memory," mimeo., 1979, quoted in Roszak, *The Cult of Information,* 140.

5. Ivan Illich, *Tools for Conviviality* (London: Calder and Boyars, 1973), quoted in Levy, *Hackers,* 181.

6. Published in *The Pill versus the Springhill Mime Disaster* (New York: Dell/Laurel), quoted in Roszak, *The Cult of Information,* 147.

7. Ibid., 214.

8. Ibid., 272.

9. Quoted in Allucquère Rosanne Stone, "Will the Real Body Please Stand Up? Boundary Stories about Virtual Cultures," in *Cyberspace: First Steps,* ed. Michael Benedikt (Cambridge, Mass.: MIT Press, 1991), 90.

10. Quoted in Howard Rheingold, *The Virtual Community: Homesteading on the Electronic Frontier* (New York: Harper Collins, 1994), 135.

11. Allucquère Rosanne Stone, "What Vampires Know: Yranssubjection and Transgender in Cyberspace" (paper presented at Graz Symposium, Austria, May 1993). Available at http://www.eff.org/pub/Security/se . . . der_issues.

12. See Todd Gitlin, *The Sixties: Years of Hope, Days of Rage* (New York: Bantam Books, 1987), 207.

13. Quoted in Paul Keegan, "The Digerati," *New York Times Magazine,* 21 May 1995, 42.

14. Steward Brand, "Personal Computers," *Co-evolution Quarterly* (Sausalito, Calif.), Summer 1975, 136.

15. He wrote, "This generation swallows computers whole, just like dope." *San Francisco Focus Magazine,* February 1985, 107.

16. Steward Brand, "Point the Institution: Verbal Snapshots from the Last Quarter Century," *Whole Earth Review,* May 1985.

17. Steward Brand, *Whole Earth Software Catalog* (Sausalito, Calif.: Doubleday, 1984), 139.

18. See Lawrence Brilliant, "Computer Conferencing: The Global connection," *Byte,* December 1985, 174.

19. Ibid.

20. Howard Rheingold, "Virtual Communities," *Whole Earth Review,* Summer 1987, 79.

21. Kevin Kelly, "Tales from Two Communities," *Whole Earth Review,* Autumn 1988, 84.

22. Mathew McClure (1985–1986), Cliff Figallo, and John Coate (1986–1991).

23. Quoted in Katie Hafner, "The Epic Saga of The Well," *Wired,* May 1997, 11–29.

24. A paragraph on The Well in Bruce Sterling, *The Hacker Crackdown* (New York: Bantam, 1993), 224, carries the heading "Whole earth = computer revolution = Well."

25. Quoted in John Coate, "A Village Called The Well," *Whole Earth Review*, Autumn 1988, 86. This theme of the electronic public sphere was already present in a book on computer-aided teleconferences: "Computerized conferencing may provide central plazas, reminiscent of Italian cities on Sunday afternoon. (Other analogies might be the Viennese cafe and the French salon)." Hiltz and Turoff, *The Network Nation*, 429.

26. Hafner, "The Epic Saga of The Well," 10–29.

27. Sterling, *The Hacker Crackdown*, 227–232.

28. Coate, "A Village Called The Well," 87. See also Sterling, *The Hacker Crackdown*, 226.

29. Quoted in Marc Smith, *Voices from The Well: The Logic of the Virtual Common*, 1992, 20. Available at http://netscan.sscnet.ucla.edu/csoc/papers/voices/Voices.htm.

30. Rheingold, "Virtual Communities," 79.

31. Quoted in Smith, *Voices from The Well*, 25.

32. Ibid., 26.

33. Rheingold, *The Virtual Community*, 61.

34. Hafner, "The Epic Saga of The Well," 23–29. In May 1991 Judith Moore wrote in the *Los Angeles Reader*: "The Well has become my soap opera, a day-to-day drama in which I am also an actor."

35. Ward Christensen and Randy Suess, "Hobbyist Computerized Bulletin Boards," *Byte*, November 1978, 150.

36. The authors' underlining.

37. Ibid., 151.

38. Tom Jennings, *History of Fidonet. Part I*, February 1985, 1. Available at http://www.scms.rgu.ac.uk/students/cs_yr94/lk/fido/fhist.html. Fidonet was first tested in December 1983.

39. Ibid., 3.

40. Tom Jennings, *Artist Statement*, October 1998. Available at http://www.wps/about-WPS.html.

41. Randy Bush, *A History of Fidonet*, 1993, 6. Available at http://www.well.com/user/vertigo/history.html.

42. Carol Anne Dodd, "What Is Fidonet? Discussion of the Growth and Development of an Amateur Computer Network," 1992, 6. Available at http://www.ca/~jweston/papers/0992/dod.

43. See Paulina Borsook, "The Anarchist," *Wired*, April 1996.

44. Michael Shamberg, *Guerilla Television* (New York: Holt, Rinehart and Winston, 1971), part II, 9.

45. Interview with John Reilly, *Video Info*, no. 3 (1973): 39.

46. See John Hopkins et al., *Video in Community Development* (London: Center for Advanced Television Studios, 1972).

47. Monroe E. Price and John Wicklein, *Cable Television: A Guide for Citizen Action* (Philadelphia: Pilgrim Press, 1972), quoted in Stephen Doheny-Farina, *The Wired Neighborhood* (New Haven: Yale University Press, 1996), 163–164. These themes of active society were also developed by Amitai Etzioni, *The Active Society: A Theory of Societal and Political Processes* (New York: Free Press, 1968).

48. For a description of the experiment, see Tom Grundler and Robert Garrett, "Interactive Medical Telecomputing: An Alternative Approach to Community Health Education," *New England Journal of Medicine* 10 (April 1986): 982–985.

49. "Background and Concept," *NPTN Blue Book*, chapter 1, 1993. Available at http://www.vcn.bc.ca/sig/comm-nets/bluebook.

50. Jay Hauben, "A Brief History of Cleveland Free-Net," *Amateur Computerist* 7, no. 1 (1994).

51. Ibid., editorial by Tom Grundler.

52. Vicky Reich and Mark Weiser, "Libraries Are More Than Information: Situational Aspects of Electronic Libraries," *Serials Review* 20, no. 3 (1994); reprinted in Stefik, *Internet Dreams*, 85.

53. Quoted in Michael Strangelove, "Free-Nets: Community Computing Systems and the Rise of the Electronic Citizen," *Online Access*, Spring 1993.

54. Tom Grundler, "Seizing the Infosphere: Toward the Formation of a Corporation for Public Cybercasting" (paper presented at DIAC '94, Cambridge, Mass.). My underlining.

55. Presentation of Dave Hughes on the online service *The Source*, 1983, quoted in Rheingold, *The Virtual Community*, 242.

56. Jacques Leslie, "The Cursor Cowboy," *Wired*, May–June 1993, 63.

57. Dave Hughes, "The Electronic Democracy Debate," Meta-Net BBS, Old Salon, Topics 121, 153, 288, 372, 1987–1989; New Salon 3, quoted in Willard Uncapher, "Electronic Homesteading on the Rural Frontier. Big Sky Telegraph and Its Community," in *Communities in Cyberspace,* ed. Marc Smith and Peter Kollock (New York: Routledge, 1999), 267.

58. Frank Odasz, "Issues in the Development of Community Cooperative Networks" (paper presented at Harvard University, May 1993), quoted in Kahin and Keller, *Public Access to the Internet*, 127.

59. Anne Beamish, *Communities Online: Community-Based Computer Networks,* Appendix 4. Available at http://sap. mit.edu/anneb/cn-thesis/html.

60. Pamela Varley, "Electronic Democracy," *Technology Review*, November–December 1991, 46.

61. Quoted in Joan Van Tassel, "Yakety-Yak, Do Talk Back! PEN, the Nation's First Publicly Funded Electronic Network, Makes a Difference in Santa Monica," *Wired*, January 1994, 78–80.

62. Varley, "Electronic Democracy," 51.

63. Van Tassel, "Yakety-Yak, Do Talk Back!" 80.

64. Steven Clift, *Minnesota E-Democracy Information*, 10 August 1994, § 2. Available at http://www.e-democracy.org/mn-politics-archive/0894/0007.html. The reader is also referred to G. Scott Aikens, "A History of Minnesota Electronic Democracy 1994." Available at http://www.firstmonday.dk/issues/issue5/index.html.

65. Clift, *Minnesota E-Democracy Information*, § 1.

66. Borsook, "The Anarchist."

67. Jack Rickard, "Home-Grown BBS," *Wired*, September–October 1993; Bush, *A History of Fidonet*.

68. See René Plaetevoet, "The National Public Telecomputing Network: A Mission toward Establishing Free and Open-Access Computing Systems," *Working Papers in Public Access Networks* (Carleton University), no. 10 (March 1992). Available at http://www.vcn.bc.ca/sigs/comm-nets/wp10.txt.

69. Mario Morino, "Assessment and Evolution of Community Networking" (paper presented at "The Ties That Bind," Apple Conference on Building Community Computing Networks, Cupertino, Calif., 5 May 1994), 7. Available at http://ifla.inist.fr/documents/infopol/community_networks/morino01.txt.

70. Hafner, "The Epic Saga of The Well," 10–29.

71. Patrice Flichy, "Technologies fin de siècle, Internet et la radio," *Réseaux*, no. 100 (2000): 249–271.

Chapter 4   From Internet Myth to Cyber-*Imaginaire*

1. Any computer linked to a network at a given point in time is considered a host.

2. Internet Society.

3. For a statistical measurement of this phenomenon, see the graph at the end of chapter 1.

4. Everett Rogers, *Diffusion of Innovations* (New York: Free Press, 1993). For a critical analysis, see Flichy, *L'Innovation technique*.

5. An earlier version of this chapter was presented at the seminar "The Social Sustainability of Technological Networks," Wagner Graduate School of Public Service, New York University, 18–20 April 2001. Patrice Flichy, "Internet: The Social Construction of a 'Network Ideology,'" in *Sustaining Urban Networks:*

The Social Diffusion of Large Technical Systems, ed. Olivier Coutard, Richard Hanley, and Rae Zimmerman (London: Routledge, 2005), 103–116.

6. Following this article, *The Well* hosts received many messages asking: "Is this the cyberspace?" Mark Dery, *Flame Wars* (Durham, N.C.: Duke University Press, 1994), 6–7.

7. Philip Elmer-Dewitt, "Cyber Punk," *Time,* 8 February 1993, 60.

8. Barbara Kantrowitz, "Live Wires," *Newsweek,* 6 September 1993, 42–49.

9. At first 35,000 copies were printed. The following year, the book was printed in paperback.

10. An expression found in one of the critiques in the presentation of his book on the site Amazon.com.

11. Hafner, "The Epic Saga of The Well," 100.

12. Brendan Kehoe, *Zen and the Art of the Internet: A Beginner's Guide to the Internet* (Englewood Cliffs, N.J.: Prentice Hall, 1992), 3.

13. Ed Krol, *The Whole Internet. User's Guide & Catalog* (Sebastopol, Calif.: O'Reilly & Associates, 1992), xix–xx.

14. A far shorter version of this guide had been published in 1989 under the title *The Hitchhiker's Guide to the Internet,* in the framework of Requests for Comments, no. 1118, on the Internet.

15. Krol, *The Whole Internet,* 2.

16. Tracy LaQuey and Jeanne Ryer, *The Internet Companion: A Beginner's Guide to Global Networking* (Reading, Mass.: Addison-Wesley, 1993), 9.

17. Adam Engst, *Internet Starter Kit for Macintosh* (Indianapolis: Hayden Books, 1993), 13.

18. T. LaQuey and Ryer, *The Internet Companion,* vi.

19. Ibid., ix.

20. Adam Gaffin and Mitchell Kapor, *Big Dummy's Guide to the Internet,* 1991, 8–9. Available at http://www.thegulf.com/InternetGuide.html. This guide was published in the form of a book under the title *Everybody's Guide to the Internet* (Cambridge, Mass.: MIT Press, 1994).

21. Evan Schwartz, "The Cleavers Enter Cyberspace," *Business Week,* 11 October 1993, 142.

22. Elmer-Dewitt, "First Nation in Cyberspace," 62.

23. Edward Baig, "Ready to Cruise the Internet?" *Business Week,* 28 March 1994, 180.

24. *Business Week,* 11 October 1993, 142.

25. *Time,* 6 December 1993, 62.

26. Philip Elmer-Dewitt, "Battle for the Soul of the Internet," *Time,* 25 July 1994, 53.

27. In March 1995, *Time* published another special issue entitled "Welcome to Cyberspace" featuring an article by Stewart Brand with the title "We Owe It All to the Hippies" and the subtitle "Forget antiwar protests, Woodstock, even long hair. The real legacy of the 1960s generation is the computer revolution."

28. *Time*: 9 articles, of which 3 are on sex and 2 are on pirating. *Newsweek*: 14 articles, of which 1 is on sex and 6 are on pirating. *Business Week*: 8 articles, of which 1 is on pirating.

29. *Business Week*, 28 March 1994, 180.

30. Katie Hafner, "Making Sense of the Internet," *Newsweek*, 24 October 1994, 46.

31. See, for example, Rheingold, *The Virtual Community*, 276–278.

32. Data on online services are drawn from Philip Elmer-Dewitt, "Hooked Up to the Max: Will America Online, Prodigy and CompuServe Lose Their Clout When the Internet Comes to Town?" *Time*, 26 September 1994, 58–60, and Paul Eng, "On-Ramps to the Info Superhighway: CompuServe and Its Rivals Are Seeing Bumper-to-Bumper Traffic," *Business Week*, 7 February 1994, 108–109.

33. "Aliens among Us," *Internet World*, November–December 1994, 82–84.

34. Dern, "Painting the Right Picture," 99–101.

35. Michael Wolf, *Net Guide* (New York: Random House, 1994), 1.

36. Ibid., 10.

37. Norman Shapiro and Robert Anderson, *Toward an Ethics and Etiquette for Electronic Mail* (Santa Monica, Calif.: Rand Corporation, 1985), 4.

38. One of the first presentations on paper of these rules is found in Quarterman, *The Matrix*, 34–37.

39. Arlene Rinaldi, *The Net: User Guidelines and Netiquette*, July 1992. Available at http://www.listserv.acsu.buffalo.edu/c . . . A2=ind9207&L–ettrain&F=& S=&P=1383.

40. Kehoe, *Zen and the Art of the Internet*, 43.

41. Virginia Shea, *Netiquette* (San Francisco: Albion Books, 1994), 19.

42. Krol, *The Whole Internet*, 35.

43. Ibid., 36.

44. Ibid., 37.

45. Smileys, symbols indicating the emotive weight of a word, were another way of showing one's familiarity with the Internet.

46. This argument is defended by Michel Marcoccia, "La normalisation des comportements communicatifs sur Internet: étude sociopragmatique de la netiquette," in *Communication, société et Internet*, ed. Nicolas Gueguen and Laurence Tobin (Paris: L'Harmattan, 1998), 15–32.

47. Quoted in John Brockman, *Digerati: Encounters with the Cyber Elite* (San Francisco: Hardwired, 1996), 221.

48. John Schwartz, "Propeller Head Heaven: A Techie Rolling Stone" *Newsweek*, 18 January 1993, 62.

49. Paul Keegan, "The Digerati! Wired Magazine Has Triumphed by Turning Mild-Mannered Computer Nerds into a Super-Desirable Consumer Niche," *New York Times Magazine*, 21 May 1995, 39.

50. On this point, see Jack Boulware, "*Mondo 1995*: Up and Down with the Next Millennium's First Magazine," *SF Weekly* 14, no. 35 (11 October 1995).

51. R. U. Sirius, "NEW World Disorder: All Is NOT One," *Mondo 2000* (date?), no. 4, 9.

52. "What Have They Been Smoking," *Wired*, September 1997, 53–56.

53. Quoted in Keegan, "The Digerati!" 39.

54. Kevin Kelly, interview with Alvin Toffler, "Anticipatory Democracy," *Wired*, July 1996.

55. Quoted in Keegan, "The Digerati!" 40.

56. Quoted in Schwartz, "Propeller Head Haven," 62.

57. Barbara Kantrowitz, "Happy Birthday: Still Wired at One," *Newsweek*, 17 January 1994, 38.

58. Keegan, "The Digerati!" 39.

59. *San Francisco Chronicle*, 8 May 1998, A20.

60. The average reader was thirty-seven years old and had an income of US$122,000 (*San Francisco Weekly*, 1996).

61. Dan Simpson, quoted in Joel Garreau, "Conspiracy of Heretics," *Wired*, November 1994, 157.

62. John Gilmore was one of the first employees of the computer company Sun Microsystems, and was paid mostly in stock options. A few years later he sold his shares and was able to live off the interest.

63. Electronic Frontier Foundation, *Mission Statement*. Available at http://www .eff.org/EFFdocs/about_eff.html.

64. Bruce Sterling, *The Hacker Crackdown* (New York: Bantam, 1993), 238. On the history of the Electronic Frontier Foundation, see also Rheingold, *Tools for Thought*, 256–260.

65. Quoted in Joshua Quittner, "The Merry Pranksters Go to Washington," *Wired*, June 1994, 140.

66. Quoted in Brockman, *Digerati*, xxxi.

67. See, for example, "The Net 50." "They're Supplying the Vision, the Rools and the Content That Are Getting Millions of People to Turn on Their Modems," *Newsweek*, 25 December 1995, 42–46.

68. *Newsweek*, special double issue, 2 January 1996.

Chapter 5   Dawn of a New Communication Age

1. In order of appearance: Bruce Sterling (twice), William Gibson (twice), Alvin Toffler, Neal Stephenson, Richard Dawkins, Nicholas Negroponte, Marshall McLuhan, George Gilder, and Sherry Turkle. Entrepreneurs and artists are also present in lead-story articles, in 22 percent of the cases for each category.

2. Not present in a cover story.

3. Not present in a cover story.

4. Clifford Stoll, *Silicon Snake Oil: Second Thoughts on the Information Highway* (New York: Doubleday, 1995).

5. See, in particular, Jon Katz, "Return of the Luddites," *Wired*, June 1995, 162–165.

6. See Flichy, *L'Innovation technique*, 180–183.

7. Steward Brand, interview with Camille Paglia, "Paglia: Brash, Self-Promoting and Possibly the Next Marshall McLuhan," *Wired*, March 1993, 52.

8. Gary Wolf, "Channelling McLuhan: The *Wired* Interview with *Wired's* Patron Saint," *Wired*, January 1996, 129.

9. Hence, the most cited of McLuhan's writings was also one of his last: Marshall McLuhan and Quentin Fiore, *The Medium Is the Message: An Inventory of Effects* (New York: Bantam Books and Random House, 1967).

10. Gary Wolf, "The Wisdom of Saint Marshall, the Holy Fool," *Wired*, January 1996, 186.

11. Marshall McLuhan, interview in *Playboy*, March 1969, 76.

12. *Wired*, March–April 1993, 6–10.

13. Ibid., 74.

14. McLuhan and Fiore, *The Medium Is the Message,* 41.

15. Burr Snider, interview with Jaron Lanier, "Jaron," *Wired*, May–June 1993, 80.

16. He cites him repeatedly in *The Gutenberg Galaxy* (Toronto: University of Toronto Press, 1962).

17. Jennifer Cobb Kreisberg, "A Globe Clothing Itself with Brain," *Wired*, June 1995, 108.

18. John Perry Barlow, "The Great Work," Electronic Frontier Foundationeditorial, *Communications of the ACM*, January 1992.

19. Quoted in Mark Dery, *Escape Velocity: Cyberculture at the End of the Century* (New York: Grove Press, 1996), 47–48.

20. Ibid.

21. Keegan, "The Digerati!" 42.

22. David Hudson, interview with Louis Rossetto, in *Rewired* (Indianapolis: Macmillan Technical Publishing, 1997), 241.

23. Marshall McLuhan, interview in *Playboy*, March 1969, 72.

24. Al Gore, in his book on ecology (*Earth in the Balance*), also cites Teilhard de Chardin but retains his spiritual perspective.

25. "Teilhard [de Chardin] helps us understand the importance of faith in the future" (Kreisberg, "A Globe Clothing Itself with Brain").

26. Interview with Marshall McLuhan, *Playboy*, March 1969; see the conclusion of his interview.

27. Peter Schwartz, interview with Alvin Toffler, "Shock Wave (Anti)warrior," *Wired*, November 1993, 62.

28. Alvin Toffler, *The Third Wave* (London: Collins, 1980).

29. *Wired*, November 1993, 63.

30. Dan Sicko, "The Roots of Techno," *Wired*, July 1994, 97.

31. Mark Nollinger, "America Online," *Wired*, September 1995, 199.

32. Toffler, *The Third Wave*, 181.

33. Ibid., 194.

34. In 1998, for the magazine's fifth anniversary, he published an article entitled "Happy Birthday *Wired*."

35. George Gilder, *Life After Television* (New York: Norton, [1990] 1994).

36. Ibid., 16.

37. Michael Crighton, "The Mediasaurus," *Wired*, September 1993, 57.

38. Gilder, *Life After Television*, 204.

39. Ibid., 68.

40. Ibid., 189.

41. Thomas Bass, interview with Nicholas Negroponte, "Being Nicholas," *Wired*, November 1995, 202.

42. Toffler, *The Third Wave*, 248.

43. "If Marshall McLuhan is *Wired*'s patron saint, then Peter Drucker should be its official oracle." Kevin Kelly, "Wealth Is Overrated" *Wired*, March 1998.

44. Peter Drucker, *The New Realities: In Government and Politics, in Economics and Business, in Society and World View* (New York: Harper & Row, 1989), 203.

45. Peter Schwartz and Kevin Kelly, "The Relentless Contrarian," *Wired*, August 1996. Negroponte believed that "digitization flattens organizations" (*Wired*, November 1995, 204).

46. Kevin Kelly, interview with John Naisbitt, "Mr. Big Trend, Futurologist John Naisbitt, on Why Small Is Not Only Beautiful, but Powerful," *Wired*, October 1994, 114.

47. Kevin Kelly, interview with Derrick de Kerckhove, "What Would McLuhan Say?" *Wired*, October 1996.

48. Ibid., 385.

49. Bass, "Being Nicholas," 200.

50. Gilder, *Life After Television*, 61–62.

51. Kelly, "Anticipatory Democracy."

52. Toffler, *The Third Wave*, 375.

53. Nicholas Negroponte, *Being Digital* (New York: Alfred Knopf, 1995).

54. This thesis was also defended by Gilder (Gilder, *Life After Television*, 164–165).

55. See Nicholas Negroponte, "Bits and Atoms," *Wired*, January 1995, 176.

56. Nicholas Negroponte, "The Fax of Life: Playing a Bit Part," *Wired*, January 1995, 176.

57. Nicholas Negroponte, "HDTV/What's Wrong with This Picture?" *Wired*, March 1993, 112.

58. Nicholas Negroponte, "Bit by Bit on Wall Street: Lucky Strikes Again," *Wired*, May 1994, 144.

59. Bass, "Being Nicholas," 204.

60. Nicholas Negroponte, "Less Is More: Interface Agents as Digital Butlers," *Wired*, June 1994, 142.

61. Negroponte, *Being Digital*, 6.

62. Nicholas Negroponte, "Learning by Doing: Don't Dissect the Frog, Build It," *Wired*, July 1994, 144.

63. Sterling, *The Hacker Crackdown*, 140.

64. Sterling presented *The Third Wave* as "a bible to many cyberpunks." See the preface to *Mirrorshades: The Cyberpunk Anthology*, ed. Bruce Sterling (New York: Arbor House, 1986).

65. Ibid.

66. Ibid.

67. Bruce Sterling, preface to William Gibson, *Burning Chrome* (New York, Arbor House, 1986), 3.

68. Alan Kay and Danny Hills, "Kay-Hillis," *Wired*, January 1994, 148.

69. Terry Gross, interview with William Gibson, *Fresh Air*, National Public Radio, 31 August 1993, quoted in Dery, *Escape Velocity*, 107.

70. Erik Davis, "TechGnosis: Magic, Memory, and the Angels of Information," in Dery, *Flame Wars*, 30.

71. The term is present in several of Gibson's writings: *Neuromancer* (New York: Ace Books, 1984), 67, and *Count Zero* (New York: Arbor House, 1986), 44. In *Burning Chrome*, Gibson uses the term "consensus-hallucination" (178).

72. Gibson, *Neuromancer*, 67.

73. Gibson, *Count Zero*, 136.

74. Gibson, *Burning Chrome*, 178.

75. William Gibson, *Mona Lisa Overdrive* (Toronto: Bantam Books, 1988), 64.

76. Gibson, *Count Zero*, 131.

77. Ibid., 240

78. Gibson, *Mona Lisa Overdrive*, 220.

79. Ibid.

80. Gibson, *Neuromancer*, 97.

81. Gibson, *Burning Chrome*, 149.

82. Gibson, *Count Zero*, 15.

83. Ibid., 2

84. Gibson, *Mona Lisa Overdrive*, 162.

85. Gibson, *Neuromancer*, 67.

86. Ibid., 71.

87. Quarterman, *The Matrix*. In the preface he thanks Gibson, from whom he borrowed this title.

88. Elmer-Dewitt, "Cyberpunk," 60.

89. Bruce Sterling, "War Is Virtual Hell," *Wired*, March 1993, 46–51.

90. Fred Hapgood, "Simnet," *Wired*, April 1997. Note that the project leader was with BBN, the company that built Arpanet, and was also a member of the Society of American Magicians.

91. Bruce Sterling, "Greetings from Burning Man," *Wired*, November 1996.

92. Bruce Sterling, "Triumph of the Plastic People," *Wired*, January 1995.

93. William Gibson, "Disneyland with the Death Penalty," *Wired*, September–October 1993.

94. Neal Stephenson, "Mother Earth, Mother Board," *Wired*, December 1996.

95. William Gibson and Bruce Sterling, *The Difference Engine* (New York: Bantam Books, 1991).

96. Bruce Sterling, "The Dead Media Project: A Modest Proposal and a Public Appeal." (paper presented at "The Life and Death of Media," the sixth International Symposium on Electronic Art, Montreal, 19 September 1995). Available at http://www.wps.com/dead-media.

97. William Gibson, conversation with Timothy Leary, "High Tech High Life," *Mondo 2000*, no. 7 (1989).

98. Bruce Sterling, "Short History of the Internet," *Magazine of Fantasy and Science Fiction*, February 1993.

99. David Tomas, "Old Rituals for New Space: Rites de Passage and William Gibson's Cultural Model of Cyberspace," in Benedikt, *Cyberspace*, 46.

100. Allucquère Rosanne Stone, "Will the Real Body Please Stand Up? Boundary Stories about Virtual Cultures," in Benedikt, *Cyberspace*, 95.

Chapter 6 The Body and Virtual Reality

1. Ted Nelson, *The Home Computer Revolution*, 1977, quoted in Howard Rheingold, *Virtual Reality* (New York: Summit Books, 1991), 92.

2. Ivan Sutherland, "Graphic Control," ARPA, 1965, quoted in Norberg and O'Neill, *Transforming Computer Technology: Information Processing for the Pentagon, 1962–1986* (Baltimore, Md.: Johns Hopkins University Press, 1996), 129.

3. Ivan Sutherland, "The Ultimate Display," *Proceedings of the IFIPS Congress* 2 (1965): 506–508.

4. Thomas Furness, "Harnessing Virtual Space," in *Proceedings of SID International Symposium Digest of Technical Papers*, 1988, 5.

5. Sterling, "War Is Virtual Hell," 102. Similar comments on virtual war are found in an article by Mark Thomson, "Onward Cyber," *Time*, 21 August 1995, 41–46.

6. Quoted in Frank Barnaby, *The Automated Battlefield* (New York: Free Press, 1986), 1.

7. Nicholas Negroponte, "Virtual Reality: Oxymoron or Pleonasm?" *Wired*, December 1993, 136.

8. Myron Krueger, *Artificial Reality* (Reading, Mass.: Addison-Wesley, 1983).

9. Ted Nelson, "Interactive Systems and the Design of Virtuality," *Creative Computing*, November 1980, 56–62, quoted in Rheingold, *Virtual Reality*, 177.

10. Brenda Laurel, *Computers as Theatre* (Menlo Park, Calif.: Addison-Wesley, 1992), 205.

11. Brenda Laurel, "Art and Activism in VR," (paper presented at the Virtual Reality Symposium, San Francisco, 1991), 3. Available at http://www.tauzero.com/Brenda_Laurel/Severed_Heads/art_and_Activism.html.

12. Quoted in Dery, *Escape Velocity*, 119.

13. Mark Pauline, quoted in Dery, *Escape Velocity*, 121.

14. Mark Pauline, in "Out of Control: A Trialogue on Machine Consciousness with Mark Pauline, Manuel De Landa, and Mark Dery," *Wired*, September 1993, 71.

15. Bruce Sterling, "Is Phoenix Burning?" *Wired*, July 1996.

16. Dery, *Escape Velocity*, 128.

17. Quoted in Ibid., 80.

18. Ibid., 82.

19. Ibid., 83.

20. *Time*, in its special issue "Welcome to Cyberspace," reported this concert: Ginia Bellafante, "Strange Sounds and Sights," 14.

21. Quoted in Steward Brand, *The Media Lab: Inventing the Future at MIT* (New York: Penguin, 1988), 108–109.

22. Kevin Kelly, "Genetic Images," *Wired*, September 1994, 115.

23. John Walker, "Through the Looking Glass," in *The Art of Human-Computer Interface Design*, ed. Brenda Laurel (Menlo Park, Calif.: Addison-Wesley, 1990).

24. Randal Walser, "Elements of a Cyberspace Playhouse," in *Virtual Reality, Theory Practice and Promise*, ed. Sandra Helsel and Judith Roth (Westport: Meckler, 1991), 51.

25. Brenda Laurel, "Imagery and Evolution" (paper presented at SIGGRAPH '94, Orlando, Fla.). Available at http://www.tauzero.com/Brenda_Laurel/Severed_Heads/Imagery_and_Evolution.html.

26. Laurel, *Computers as Theatre*, 135.

27. Ibid.

28. Brenda Laurel, Rachel Strickland, and Rob Tow, "Placeholder: Landscape and Narrative in Virtual Environments," *ACM Computer Graphics Quarterly* 28, no. 2 (1994).

29. Quoted in Susan McCarthy, "Techno Soaps and Virtual Theatre. Brenda Laurel Can Blow Anything Up," *Wired*, May 1993, 41.

30. Eric Gullichsen and Randal Walser, "Cyberspace: Experiential Computing," *Nexus 89 Science Fiction and Science Fact*, quoted in Rheingold, *Virtual Reality*, 205.

31. Interview with Jaron Lanier, in *Clicking In: Hot Links to a Digital Culture*, ed. Lynn Hershman Leeson (Seattle: Bay Press, 1996), 48.

32. Interview quoted in Heather Bromberg, "Are MUDs Communities? Identity, Belonging and Consciousness in Virtual Worlds," in *Culture of Internet*, ed. Rob Shields (London: Sage, 1996), 149–150.

33. Levy, *Hackers*, 18.

34. Ibid., 126.

35. Ibid.

36. Gareth Branwyn, "The Desire to Be Wired: Will We Live to See Our Brains Wired to Gadgets? How about Today?" *Wired*, September 1993, 64.

37. Ibid.

38. Elmer-Dewitt, "Cyberpunk," 60.

39. Barbara Kantrowitz, "Computers as Mind Readers," *Newsweek*, 30 May 1994, 68.

40. Ed Regis, "Meet the Extropians," *Wired*, October 1994, 105.

41. Ibid., 104.

42. Ibid.

43. Douglas Cooper, interview with David Rokeby, "Very Nervous System," *Wired*, March 1995, 135.

44. Yiannis Melanitis, interview with Stelarc, *Journal of Art, Research and Critical Curating*, November 1999. Available at http://a-r-c.gold.ac.uk/reference .html#articles.

45. Stelarc, "Prosthetics, Robotics and Remote Existence: Postevolutionary Strategies," *Leonardo* 24, no. 5 (1991): 594.

46. Stelarc, "Parasite Visions: Alternate, Intimate and Involuntary experiences." Available at http://www.stelarc.va.com.au/articles/index.html.

47. Stelarc, "Detached, Breath/Spinning Retina," *High Performance*, no. 41–42 (1988): 70.

48. William Gibson, *Neuromancer* (London: Grafton Books, 1986), 12.

49. Ibid., 58.

50. Ibid., 20.

51. Ibid., 76.

52. Pat Cadigan, *Synners* (New York: Bantam Spectra, 1991), 239.

53. Ibid., 400.

54. Ibid., 234.

55. Anne Balsamo, "Feminism for the Incurably Informed," in Dery, *Flame Wars*, 137.

56. Ibid., 147.

57. Kevin Kelly, interview with Vernor Vinge, "Singular Visionary," *Wired*, June 1995, 160–161.

58. Vernor Vinge, "The Digital Gaia: As Computing Power Accelerates, the Network Knows All—and It's Everywhere," *Wired*, January 2000, 75.

59. Ibid., 76.

60. Ibid., 204.

61. Manuel De Landa, *War in the Age of Intelligent Machines* (New York: Zone Books, 1991), 21.

62. Hans Moravec, *Mind Children: The Future of Robot and Human Intelligence* (Cambridge, Mass.: Harvard University Press, 1988), 112.

63. Ibid.

64. Ibid., 149.

65. Ibid., 204.

66. Moravec, *Mind Children*, 112.

67. Susan Stryker, interview with Allucquère Rosanne Stone, "Sex and Death among the Cyborgs," *Wired*, May 1996, 136.

68. Allucquère Rosanne Stone, *The War of Desire and Technology at the Close of the Mechanical Age* (Cambridge, Mass.: MIT Press, 1995), 34.

69. Ibid., 39.

70. Sherry Turkle, "Who Am We?" *Wired*, January 1996, 151.

71. Heather Bromberg, "Are MUDs Communities? Identity, Belonging and Consciousness in Virtual Worlds," in Shields, *Cultures of Internet*, 144.

72. Ibid.

73. Kevin Kelly and Howard Rheingold, "The Dragon Ate My Homework," *Wired*, July 1993, 69.

74. Quoted in part from Joshua Quittner, "Johnny Manhattan Meets the Furry Muckers: Why Playing MUDs Is Becoming the Addiction of the '90s," *Wired*, March 1994, 95.

75. Sherry Turkle, *Life on the Screen* (New York: Touchstone, 1997), 184.

76. Ibid., 185.

77. Turkle, "Who Am We?" 194.

78. Turkle, *Life on the Screen*, 89.

79. Andrew Leonard, "Bots Are Hot!" *Wired*, April 1996, 166.

80. Ibid.

81. Kelly and Rheingold, "The Dragon Ate My Homework," 69.

82. Turkle, "Who Am We?" 197.

83. Quittner, "Johnny Manhattan Meets the Furry Muckers," 95.

84. Gerard Van der Leun, "This Is a Naked Lady: Behind Every New Technology Is . . . Sex?" *Wired*, March 1993, 74–75.

85. Paulina Borsook, "Love over the Wires," *Wired*, September 1993, 97–112.

86. Richard Kadrey, "alt.sex.bondage," *Wired*, June 1994, 40–43.

87. Robert Rossney, "The Next Best Thing to Being There," *Wired*, May 1995, 98–105.

88. Frank Rose, "Sex Sells," *Wired*, December 1997, 218–223, 276–284. The author notes that in 1996 the turnover of sex-related sites on the Internet was bigger than that of chatlines. The turnover of these two industries combined was 80 percent that of strip-tease clubs and 33 percent that of porn videos. Cybersex accounts for a quarter of all Internet traffic. It is the main object of residential use (a quarter of all pages viewed) and the second main use in the workplace (20 percent of all pages viewed). See Michel Gensollen, "La création de valeur sur Internet," *Réseaux* 17, no. 97 (1999): 23.

89. *Mondo 2000: A User's Guide to the New Edge* (New York: HarperPerennial, 1992), 272, quoted in Dery, *Escape Velocity*, 217.

90. Interview with R. U. Sirius, in Leeson, *Clicking In*, 60.

91. Rheingold, *Virtual Reality*, 346.

92. Ibid.

93. George Gilder, *Life After Television* (New York: Norton, 1994), 65.

94. Brenda Laurel, "The L Is for Location," in *Location Based Entertainment Panel Speech* (Beverly Hills: Digital World, 1992). Available at http://www.tauzero.com/Brenda_Laurel/Severed_Heads/L_is_for_Location.html.

95. Ibid.

96. Manfred Clynes and Nathan S. Kline, "Cyborgs and Space," *Astronautics*, September 1960, 26–27, 74–75.

97. Donna Haraway, *Simians, Cyborgs, and Women: The Reinvention of Nature* (New York: Routledge, 1991), 180.

98. Ibid., 177.

99. Ibid., 181.

100. Ibid., 149.

101. Hari Kunzru, "You Are Cyborg: For Donna Haraway, We Are Already Assimilated," *Wired*, February 1997.

102. Ibid., 164.

Chapter 7   The End of Politics

1. Rheingold, *The Virtual Community*, 14.

2. Kelly, "Anticipatory Democracy."

3. Quoted in Kenneth Hacker, "The Role of the Clinton White House in Facilitating Electronic Democratization and Political Interactivity," *Political Communication Division of the Speech Communication Association*, November 1996, 6. Available at http://Web.nmsu.edu/~comstudy/pc1.htm. On this subject, the reader is also referred to Evan Schwartz, "Power to the People," *Wired*, December 1994, 88–93.

4. Quoted in Mark Lewyn and John Carey, "Will America Log on to the Internet?" *Business Week*, 5 December 1994, 38.

5. Kevin Phillips, "Virtual Washington," *Time*, Spring 1995, special issue, 65–66.

6. Robert Wright, "Hyperdemocracy," *Time*, 23 January 1995, 15–21.

7. Mitchell Kapor, "Where Is the Digital Highway Really Heading? The Case for a Jeffersonian Information Policy," *Wired*, July–August 1993, 53.

8. Jon Katz, "The Age of Paine," *Wired*, May 1995, 154.

9. Ibid., 156.

10. Ibid., 210.

11. This thesis is also developed by John Perry Barlow, for example, in "The Powers That Were," *Wired*, September 1996, 197.

12. Interview with Jaron Lanier, in *Clicking In*, 53.

13. Rheingold, *The Virtual Community*, 281.

14. Beth Kolko and Elizabeth Reid, "Dissolution and Fragmentation: Problems in Online Communities," in *Cybersociety 2.0*, ed. Steven Jones (Thousand Oaks, Calif.: Sage, 1998), 216.

15. Mark Poster, "The Net as a Public Sphere?" *Wired*, November 1995, 135–136. A scientific and more in-depth version of this analysis can be found in Mark Poster, "Cyberdemocracy: The Internet and the Public Sphere," in *Virtual Politics, Identity and Community in Cyberspace*, ed. David Holmes (London: Sage, 1997), 212–228.

16. In Internaut's language, the acronym IRL (in real life) is used to denote the outside world.

17. John Perry Barlow, "A Cyberspace Independence Declaration," newsgroup message posted on 9 February 1996.

18. Ibid.

19. John Perry Barlow, "Declaring Independence," *Wired*, June 1996, 122.

20. Barlow, "A Cyberspace Independence Declaration."

21. Ibid.

22. Todd Lappin, interview with David Post, "The Missing Link," *Wired*, August 1998, 121.

23. David Johnson and David Post, "Law and Borders: The Rise of Law in Cyberspace," *Stanford Law Review*, 1996, 17. Available at http://www.cli.org/X0025_LBFIN.html.

24. David Johnson and David Post, "The New 'Civic Virtue' of the Internet," *First Monday* 3, no. 1 (1998): 19.

25. Lawrence Lessig, "Tyranny in the Infrastructure," *Wired*, July 1997, 96.

26. Lawrence Lessig, *Code, and Other Laws of Cyberspace* (New York: Basic Books, 1999), 30.

27. Ibid., 19–20.

28. Ibid., 220.

29. David G. Post, "What Larry Doesn't Get: Code, Law, and Liberty in Cyberspace," *Stanford Law Review* 52 (May 2000): 1440.

30. John Perry Barlow, "Thinking Locally, Acting Globally," *Time*, 15 January 1996.

31. Esther Dyson, George Gilder, George Keyworth, and Alvin Toffler, "Cyberspace and the American Dream: A Magna Carta for the Knowledge Age," The Progress and Freedom Foundation, August 1994. Available at http://www.pff.org/position.html.

32. Jon Katz, "Birth of a Digital Nation," *Wired*, April 1997, 49.

33. Ibid., 190.

34. Ibid., 52.

35. Jon Katz, "The Digital Citizen," *Wired*, December 1997, 71–72.

36. Interview with Arthur Kroker, *Radio Canada*, 23 July 1995. Available at http://uregina.ca/~gingrich/kintvw.htm. There is also a short interview with him in *Wired*: Jean-Hughes Roy, "Way New Leftists," *Wired*, February 1996, 109. The reader is furthermore referred to Arthur Kroker and Michael A. Weinstein, *Data Trash: The Theory of the Virtual Class* (Montreal: New World Perspectives, 1994).

37. Dyson, Gilder, Keyworth, and Toffler, "Cyberspace and the American Dream," 11.

38. David Hudson, interview with Louis Rossetto, "What Kind of Libertarian," in *Rewired*, 255.

39. Lewis J. Perelman, "School's Out," *Wired*, March 1993, 71.

40. Ibid., 104.

41. Hudson, *Rewired*, 253.

42. Robert Nozick, *Anarchy, State and Utopia* (New York: Basic Books, 1974).

43. Paulina Borsook, "Cyberselfish," *Mother Jones Interactive*, July-August 1996. Available at http://www.mother-jones.com/mother_jones/JA96/borsook_jump .html.

44. Richard Barbrook and Andy Cameron, "The Californian Ideology," 1. Available at http://www.wmin.ac.uk/media/HRC/ci/calif5.html.

45. Ibid., 7.

46. *The Open Platform: A Proposal for a National Telecommunications Infrastructure* (Washington, D.C.: Electronic Frontier Foundation, 1992), also quoted in Kahin, *Information Infrastructure Sourcebook*, 187–188.

47. See in *Wired*, September 1994, the free tribune of film producer George Lucas and Senator Bob Kerrey, "Access to Education." In the same issue, John Browning criticized the universal service ("Universal Service, an Idea Whose Time Is Past"). Rob Glaser answered him in the January 1995 issue ("Universal Service *Does* Matter").

48. To show his esteem for Toffler's thinking, Gingrich prefaced his book *Creating a New Civilization: The Politics of the Third Wave* (Atlanta: Turner Publishing, 1995).

49. George Keyworth, Jeffrey Eisenach, and Thomas Lenart, *The Telecom Revolution. An American Opportunity* (The Progress and Freedom Foundation, 1995).

50. Quittner, "The Merry Pranksters Go to Washington," 80.

51. On the digerati's relations with Al Gore and Newt Gingrich, see John Heilemann, "The Making of the President 2000," *Wired*, December 1995, 152–155,

and Geoff Lewis, "The Newtniks Have Seen the Future. Or So They Think," *Business Week*, 11 September 1995, 92–93.

52. "Save the Bill of Rights," *Wired*, April 1994, 40.

53. John Perry Barlow, "Jackboots on the Infobahn," *Wired*, April 1994, 46.

54. Bruce Sterling, "So, People, We Have a Fight on Our Hands," *Wired*, July 1994, 72.

55. Steven Levy, "The Encryption Wars: Is Privacy Good or Bad?" *Newsweek*, 24 April 1995, 56.

56. See Steven Levy, "Crypto Rebels," *Wired*, May–June 1993, 56.

57. "A Crypto Anarchist Manifesto," in *High Noon on the Electronic Frontier*, ed. Peter Ludlow (Cambridge, Mass.: MIT Press, 1996), 237–238.

58. Philip Zimmermann, *The Official PGP User's Guide* (Cambridge, Mass.: MIT Press, 1995), 7.

59. Steven Levy, "Anonymously Yours: How to Launder Your Email," *Wired*, June 1994, 50–51.

60. Remember that the live memory stores data while they are processed. Data in the live memory disappear when the computer is switched off, unlike the data recorded on the hard disk.

61. For a detailed presentation and critique of the White Paper, see Pamela Samuelson, "The Copyright Grab," *Wired*, January 1996, 134–138, 188–191.

62. All these actors created the Digital Future Coalition in 1995, with the Electronic Frontier Foundation, among others.

63. See Pamela Samuelson and John Browning, "Confab Clips Copyright Cartel," *Wired*, March 1997, 61–64, 178–188.

64. John Perry Barlow, "The Next Economy of Ideas: Will Copyright Survive the Napster Bomb? Nope, but Creativity Will," *Wired*, October 2000, 240.

65. Simson Garfinkel, Richard Stallman, and Mitchell Kapor, "Why Patents Are Bad for Software," *Issues in Science and Technology*, Fall 1991, 54–55.

66. *Time* published an article on the topic in 1993 ("Orgies Online," 31 May 1993) and *Newsweek* in 1994 ("Child Abuse in Cyberspace," 18 April 1994). But in 1995 *Time* published both an article by Philip Elmer-Dewitt ("Snuff Porn on the Net"), on 20 February and, more significant, a cover story entitled "Cyberporn," on 3 July. On the same day *Newsweek* published a far more moderate cover story: "No Place for Kids? A Parent's Guide to Sex on the Net," by Steven Levy. The same journalist tried to close the debate in an editorial on 16 October entitled "Stop Talking Dirty to Me."

67. See Philip Elmer-Dewitt, "Censoring Cyberspace: Carnegie Mellon's Attempt to Ban Sex from Its Campus Computer Network," *Time*, 21 November 1994, 102–104.

68. Quoted in Steven Levy, "A Bad Day in Cyberspace," *Newsweek*, 26 June 1995, 47.

69. Mike Godwin, "alt.sex.academic.freedom," *Wired*, February 1995, 72.

70. Text of Court Decision—CDA Case, 11 June 1996, 56. Available at http://www
.ciec.org/decision_PA/decision_text.html.

71. Katz, "Birth of a Digital Nation," 191.

72. Jay Kinney, "Anarcho-Emergentist-Republicans," *Wired*, September 1995, 95.

73. Quoted in Ibid., 94.

Chapter 8   The New Economy

1. A first version of this text was presented in a seminar in Paris and published in *The Economics of the Internet*, ed. Eric Brousseau and Nicholas Curien (Cambridge: Cambridge University Press, 2005).

2. Richard Stallman, "Original Announcement of the GNU Project," 27 September 1983. Available at http://www.gnu.org/gnu/initial-announcement.html.

3. In a document in which Stallman explains his disagreement with his colleagues at MIT, he associates acceptance of a license with fascism (quoted in Levy, *Hackers*, 425).

4. Richard Stallman, "The GNU Project," 1998. Available at http://www.gnu.org/gnu/the-gnu-project.html.

5. Ibid.

6. GNU General Public License, Version 2, June 1991.

7. Preamble in Ibid.

8. Stallman, "The GNNU Project."

9. David Betz and Jon Edwards, interview with Richard Stallman, *Byte*, July 1986. Available at http://www.gnu.org/gnu/byte-interview.html.

10. Richard Stallman, "The GNU Manifesto," *Dr. Dobb's Journal*, March 1985.

11. Joe Barr, interview with Richard Stallman, *Linux World Today*, n.d. Available at http://www.linuxworldtoday.com/f_lwt-indepth7.html.

12. Simson Garfinkel, "Is Stallman Stalled?" *Wired*, March 1993, 34 and 108.

13. Eben Moglen, "Anarchism Triumphant: Free Software and the Death of Copyright," *First Monday* 4, no. 8 (August 1999). Available at http://www.first monday.dk.

14. Glyn Moody, "The Greatest OS That Never Was," *Wired*, August 1997, 156. In some cases, such as web servers, freeware (Apache) accounts for roughly 60 percent of the market.

15. Ibid., 155.

16. Jesse Freund and Chip Bayers, "Hacker-Philosopher," *Wired*, May 1998, 45.

17. Eric Raymond, "The Cathedral and the Bazaar," *First Monday* 3, no. 3 (March 1998): § 4. Available at http://www.firstmonday.dk.

18. Moody, "The Greatest OS That Never Was," 123.

19. Raymond, "The Cathedral and the Bazaar," § 10.

20. Ibid., 154.

21. See G. Hardin, "The Tragedy of Commons," *Science*, no. 162 (1968): 1243–1248.

22. Eric Raymond, "The Magic Cauldron," June 1999. Available at http://www.tuxedo.org/.

23. Thomas Malone and Robert Laubacher, "The Dawn of the E-lance Economy," *Harvard Business Review*, September–October 1998, 146.

24. Kahin, *Information Infrastructure Sourcebook.*

25. R. Wessen, "Canter & Siegel: Stop Them before They Spam Again!" *Netsurfer* 0, no. 1 (24 June 1994). Available at http://earthsci.unimelb.edu.au/~awatkins/CandS.html.

26. L. Canter and M. Siegel, *How to Make a Fortune on the Information Superhighway* (New York: Harper-Collins, 1994).

27. Ibid., 192.

28. Ibid., 12.

29. J. and M. V. Ellsworth, *The Internet Business Book* (New York: Wiley, 1994).

30. In 1994 and 1995, *Time*, *Newsweek*, and *Business Week* published two, two, and four articles on the subject, respectively.

31. Elmer-Dewitt, "Battle for the Soul of the Internet," 56.

32. J. Verity, "Truck Lanes for the Info Highway: CommerceNet, a Bazaar for Silicon Valley, May Help Shape a Far Larger Business Infrastructure," *Business Week*, 18 April 1994, 113.

33. J. Verity and R. Hof, "The Internet: How It Will Change the Way You Do Business," *Business Week*, 14 November 1994, 81.

34. Canter and Siegel, *How to Make a Fortune on the Information Superhighway*, 118.

35. J. Castro, "Just Click to Buy: Madison Avenue Meets the Online World and Neither Will Be the Same Again," *Time*, special issue "Welcome to Cyberspace," March 1995, 74–75.

36. Quoted in K. Kelly and G. Wolf, "Push," *Wired*, March 1997, 17.

37. N. Weintraut, quoted in A. Cortese, "A Way Out of the Web Maze," *Business Week*, European edition, 24 February 1997, 42.

38. Cortese, "A Way Out of the Web Maze," 41.

39. Steven Levy, "The Year of the Internet," *Newsweek*, 25 December 1995, 28.

40. Quoted in C. Bayers, "The Great Web Wipeout," *Wired*, April 1996, 128.

41. D. Peppers and M. Rogers, *The One to One Future: Building Relationships One Customer at a Time* (New York: Currency Doubleday, 1993).

42. D. Peppers and M. Rogers, "Let's Make a Deal," *Wired*, February 1994, 74, 126.

43. M. Schrage, "Is Advertising Finally Dead?" *Wired*, February 1994, 71.

44. Ibid., 74.

45. E. Schwartz, "Advertising Webonomics 101," *Wired*, February 1996.

46. Schwartz was to develop his theses in a book published in the following year: *Webonomics: Nine Essential Principles for Growing Your Business on the World Wide Web* (New York: Broadway Books, 1997).

47. John Hagel and Arthur Armstrong, *Net Gain: Expanding Markets through Virtual Communities* (Boston: Harvard Business School Press, 1997).

48. K. Kelly, "It Takes a Village to Make a Mall: *Net Gain*'s John Hagel on the Prerequisite for Net Commerce: Community," *Wired*, August 1997, 84.

49. Hagel and Armstrong, *Net Gain*, 13.

50. Ibid., xii.

51. Ibid., xiii.

52. Ibid., 142.

53. Ibid., 170.

54. "Internet Communities," *Business Week*, European edition, 5 May 1997.

55. Chip Morningstar and Randall Farmer, "The Lessons of Lucasfilm's Habitat," in *Cyberspace First Steps*, ed. Michael Benedikt (Cambridge, Mass.: MIT Press, 1993), 273–301.

56. Hof, "Special Report," in Benedikt, *Cyberspace*, 42.

57. C. Figallo, former leader of a hippie commune and then of The Well (see chapter 3), also published a book on this subject: *Hosting Web Communities: Building Relationships, Increasing Customer Loyalty, and Maintaining a Competitive Edge* (New York: Wiley, 1998).

58. R. Hof, "The 'Click Here' Economy," *Business Week*, European edition, 22 June 1998, 65.

59. Quoted in Paul Keegan, "The Digerati! *Wired Magazine* Has Triumphed by Turning Mild-Mannered Computer Nerds into a Super-Desirable Consumer Niche," *New York Times Magazine*, 21 May 1995, 42.

60. In a note to a new edition in 1996, we learn that this text is not a solitary contribution but the fruit of a debate with certain authors of *Wired*, some of whom were also members of the Electronic Frontier Foundation (Pamela Samuelson, Kevin Kelly, Mitch Kapor, Mike Godwin, Stewart Brand) and with Alvin Toffler; see Leeson, *Clicking In*.

61. John Perry Barlow, "The Economy of Ideas: A Framework for Rethinking Patents and Copyrights in the Digital Age," *Wired*, March 1994, 86.

62. Ibid., 90.

63. The previous year Richard Stallman had suggested authorizing copies of musical recordings and remunerating the musicians through a tax on machines used to make copies. See R. Stallman, "Copywrong," *Wired*, July 1993, 48–49.

64. Ibid., 126.

65. Ibid., 128.

66. "The (Second Phase of the) Revolution Has Begun," interview with Jim Clark by Michael Goldberg, *Wired*, October 1994, 156.

67. Esther Dyson, interview with Jim Barksdale, "Netscape's Secret Weapon," *Wired*, March 1996, 207.

68. Esther Dyson, "Intellectual Value," *Wired*, July 1995, 138.

69. Ibid., 139.

70. Ibid., 182.

71. Ibid., 183.

72. Ibid., 184.

73. Dyson's thesis was to be adopted by various authors. It was, for example, the basis for the argument put forward by Andrew Odlyzko "The Bumpy Road of Electronic Commerce." Available at http://curry.edschool.virginia.edu/aace/conf/webnet/html/ao/htm.

74. Network Wizard/SRI International.

75. Michel Gensollen, "Creation of Value on the Internet," 1999. Available at http://www.gensollen.net.

76. Michael Mandel, "The Triumph of the New Economy: A Powerful Payoff from Globalization and the Info Revolution," *Business Week*, 30 December 1996.

77. Kevin Kelly, "New Rules for the New Economy," *Wired*, September 1997.

78. Kevin Kelly, *New Rules for the New Economy: Ten Radical Strategies for a Connected World* (New York: Viking, 1998). The *Harvard Business Review* reviewed it at length, although critically. See Peter Bernstein, "Are Networks Driving the New Economy?" *Harvard Business Review*, November–December 1998, 159–166.

79. Ibid., 142.

80. Kevin Kelly, "The Economics of Ideas," *Wired*, June 1996, presentation of Paul Romer's theses; Kevin Kelly, interview with Michael Cox, "Wealth If You Want It," *Wired*, November 1996.

81. Kevin Kelly, *Out of Control: The Rise of Neo-Biological Civilization* (Reading, Mass.: Addison-Wesley, 1994).

82. Kelly, *New Rules for the New Economy*, 194.

83. Ibid., 196.

84. Paul Kedrosky, interview with Brian Arthur, "The More You Sell," *Wired*, October 1995, 132–133.

85. John Browning and Spencer Reiss, "Encyclopedia of New Economy," *Wired*, March, April, and May 1998.

86. *Wired*, March 1998, 106.

87. Ibid., 107.

88. *Wired*, April 1998, 100.

89. Ibid., 93.

90. Ibid., 100.

91. Ibid., 102.

92. *Wired*, May 1998, 109.

93. *Wired*, April 1998, 96.

94. *Wired*, May 1998, 108.

95. Stephen Shepard, "The New Economy: What It Really Means," *Business Week*, 17 November 1997, 48–49.

96. Chip Bayers, "Capitalist Econstruction," *Wired*, March 2000.

97. Kevin Kelly, "Prophets of Boom: Harry Dent, Jr.," *Wired*, September 1999.

98. Kevin Kelly, "The Roaring Zeros," *Wired*, September 1999.

99. Warren Frey, "The Zero Effect," Rants and Raves, *Wired*, December 1999.

100. Peter Schwartz, "The Future of the Newconomy," *Red Herring*, July 2000.

101. Kevin Kelleher, "Death of the New Economy, R.I.P.," *Wired*, November 2001. Available at http://www.wired.com/wired/archive/9.11/change.html.

102. James Surowiecki, "The New Economy Was a Myth, Right?" *Wired*, July 2002. Available at http://www.wired.com/wired/archive/10.07/myth.html.

103. J. Bradford DeLong, "Don't Worry About Deflation," *Wired*, August 2003. Available at http://www.wired.com/wired/archive/11.08/view.html?pg=5.

104. Carl Shapiro and Hal R. Varian, *Information Rules: A Strategic Guide to the Network Economy* (Boston: Harvard Business School Press, 1998).

105. Ibid., x.

106. One year before Kelly's article, the magazine had published an interview with Brian Arthur in which he explained the principles of increasing returns and technological lock-in. See Kedrosky, "The More You Sell," 133.

107. Shapiro and Varian, *Information Rules*, 18.

108. Ibid., 14.

Conclusion

1. For a comparison between the history of radio and that of the Internet, see Flichy, "Technologies fin de siècle, Internet et la radio," 249–271.

2. Ricœur, *Lectures on Ideology and Utopia*, 311.

3. Michel de Certeau, *L'Invention du quotidian: I. Arts de faire* (Paris: Gallimard-Folio, 1998), 185 (our translation).

4. Alexis de Tocqueville, *De la démocratie en Amérique* (Paris: Gallimard, "La Pléiade," 1992), 612 (our translation).

5. Ana Maria Fernandez-Madonado, "The Diffusion of Information and Communication Technologies in Lower-Income Groups: *Cabinas De Internet* in Lima Peru," in *Sustaining Urban Networks: The Social Diffusion of Large Technical Systems,* ed. Olivier Coutard, Richard Hanley, and Rae Zimmerman (London: Routledge, 2005), 1117–1134.

Index

Made in United States
Orlando, FL
22 March 2026

79568180R00152